Frederick Andrew Inderwick

The interregnum:

Studies of the commonwealth, legislative, social, and legal

Frederick Andrew Inderwick

The interregnum:
Studies of the commonwealth, legislative, social, and legal

ISBN/EAN: 9783744715355

Printed in Europe, USA, Canada, Australia, Japan

Cover: Foto ©Suzi / pixelio.de

More available books at **www.hansebooks.com**

A Twenty Shilling Piece or Broad, A.D. 1653.

A Twenty Shilling Piece or Broad,
issued by the Protector, A.D. 1656.

THE
INTERREGNUM

(A.D. 1648—1660)

STUDIES OF THE COMMONWEALTH

LEGISLATIVE, SOCIAL, AND LEGAL

BY

F. A. INDERWICK, Q.C.,

AUTHOR OF "SIDELIGHTS ON THE STUARTS," ETC., ETC.

LONDON

SAMPSON LOW, MARSTON, SEARLE & RIVINGTON

Limited

St. Dunstan's House

FETTER LANE, FLEET STREET, E.C.

1891

PREFACE.

"Have I three kingdoms," said King James to the fly, "and thou must needs fly into my eye?" To which the fly might have replied, had he been ready-witted, that His Majesty's eye was as open to him as any other spot in his royal dominions. The same question, with the same reply, may be put to the writer who, having open to him the whole world of history, archæology, and romance, wantonly intrudes into the public eye a subject well worn and discussed, and an epoch dark with dulness and disputes. The Interregnum was truly an age of experiment and of transition, but it was also one of the turning points of our national life, and the more fully its details are investigated and published, the more surely will the country appreciate the patriotic devotion and the unselfish aims that underlay the evils and the eccentricities of the time. The more clearly, also, will it realize how the great reforms of the present century had their origin during the few years of the Interregnum, when religion seemed to have gone mad and chaos to have possessed itself of our domestic affairs. For then it was that the sentiments of religious liberty matured with the uninterrupted multiplication of religious sects, that the tree of constitutional freedom was planted in the acknowledged supremacy of Parliament, that the principles of a firm and equal administration of justice were expounded in Ordinances and Statutes, and that the scheme of our most recent reforms was enacted in the provisions for popular representation. Some of the difficulties of such an investigation are pointed out in the text, but the greatest obstacle is to be encountered in the fact that a complete copy of the Acts and Ordinances, from the opening of the Long Parliament to the death of the Protector, does not exist, unless indeed it is hidden away in some library inaccessible to the public. The authorised, and best known collection, that of Henry Scoble, Clerk of the Parliament after the death of Thomas May, professes only to give the Acts and Ordinances that were in force at the end of the Parliamentary Session of 1656. Authentically recorded details of the various experiments in legislation during this period are thus wanting, and they have to be sought in the contemporary newspapers, not always impartial or well informed, in the conflicting and inaccurate accounts of the Cavalier and Roundhead presses, or in the chance and not easily discoverable store of some private collector. From such a thicket of embrangled briars it is not easy to pluck the flower of accuracy, but I have striven to do so, and in the hope that I may have succeeded have sent these pages to the press.

F. A. INDERWICK.

WINCHELSEA,
    October, 1890.

CONTENTS.

A

CHAPTER II.

THE PEOPLE'S COMPENSATION FOR THE ABOLITION OF ROYALTY.

CHAPTER III.

THE GERM OF RELIGIOUS TOLERATION.

CHAPTER IV.

THE ADMINISTRATION OF JUSTICE AND REFORMS OF THE LAW.

I.—*The Administration of Justice.*

II.—*Reforms of the Law.*

CHAPTER V.

THE HIGH COURTS OF JUSTICE.

CHAPTER VI.

CELEBRATED TRIALS UNDER THE COMMONWEALTH.

I.—The Trials of John Lilburn for Seditious Libels.

THE INTERREGNUM.

CHAPTER I.

EXPERIMENTS IN LEGISLATION.

THE battle had been won. The great struggle against sacerdotalism, autocracy and intolerance had run its course, had culminated in the triumph of the more advanced and resolute section of the party of Nonconformists; and had resulted in the most complete victory ever yet accomplished by the friends of liberty over the champions of arbitrary government. Each party had in turn invoked the Almighty Disposer of Events, had used His name as a talisman, and had vouched Him as a champion. The image and superscription of the King stamped upon the national coinage called upon the Deity to rise in His strength and scatter the enemies of the truth. "Exurgat Dominus dissipientur inimici" was the last cry of the Monarch issued into every household that could boast of a golden sovereign, an angel, or a crown. But the God of Battles had declared against him. "The Lord of Hosts" was the national war-cry at Worcester and Dunbar, and "God with us" was the exulting and victorious motto of the Commonwealth as they entered into their kingdom and proceeded to realize the objects of their strife. When, however, the tumult

B

of war had subsided, when the destructive tactics of
the soldier gave place to the constructive abilities of
the statesman, and the Commonwealth proceeded to
the reformation of the kingdom, difficulties far
greater than those of arms rose up before them.   The
first great work, pressed upon them alike by the army and
by their own repeated declarations, was the reform of
the law, and the reconstitution of the magistracy on a
sound and impartial basis.   Included in this, and even
more specially needed, was the reform of the existing legal
procedure, involving as it did delay, uncertainty and suspicion of corruption, and of permitting if not encouraging a
disregard of legal obligations by the rich to the derogation
or the ruin of the poor.   Throughout the country districts
where justices of quarter sessions and of other inferior
tribunals held courts and exercised judicial functions,
trying small actions of debt and of trespass, the tediousness
and cost were almost unbearable.   I have seen in some of
the records of these courts during the first half of the seventeenth century numerous cases where the action having
been brought for a sum under £10 there have been from
ten to fifteen adjournments; while in the great majority
of such suits the delay and cost of the proceedings compelled
the plaintiff to forego his claim and agree to a settlement
in derogation of his rights.   In the superior courts matters
were even worse.   Over twenty thousand causes, it was
said, were standing for judgment in the Court of Chancery,
some of them even ten, twenty, and thirty years old, and
in some not less than five hundred orders had been made.[1]
The Bishops holding courts at Durham, at York, and at
Ely, each, within his see, claiming, like a Pope, to exercise
temporal as well as spiritual jurisdiction, and the Palatine
Courts at Lancaster and Chester, permitted their causes to
be sent to London, where they were out of reach of all but

[1] Parliamentary History, Vol. 3, p. 1412.

wealthy litigants. Judges and their marshals,[1] clerks, and sheriffs, everyone connected with Courts of Justice, exacted exorbitant fees, and gave preference in the cause list to those suitors who paid them best. Courts of Chancery, of Common Law, and of Admiralty sometimes out of jealousy of their respective jurisdictions, sometimes to bring causes from the country to London, sometimes for mere gain to the judges, issued prohibitions and injunctions against each other, and often dissolved them, as they had issued them, in collusion. Appeals lay in every civil cause from court to court, and pleadings were technical and prolix and drawn in a language neither spoken nor understood by any but the lawyers themselves. The very writing of legal documents, orders, and indictments was in a text long since forgotten, and disused by the public. Fees and costs in small cases often amounted to double the amount recovered, and the prisons of the State were crowded with unhappy debtors overwhelmed with huge accumulations of interest and costs, unable to pay the demands of their gaolers or to obtain any order of release. Under the careful and personal rule of the Tudors the industries of the country had been safeguarded. Trade had been protected, prices had been regulated for all the necessaries of life, and laws had been passed, which, endeavouring to give a just influence to capital, were directed at the same time to secure to the artificer, the labourer, and the husbandman a fair day's wage for a fair day's work. But wars, which bring glory to commanders and desolation to countries, had combined with the apathy of the Stuarts and the power of the plutocracy to deprive the great bulk of the nation of the benefit of this even-handed legislation, and had tended to obliterate from the minds of the people the recollection that such laws had

---

[1] State Papers, Vol. 124.

ever existed. They knew only by experience the repressive clauses of the various Acts originally passed for their benefit. While the wages they were to receive were fixed by their employers in Quarter Sessions at the lowest figure possible to sustain life, they were powerless to uphold their rights against those who enhanced by fraudulent contrivance the price of the necessaries of existence. "Your balms," they may have said with the Psalmist, "have broken our heads," as, owing to the infinity of small duties to which they were liable, they found themselves by virtue of these very laws harassed by informers and dragooned by Justices of the Peace.[1]

The cleansing of the judicial stable and the resuscitation of the old popular laws were in due course taken in hand, but in the meantime the temper of the victorious party compelled the immediate discussion of certain questions upon which the mind of Parliament and the country was for the moment intently fixed. We may judge of a man, it is commonly said, by the company he keeps, and we have been told that we may discover the moral type of the ancient Jew by studying the list of hideous offences which he was forbidden to commit. If we apply this test to the English people at the time of the Commonwealth, we might conclude that the land was free from the disfigurements of felonies and misdemeanours, that the thief and the man-slayer were no longer in the midst, but that all classes of the community were given over to continuous breaches of the Seventh Commandment, to habitual drunkenness, profanity, Sabbath-breaking and oaths. That this was so I have no reason to suppose, but constant and vigorous preaching against social offences, such as drinking, swearing, incontinence and Sabbath-breaking had led the people

---

[1] In a small corporate town in the south of England I found that in 1650 the Grand Jury had presented six widows for buying butter and eggs of their neighbours to sell again in the market. They were all fined for breaking the law by forestalling the market.

to regard these as the great sins of the nation that had
brought God's judgment upon them, and to believe that
if they were rooted out from the land a new era of
prosperity would arise. They were also taught by
agitators, and they believed that these were the special
sins of people in high places, and that against them
the law should mainly be invoked. But it happened,
as it has always happened when legislation proceeds on
these assumptions, that the people were alike misled
in their view of the present and in their forecast of the
future, for the penalties of the laws that they afterwards
enacted were, with scarcely a single exception, enforced
against and suffered by the very class of the community
which had been most loud in their invocation. These
sentiments, however, of which it was necessary immediately to take account, resulted in a course of what I
will venture to describe as experiments in legislation.
Not that any legislation of the Commonwealth was
intended to be purely experimental or temporary, but
their Acts were in some instances of a character never
yet attempted in England, of which the details had
not been sufficiently considered, and of which the results
were indefinite and unsuccessful. Experiments in
legislation partake very much of the character of experiments in husbandry. They require for their successful
prosecution a propitious climate, a soil prepared
to receive them, and many revolutions of the seasons to test
their effect. For these experiments of the Commonwealth
the country and the times were hardly ripe, while the
biting frost on all liberal reforms which followed the sudden
death of the Protector, set back for many recurring
summers the swelling buds that were just bursting into
bloom. And thus it happened that the seeds of reform
gathered at the Commonwealth like the grains of wheat in
the folds of the Egyptian mummy, remained living in
themselves, but encompassed by the shroud of ignorance

and bigotry, till succeeding generations brought them forth once more to enrich the earth with the golden products of bygone ages.

To make men religious, temperate, or chaste by Act of Parliament is almost as impossible as to regulate by legislation the caste of their features, or the length of their limbs. But it can hardly be denied that by prudent and tentative measures, decreasing the opportunities of vice and encouraging the practice of the opposite virtues, much may be done to repress existing immorality, and to improve the tone and habits of a nation. Whatever, therefore, of benefit, —and there was very much,—accrued to the nation under the Commonwealth, was derived from the temperate prosecution of this course, and the ultimate failure of repressive laws, followed, as they were, by a reaction in favour of vice and immorality, arose from the absence of that virtue recognised as indispensable to progress by practical statesmen, but regarded as detestable and abominable by the zealous social reformer, and as stinking in the nostrils of every fanatical enthusiast—moderation.

The Commonwealth having abolished King and House of Lords, found themselves face to face with a position in which power was for the first time in history deposited in the hands of a Parliament consisting solely of a House of Commons, which could only be dissolved by its own consent. After less than five years they returned almost in despair to government by a supreme authority in the person of a Lord Protector, with a House of Lords summoned by the Protector's writ; but in the meanwhile the existing difficulty had to be met, and the great experiment of ruling with one chamber had to be tried. Such an experiment from the very first was doomed to failure. Making bricks without straw was found by the result not to have been an impossible task, but the attempt to construct a republic without republicans would have taxed to the utmost the ingenuity of an Egyptian overseer. We have the Lord

Commissioner's account of the conference,[1] at which he was present, together with the Speaker, Cromwell, Harrison, Fleetwood, Desborough, Whalley, Sir Thomas Widdrington, Chief Justice St. John, and many others as to the settlement of a government for the country. We know from him that Cromwell, Whitelock, Lenthall, Widdrington, and St. John declared openly in favour of a limited monarchy, while Colonels Desborough and Whalley alone of all the assembled company spoke up for a republic. And this, I imagine, fairly represented the proportion of republicans to the great body of educated people. Whitelock, however, adds that the army were generally against anything of a monarchy and the lawyers generally for it, and concludes that much discourse came to nothing. In this, however, I can hardly agree, for this most important meeting clearly showed the inclination of the army, then the most powerful body in the State, and rendered any steps towards the reconstruction of a monarchy under any conditions at that time impossible. But a pure republic organized by and in the hands of Cromwell as chief constructor, St. John as one of the chiefs of the law, Whitelock and Widdrington holding the Great Seal, and Lenthall as Speaker of the only House of Parliament, would have been equally impossible, and the enterprise eventuated in a hybrid form of government, the result of a compromise incapable of performance. A republic pure and simple, with a First Consul or a President, with a Senate and a House of Assembly elected by popular vote, and holding office for a limited period, might have been practicable and would probably have been successful. A monarchy, be the monarch whomsoever they would, with any constitutional checks that might have been devised, would probably also have been a permanent and successful arrangement, and in the almost parallel case of Napoleon a somewhat similar scheme did

[1] Whitelock, Vol. 3, p. 372.

actually succeed. But a constitution where neither republic
nor monarchy was actually established, but something
betwixt and between, where the supreme power was to be
lodged in the hands of a numerous and varying body of
persons, was never seen or heard of by England before or
since, and was manifestly incapable of bearing the strain of
practical working. A form of government with something
of the monarchy about it was condemned and one with
something of the republic about it was accepted, with the
result that the something of the monarchy speedily came to
the top and the something of the republic gradually sank to
the bottom, with the general assent and goodwill of the kingdom. Meantime, the solemn engagement, " I do declare and
promise that I will be true and faithful to the Commonwealth
of England as the same is now established without a King
or House of Lords," was in course of being taken by all
persons in authority, from the Lords Commissioners of the
Great Seal to the lowliest of parish constables. And then,
as if in mockery of the Chamber they had dissolved, and of
the engagement which they were about to make of universal
obligation, the Commonwealth proceeded to elect a body
more powerful than the House of Lords, whose dominion
became actually though not nominally supreme over Parliament itself, which issued its orders and its edicts, summoned persons before it and committed them for contempt, and, though professing to attend the decisions of
Parliament, did in fact transact the entire business of
the nation. The Council of State, known at first by the
high-sounding title of the Lords States General,[1] in
whose records, far more than in those of Parliament, is
to be found the full history of the times, was constituted
in February, 1648-9, and consisted of forty-one members,
of whom nine were a quorum.[2] They had the dignity of
a House of Parliament; a Great Seal of their own; their

---

[1] History of Independency, Pt. 2, p. 128.
[2] The number varied in different councils.

officer carried a mace similar to that of the House of
Commons ; they elected their own Speaker or President,
their own chaplain,[1] and their own serjeant-at-arms.
Their number also comprised many of those very persons of
whom it is now the fashion to say that a model second
chamber should consist. The Lords Commissioners of the
Great Seal, the Chief Justices of the Upper Bench and of
the Common Pleas, the Chief Baron of the Exchequer, the
heads of the various departments of the State, the Lord
President Bradshaw, Lord Pembroke, Lord Salisbury, the
Lord Mayor of London, Sydenham, the father of medicine,
the commanders of the army, Fairfax and Cromwell,
General Skippon who commanded the troops in the
Metropolitan district ; these, together with others of the
most eminent and statesmenlike men of the period, some
of them peers, some of them members of the House of
Commons, some of them private gentlemen, composed
the Council of State. To these councillors, while
directed to act according to the instructions of the
House of Commons, the following among other independent
functions were committed.[2] They had the absolute
power and command of the army and navy, and of all
militias and forces by sea and land ; of all military and
naval stores, and of all recruiting of soldiers and sailors,
and building of ships of war,[3] together with all the power
and authority of the Lord High Admiral or the Commissioners of the Admiralty. They were charged with the
protection and encouragement of trade. They were

---

[1] The Reverends Goodwin and Sterry were the first chaplains
appointed at a salary of £200 a year each and lodgings. State Papers,
2nd Nov., 1649.

[2] Instructions to the Council of State, Hansard's Parliamentary
History, Vol. 3, p. 1218. At a later period other duties were from
time to time added to the above.

[3] The British ships of war, during the Interregnum, carried a red
cross on a white flag, quite through the flag. On the stern they
had the red cross on one escutcheon, and the harp on the other.

entrusted with all diplomatic negotiations with foreign countries, and with the appointment and reception of ambassadors and foreign ministers. They were empowered to send for all persons whomsoever, including the judges, who were frequently consulted, to advise with them as to their course of proceeding, and they could compel the production of records, books, papers, and writings. They had power to administer oaths, and to bind over or imprison those who disobeyed their orders, or were guilty of contempt. And finally, they were authorized to charge all necessary expenses and salaries upon the public revenue. In one other important respect, also, they discharged the functions of a House of Parliament, for they drew Bills of which they settled the details, and then submitted them to be passed by the House of Commons. In the year 1649 alone I find from the Daily Proceedings of the Council of State[1] that on the 12th May the President was ordered to bring in an Act prohibiting the printing of seditious and scandalous pamphlets, and to read it a first time on a Saturday in August, 1649. On the 14th August, an Act for regulating the manufacture of woollen cloth was ordered to be considered by them on Saturday next. On the 26th December, 1649, an Act for putting cavaliers out of the town was ordered to be reported to the House by the Earl of Pembroke. In January, 1649-50, a Landlord and Tenant Act, presented to the Council by the President, was sent by them to the Lords Commissioners of the Great Seal for their report. I find in addition that the following among other Bills were sent by Parliament to the Council of State in June, 1649 : A Bill for levying money by assessments, etc.; a Bill for a general pardon ; a Bill to prohibit the exportation of wool and fuller's earth ; a similar Bill as to gold and silver ; a Bill for the relief of tenants from malignant landlords ; a Bill to regulate the press and to prevent the publication of scandalous and seditious pamphlets ; a Bill

---

[1] State Papers, 12th May and August, 1649.

for the relief of poor prisoners not able to pay their debts; a Bill to provide for the probate of wills and granting of letters of administration. Thus was conferred upon the Council of State the power of transacting nearly the whole business of the country, for although the House of Commons had nominally retained to itself the right of legislation, yet a power of independent legislation was indirectly given to the Council of State when they were authorized to make orders without appeal, and were further armed with executive powers which enabled them to carry their orders into effect. The Council, in truth, occupied towards Parliament the position of a powerful and strong-minded wife, who, although supposed to be with her husband of one mind and together with him to constitute but one person, does in fact by her strength of will control the household and regulate the expenditure. And this Council of State, re-appointed from time to time on nine different occasions, with certain necessary modifications, continued to transact every important matter of business during the twelve years of the Commonwealth, including the period of Cromwell's protectorate. Our own system of an Upper House, composed with rare exceptions of persons sitting by hereditary right alone, though consecrated by the prescription of many centuries, is perhaps in theory one of the most illogical and unworkable that can well be conceived. The mere existence of an hereditary chamber would seem to be inconsistent with the instincts of a free people. And yet the Peers were and are by no means unpopular. Their titles were retained and their hereditary succession was acknowledged under the Commonwealth as they had been under the King, and no attempt was made to abolish the peerage or to lower its dignity. This vitality of the House of Lords, which in a remarkable manner survived the Commonwealth, doubtless, arises in a great measure from its constant accession of recruits, sometimes the nominees of the sovereign, but generally the partisans of a

Prime Minister anxious to promote or consolidate his position in that assembly. It is also, to some extent, owing to the fact that most of the Peers who take part in public business have received their early political training in the Lower House, and that the Lords have on many occasions in the history of our country stood forth on behalf of popular rights. That the system has worked fairly well, in spite of its anomalies, says much for our House of Lords and for the business aptitude of our nobility, but it can hardly, I think, be disputed that a second Chamber, elected on the principle attempted by the Commonwealth, offers far surer guarantees of permanent success than a Chamber constituted on the present model.

During the Commonwealth, as a natural result, while the more popular Assembly troubled itself with questions of orthodoxy and of social reforms, discussed at great length an ideal form of government, and formulated many projects of law, abandoned as soon as put into print, the Council of State inquired into all the affairs of the kingdom, and made recommendations to Parliament which that House did its best to carry out. And thus the Council of State occupied a stronger and, if possible, a more independent position than the American Senate, for while Parliament, like the House of Assembly, occupied itself chiefly in debates, and was guided by and to some extent the reflex of popular sentiment and passion, the Council, sitting at the same time, devoted itself more particularly to those questions which concerned the welfare and prosperity of the country at home and abroad, without necessarily raising political or controversial storms. Without such a body as this, the government of the country could not have been carried on : with it, and with a House of Commons where the more fiery and fanatical spirits could assert their grievances and discuss popular topics, the Government was actually carried on with very remarkable success both at home and abroad, and was enabled to

originate numerous reforms in every department of the
State of which we are even now reaping the benefit, and
for which the Commonwealth has never yet received its due
acknowledgment. The Council of State met every day
except Sunday and an occasional Monday, in every week
from February, 1649, to the end of 1654. In 1655 and 1656
they met on an average twenty days in each month, and in
1656 and 1657 about twelve days in each month. A record
was kept not only of the days of meeting of the Council, but
also of the names of the Councillors who attended, and of
the period of the sitting at which they arrived, the subjects
on the agenda papers being numbered consecutively, and
each member's name being marked with the number of the
subject under consideration at the moment of his arrival.
They sat each day at 2.30 p.m., but not beyond 6.30 p.m.
unless for business of importance.[1] The orders for the regulation of their business were similar to those of the House
of Commons, but with somewhat stricter rules of debate.
Their duties were far-reaching and multifarious. They
carried on the wars with Holland and with Spain.
They inquired into the details of all plots and schemes
for the disturbance of the existing Government. They
prepared Bills and commended subjects of legislation
to the House of Commons. They undertook the providing of money for the public service by means of
assessments, of compounding with delinquents and of sales
of Crown lands and fee farm rents. They appointed judges
and arranged the circuits, they discussed and provided for
the details of every trade, craft, and handiwork of the
country, relaxing and imposing from time to time import
and export duties where necessary. Nor, while compre-
hending the broad heaven of politics, did they forbear to
inspect the mites of daily wants, for they undertook the
hunting of highwaymen and the protection of travellers.
They settled the prices of food and of drink, ordered the

---

[1] Order for business. Council of State. State Paper, May 7th, 1649

new weathercock for Whitehall,[1] and fixed the day for the
grass to be cut at Hampton Court.[2] And whatever they
took in hand they carried out with vigour, determination,
and despatch. Whitelock, speaking of the energy and the
activity of the Council of State, during the autumn of 1651,
before the battle of Worcester, says[3]: "The Council of
State during this period had almost hourly messengers
going out and returning from the several forces, carrying advice and directions to them, and bringing to
the Council an account of their motions and designs,
and of the enemy's motions. It could hardly be
that any affair of this nature could be managed with
more diligence, courage and prudence than this was;
nor was there ever so great a body of men so well armed
and provided got together in so short a time." The
Commons, on the other hand, could never work alone.
The Long Parliament, or what was left of it, after passing
some Acts and attempting many more, broke down hope-
lessly over the most crying want of the time, the reformation of the law, haggled and boggled over the day of their
own dissolution, and were at last dismissed with violence
and opprobrium, to the general delight of the community, in
the month of April, 1653.[4] Cromwell, who, in his heart,
earnestly desired to be a constitutional ruler, then tried
parliamentary government under various conditions. It is
remarkable, says Hallam, that Cromwell would neither
govern with parliaments nor without them.[5] The truth, I
take to be, that he saw the difficulty of governing with
one chamber alone, but tried with sincerity, although with-

---

[1] State Papers, Vol. 24, 13th Sept., 1653.

[2] Ibid., Vol. 203, Col. 34.

[3] Whitelock, Vol. 3, p. 332.

[4] "The nation loathed their sitting. And so far as I could discern,
when they were dissolved there was not so much as the barking of a
dog or any general and visible repining at it." Cromwell's speech to
the Parliament of 1654. Carlyle, Speech III.

[5] Constitutional History, Vol. I., p. 678.

out success, to frame a constitution that would work on such a model. His attempts failed, and the true secret of his failure is, I think, to be found well described in his own words in his own speeches. These, given *in extenso* by Carlyle, are very hard reading,[1] but in rough and rugged language they convey a very definite meaning. The Long Parliament being thus disposed of, Cromwell endeavoured by means of a Convention to combine in one House the elements of both. This Assembly, which he called together in July, 1653, had the misfortune to include in its number one Praise God Bare-bones, and the Royalists, ever on the watch for the means of bringing parliamentary government into ridicule and contempt, afterwards termed it Barebones Parliament, a name which has adhered to it ever since, and has deprived it of the consideration which it certainly merited. It was composed of one hundred and twenty persons, upon whom it was proposed to confer the supreme power of the realm, and to whom were to be confided the issues of life and death. The members of this Convention were, as White-lock tells us,[2] persons of fortune and knowledge whose attendance on Cromwell's summons was much wondered at by some people, and who might have made a respectable and useful Government had they fairly taken upon themselves the responsibilities of their position, and endeavoured to form a permanent Administration. They

---

[1] This is not rendered more easy by his mode of editing. It is a tradition of the old days of Her Majesty's buck-hounds that it was not uncommon for the pack when in full cry, and in view of the quarry, to be suddenly whipped off to give the noble master time for a sandwich and a glass of sherry. Carlyle, who must in his youth have hunted with those hounds, when the reader is approaching the point of the speech, suddenly whips him off, sometimes in the middle of a sentence, to interject some matter and criticism of his own. Having filled half a page or so with his observations, he picks up the scent and finishes the speech.

[2] Vol. IV, p. 21.

sat under the presidency of Dr. Routh, Provost of Eton, from 4th July to 13th December, 1653. Before retiring from their post, they so far recognised the national desires as to pass Acts for certain reforms in the law, a necessity which Cromwell had put in the front of his speech,[1] for the regulation and registration of civil marriages, for the reconstruction of a High Court of Justice, for continuing the Customs and Excise, altogether twenty-six Acts, including matters of minor importance. They discussed and nearly settled in committee a Bill to reform the High Court of Chancery, and they also considered the question of tithe, as to which they disagreed by a small majority with the report of their own Committee. Being thus unable by reason of their divisions to transact business, or to do any good for the country, they resigned into the hands of the Lord General the powers which he had committed to them. Whatever may have been the reasons which induced this Parliament to commit this act of suicide, its results were most unfortunate, for it induced a feeling of insecurity, tending to produce an instability of government from which, until the last years of Cromwell's Protectorate, the country never recovered. The mistake of this position they speedily realized; and in 1654 they published "*An exact relation of the Proceedings and Transactions of the Late Parliament,*" showing the various measures they had passed, enumerating other schemes they had in hand, and endeavouring to throw the whole blame of their premature dissolution upon their Speaker and a small minority of the House. Some hundred and forty years after this, the French, vainly endeavouring to tread in our footsteps, elected a National Convention. This, like the Convention of 1653, was the supreme power of the State, with power of life and death. Their ignorance of popular institutions and their inexperience of parliamentary government, led the French to believe that a great country

Carlyle, Speech 1.

could be administered and equitably governed by a number
of delegates, each equal to his fellow, and each entitled to
a vote upon every question of administration. The Convention of 1653, seeing the impossibility of government
under such conditions, speedily withdrew from the task in
order to make way for a Government by a Protector and
Parliament acting together. The Convention of 1793, bolder
but less patriotic than that of 1653, proceeded with its hopeless task, fell speedily under the domination of demagogues
and fanatics, gave its decisions, under control of the mob,
suppressed by violence and by death the moderate minority
of the Chamber, pursued a course of tyranny and butchery
unexampled in the world, and left a stain on the fair fame
of its country which can never be effaced. And in the end,
it, too, made way for a military dictator followed by a
restoration of imperial rule. Cromwell's first experiment
having thus proved a failure, the Protector, with the Council
of State, framed ordinances for the good government of the
kingdom, and amongst others issued one of incalculable
courage and value for the union of England and Scotland
under one Parliament. But the country could not subsist
on ordinances alone, and in this deadlock of government
Cromwell's Protectorate was established and assented to
by the nation. Power was quietly assumed by him, he
appointed his council, and nominated his officers, and the
judges with one accord accepted their commissions from
him and acted upon his authority. Then was formulated
by the Protector, the Council, and the army, the *Instrument
of Government*[1] under the authority of which the
Protector called his first Parliament by popular election
in September, 1654, when, for the first time in the
history of this country, the representation of the
people was put upon a uniform and popular footing.
An assimilation of the county, and borough franchise was

---

[1] Irreverently called by the Cavaliers, "The Saints' new Magna
Charta."

C

ordained. No members were given to the old and rotten
boroughs, but the counties had members in proportion to
their population, and the large towns had their fair share of
representation. Parliament was to consist of four hundred
members, and its first session was not to be of less than five
months' duration. Under this scheme, of which Clarendon
says[1] that it was generally looked upon as an alteration fit
to be more warrantably made at a better time, a Parliament
came together and was opened by the Protector on the 4th
September. It contained men of good position in the
counties and in the boroughs, and they had an absolute
legislative power without any right of veto by the Protector.
It was a moment at which all the energy and the wisdom
of a popular Parliament were required for the safety and
honour of the nation. The country was in financial difficulties, war was threatening, and it lay in the power of
Parliament to administer the affairs of the nation and to
model the constitution almost as they chose. But this
House passed its whole time in discussing the Instrument
of Government under which it had accepted its election.
While the enemy was at the gate, and the country, with
the whole Bench of Judges having accepted the form of
government, was longing for some rest and finality, it
passed not a single measure. Voting no money for the
public service, it had, in fact, put the Army upon free
quarter[2] and left the whole Civil Staff without salaries ;

---

[1] History of Rebellion, Vol. III., p. 495.

[2] Carlyle's Speech IV.   January, 1654-5.—Mr. Palgrave (*Oliver
Cromwell*, p. 50) says that this statement has, on enquiry, been found
to be untrue; and he gives it as an instance of Cromwell's deceit.
Literally it may have been inaccurate as free quarter had been
abolished and never re-enacted, but *substantially* it was true enough.
I have found among some of the papers of the Cinq-Ports for the year
1655-6 various petitions to the Protector, saying that, although free
quarter is abolished, yet the soldiers are quartered on the innkeepers
and the inhabitants, and that, as the soldiers are unable to pay for
their keep, the petitioners are in as evil a case as if free quarter were
    existing.

and its five months having expired, it was dissolved by the
Protector on the 22nd January, 1655. It had, however,
discussed the greater portion of the Instrument of Government, although eighty additional amendments were then
ready to be tendered to the Bill,[1] and had given its sanction
to the various ordinances issued by the Protector and the
Council. His second attempt had, therefore, if possible,
been more unsuccessful than the first, and the Commons,
having no counterbalancing power to keep them to work,
was likely to become not only a useless but a mischievous
machine. The Council of State, however, continued to
transact the business of the nation, and ordinances were
passed by Cromwell under the authority of the Instrument
of Government till 1656, when he summoned another
Parliament to his aid.

The position of Cromwell with regard to his Parliaments
was somewhat peculiar, the meaning of a triennial Parliament not being that commonly accepted at the present day.
The Proclamation[2] issued by the Council of State in December
1653, expressly declared the Government of the country, as
then established, to be by a *Lord Protector and successive
triennial Parliaments.* The Instrument of Government, published on the same day, declared by Clause VII. that there
should be a Parliament summoned upon the 3rd of September,
1654, and that successively a Parliament should be summoned
once in every third year, to be accounted from the dissolution of the preceding Parliament. No such Parliament was,
however, by Clause VIII. to be dissolved within five months

---

[1] *Perfect Intelligencer*, No. 267.

[2] By the Council: Whereas the late Parliament dissolving themselves and resigning their powers and authorities, the Government of
this Commonwealth of England, Scotland and Wales by a Lord
Protector and successive triennial parliaments is now established.
And whereas Oliver Cromwell, Captain General of the forces of this
Commonwealth, is declared Lord Protector of the said nations, and
hath accepted thereof, now, &c. Given at Whitehall, 16th December,
1653. Whitelock, Vol. IV., p. 72.

of its first meeting without its own consent.[1] Cromwell was, therefore, free to dispense with a Parliament until January, 1658, and had in the meantime power to give all necessary ordinances for the government of the kingdom. His speedy summoning of a second Parliament was, therefore, due to the strong feeling in favour of national representation and of popular government held by himself in common with the great body of the army. And having provided by ordinances for certain necessary reforms, he proceeded in what was undoubtedly the spirit of the new Constitution.

The Parliament of September, 1656, was summoned by the same form of writ as that used in 1654, declaring that those elected should be " such and no other as are persons of known integrity, fearing God, and of good conversation." They met on the 17th of September, when business was begun badly by the exclusion, necessary perhaps at the time, but appearing unjustifiable to us now, of some ninety members who were not considered by the Council of State to be duly qualified under the above condition. A division, however, being taken on the question of the absence of the ninety members, the rest of the House refused by 125 to 20 to condemn their forcible exclusion, and referred them to the Council for their certificates, which, in the end, they all obtained. This Parliament, in their first session, debated and settled the frame of government, and declared for a Seeond Chamber, with some sort of judicial status, to be associated with the Commons in the conduct of public affairs. They passed several Acts, and were prorogued under auspicious circumstances in June, 1657. " Somewhat to stand between me and the House of Commons " was agreeable to the well-known sentiments of the Protector, who had now to undertake the most delicate task of his time in nominating the " other House." Cromwell's views as to a Second Chamber seem to have been very

---

[1] Whitelock, Vol. IV., p. 57.

much those of the present day. "I did tell you,"[1] said
he, "that I would not undertake it unless there might be
some other persons to interpose between me and the
House of Commons, who then had the power, and prevent
tumultuary and popular spirits. . . . . Men of your
own rank and quality, who will not only be a balance unto
you, but a new force added to you, while you love England
and religion." In other words, "Unless I have some
moderating and business-like body to leaven the lump of
fractiousness in the Commons, I cannot carry on the
affairs of the nation." Cromwell's House of Lords, however, it must be admitted, was not a success, and, like
Lord Palmerston's Privy Seal, failed to make a good impression. A list of these gentlemen was published officially
in the *Mercurius Politicus*,[2] No. 394, and may be taken to

[1] Carlyle, Speech XVIII.

[2] A Catalogue of the names of those Honourable Persons who are by
writ summoned to sit in the Other House of Parliament:—
The Lord Richard Cromwell, The Lord Hen. Cromwell, Lord Deputy
of Ireland; Nathaniel Fiennes and John Lisle, Lords Commissioners
of the Great Seal; Henry Lawrence, Lord President of His Highness,
Privy Council; the Lord Charles Fleetwood, Robert, Earl of Warwick;
Edmond, Earl of Mulgrave; Edward, Earl of Manchester; William
Lord Viscount Say and Seal, Lord John Cleypole, Master of the Horse;
Philip Lord Viscount Lisle, Charles Lord Viscount Howard, Philip
Lord Wharton, Thomas Lord Fauconbridge, Lord John Disbrowe and
Lord Edward Mountague, Generals at Sea; George Lord Eure, the
Lord Whitelock, Sir Gilbert Pickering, Col. William Sydenham, Sir
Charles Wolseley, M. G. Philip Skippon, Lord Strickland, Col. Philip
Jones, Sir William Strickland, Francis Rous, Esq., John Fiennes, Esq.,
Sir Francis Russel, Sir Thomas Honywood, Sir Arthur Hesilrigg, Sir
John Hobart, Sir Richard Onslow, Sir Gilbert Gerard, Sir William
Roberts, John Glyn and Oliver St. John, Lord Chief Justices; William
Pierrepoint, Esq., John Jones, Esq., John Crew, Esq., Alexander Pop-
ham, Esq., Sir Christopher Pack, Sir Robert Tichborne, Edward
Whalley, Esq., Sir John Barkstead, Knight, Lieutenant of the Tower;
Sir Thomas Pride, Sir George Fleetwood, Richard Ingoldsby, Esq., Sir
John Hewson, James Berry, Esq., William Gosse, Esq., Thoma
Cooper, Esq., Edmond Thomas, Esq., George Monck, Commander-in-
Chief of His Highness' Forces in Scotland; David, Earle of Castils; Sir

be correct. It shows them to have been on the whole a respectable though not very aristocratic body, answering very much to the Protector's description. " I named the House," said Cromwell, " of men who shall meet you wherever you go, and shake hands with you, and tell you it is not titles, nor lands, nor parties that they value, but a Christian and an English interest."[1] But although the Lords were ready and willing to shake hands with the Commons, at least over matters of business, many of the latter would have nothing to do with the Lords, and would neither consent to meet them nor to shake hands with them when they did. The " Other House," was attacked from within and from without. The peers nominated to it refused to sit, not that they objected to a House of Lords, but they objected to the nominations, and to the company with whom they were to be associated. Some of the members of the Lower House, thinking their importance and their usefulness affected, refused to sit in the Lords, and became Opposition members of the Commons, and the members whose temporary seclusion from the House of Commons had soured them against the Government, took an early opportunity of attacking the other House. Of these Sir Anthony Ashley Cooper (afterwards Lord Shaftesbury), was perhaps the most demonstrative, certainly the most effective, and yet even he in the great speech which was published after the Restoration, and made a great effect at the time, did not impeach the policy or the necessity of a Second Chamber ; he even approved and adopted the scheme, but he directed his whole energy to attacking the individuals of whom it was com-

William Lockhart, Sir Archibald Johnson, of Warriston, William Steel, Lord Chancellor of Ireland ; The Lord Broghill, Sir Matthew Tomlinson. In number sixty. The reader is to excuse this list, if the names be not set down in their due order, because the copy came to my hand as here you see it.—*Mercurius Politicus* No. 394, pages 165-167.

[1] Carlyle, Speech XVIII.

posed. " I honour the old Lords," said he, referring to the
Lords of the Long Parliament, "and wish they were
restored,"[1] and then taking as his text the sin of Jeroboam,
who made priests of the lowest of the people, he attacked
the Lords nominatim by denouncing Fiennes, the Lord
Keeper, as a condemned coward[2], some unknown Lord as
having cheated his father ; Lord Broghill, afterwards Earl
of Orrery, as having been a cavalier, a Presbyterian, an
Independent, for a republic, for a protectorate, all in turns ;
Colonel Pride as having been a brewer ; Colonel Hewson
as having been a shoemaker, and others as having
no lands in the country but what had been obtained
as the ' price of blood. Notwithstanding this furious
invective, he and all his party agreed to act with
the Lords till the end of the Parliament. And the
same course was pursued by him and his friends with
regard to the House of Lords summoned by Richard
during his short Protectorate. When, therefore, the two
Houses met together on 20th January, 1658, the torrent
broke forth. On the 23rd January, the Lords, acting on
the melancholy precedent of many years, sent a respectful
message to the Commons by Justice Windham and Baron
Hill, who, as in former times, sat in the House of Lords as
assistants to the peers,[3] to invite them to join in an address
to the Protector to appoint a day of public humiliation.
Thereupon a debate arose in the Commons as to the form
of their reply, and it waxed hotter and hotter till the 25th,
when Cromwell himself, coming down, as he describes it,
from his watch tower[4] to advise with the Parliament,
pointed out the imminent dangers at home and abroad, the
enemy threatening war, the Army and the Civil Service

---

[1] Shaftesbury Papers, page 193.

[2] He had been sentenced to death for giving up Bristol to the King
but the Earl of Essex had him pardoned, and both Fairfax and Crom
well thought well of him.

[3] *Mercurius Politicus*, No. 399.

[4] Carlyle, Speech XVII.

unpaid, Ireland unsettled, Scotland in great suffering, England impatient for reforms, and implored of the Houses, by every sentiment of patriotism, to postpone their quarrels and proceed to business. But still in the Commons the same useless debate continued. Another respectful message from the Lords, brought by Justices Windham and Newdigate,[1] met with the same reception, and on the 4th February, this second Parliament also was dissolved. Before another Parliament could be elected, Oliver was dead, and Richard called his first and only Parliament in 1658. But here the same troubles broke out, and again were violent attacks made on the personality of his House of Lords till that Parliament also was dissolved. Then, again, after an interval of chaos, tempered only with a temporary re-instatement of the survivors of the Long Parliament, and with the Convention which effected the restoration of Charles II., we reverted to our old system of King, Lords, and Commons, with the result that the Lords henceforward assumed a greater power in the State and took a more active and direct part in public affairs, than had ever hitherto been known. During the whole of the Interregnum, therefore, owing to the want of patriotism and the impracticability of the Commons, power and authority were necessarily vested in Cromwell and his Council of State, although they both openly endeavoured to make Parliament responsible, as indeed they were, for much of the miscarriage of government business.

It may be urged with much show of reason that this experiment of governing with one Chamber alone was not tried under very favourable auspices. The Long Parliament had been forcibly shorn of many and influential members, and the residue were by no means unanimous as to the abolition of the other House. This Parliament had on several occasions expressed their loyalty to the House of Lords, and, although many of the Peers had joined the

---

[1] *Mercurius Politicus*, No. 401.

King at Oxford, yet there were always sufficient left to make a House at Westminster, and to compose what is even now an average attendance. On the 9th January, 1648-9, a division being taken as to whether the Commons should receive a message from the House of Lords, the ayes were 31 and the noes were 18, Cromwell being one of the tellers for the majority. On the 18th January a motion being put that the assent of the Lords be requested to the resolution that sovereignty resides in the Commons, 18 voted in the affirmative and 25 in the negative, Cromwell again being in favour of the resolution ; and when on the 6th February a test vote was taken on the question that the advice of the House of Lords be taken on the exercise of legislative powers, 29 members voted aye against 44 who voted no, and thus settled the question of the double Chamber. How Cromwell voted on this last occasion I know not, but I conclude from his former votes that he again voted in the minority. This number, therefore, fairly represents the divided opinion of the remnant of the Long Parliament on this very disputed question. But the Lords had refused to sanction the trial of the King, and thereupon the vote was passed that whatever is enacted for law by the Commons in Parliament hath the force of a law, though consent of King and Peers be not had thereto. This was followed by an express vote, in direct corollary to the former, that the House of Peers in Parliament is useless and dangerous, and ought to be abolished. And this again was incorporated into an Act abolishing the House of Lords, but declaring that peers should not be excluded from the Council of the Nation,[1] but have power to sit and vote in Parliament if duly elected. That course once adopted there was no harking back, and the Commonwealth was for a time adminis-tered as if the abolition of the House of Lords had been one of the main objects of the Rebellion,

---

Statutes 1648, c. 17 (19th March, 1648-9).

instead of being, as it actually was, merely an unexpected incident of the social and political warfare. It will thus be seen that the vote abolishing the House of Lords, and upon which much stress is now laid by that slowly increasing party that clamours for government by a single house of representation, was not the deliberate vote of the Commons after debate on the policy or expediency of the existence of a House of Lords. The general principle was never raised or debated, much less was there any debate as to the expediency of a second Chamber of some sort. The vote was passed in the lower House at a time of great excitement, and in order solely to remove what appeared to be an obstacle to the attainment of their wishes by the majority of Independents, who were then *de facto* the ruling party in the State. The fact, however, remains that no House of Lords as we understand the term, with hereditary Peers, and Bishops with seats as of right, did in fact exist, from 1648 to 1660, although its functions were, in a great measure, carried out by the omnipresent Council of State. Making, therefore, every allowance for the peculiar circumstances in which the Commonwealth was placed, recognising the fact that during the whole of this time there existed not only in the minds of the great leaders but of many others of the Commonwealth a feeling that no Government could be stable which had not something of a monarchical element about it, and granting that the several Parliaments were wanting in a true spirit of patriotism and contained disturbing elements which must be fairly taken into account, this first great experiment seems to me to have established two important political facts. First, that the government of Great Britain can be completely carried on, and its home and foreign interests duly safeguarded, without a House of Lords in the sense of an hereditary Chamber, and, secondly, that no government would seem to be possible in England

without the co-operation and influence of a second
Chamber, selected either by Parliament or by the supreme
authority, and not liable to the pressure or distraction
of recurrent and fluctuating popular elections. This
element was, during the Commonwealth, supplied by the
Council of State, without whose incessant labour and
moderating if not controlling influence, our country would
long before the death of Cromwell have been again
delivered up to anarchy and civil war, and have
become the prey of the expectant and ambitious foreigner.
A moderating or compensating balance in public affairs
seems to be indigenous to the views and habits of our
people. From the earliest period on record, even when the
Parliament sat in one house with the Bishops at one end
and the Barons at the other, this double representation
has been an essential portion of the constitution of our
Parliament. In all our judicial proceedings we commit
the decision of the law to the calm and indifferent mind of
the Judge, while the finding of the fact is left to the more
popular and impressionable jury. And while broad questions of fact are disposed of by Courts of Common Law,
the nicer questions of conflicting duties and obligations are
subject to the controlling influence of the Courts of Equity.
All our municipal institutions, even those recently modelled
for the various counties of Great Britain, involve the
principle of elective councillors and aldermen. And our
ecclesiastical parliament, though not a very powerful or
important factor in our constitution, bears the double
character of an Upper and a Lower House of Convocation.
Following in our footsteps, the American Commonwealth
instituted a Senate and a Chamber of Deputies, and
although in the French Republic of 1790 Government by
one Chamber was proclaimed, yet the period of that
Government was notorious for the most fearful access
of fury, savagery, and brutality that has ever disgraced
the annals of Europe. And it is now more than ever

necessary to adhere to our composite form of Government when the Lower House is becoming day by day more and more unskilled and democratic in its elements, and when its electors are now in overwhelming numerical force drawn from the least intellectual strata of the community, whose individual judgment on questions of foreign policy, fiscal arrangements, international obligations, peace or war, is utterly unreasoning, fickle, and untrustworthy, however much it may be rightly and usefully consulted on many of those social questions in which working-class electors are, of all the community, perhaps most deeply interested.

Of the various domestic Statutes passed during the early period of the Commonwealth, two have given rise to considerable discussion and misconception, viz., those against duelling and immorality. To kill another in a duel was always murder by the Common Law of England, but it was a law that had been uniformily disregarded, and public sentiment had, until the rise of Puritanism, been rather favourable than otherwise to this private wager of battle. The actual Statute against duelling was, however, the direct outcome of a fatal encounter at Southwark, in the spring of 1652, between Lord Chandois and Mr. Crompton, in which the former had killed Mr. Crompton; and in which the noble lord had, by pleading his clergy, it being his first offence, escaped without punishment. Public feeling at this time ran strongly against this form of redressing social grievances, and accordingly Parliament, on the 13th May, 1652, within a few weeks of this duel, read a second time and committed a Bill against challenges and duels and provocations thereto. In the meantime, warrants were issued, and Lord Chandois and his second, Lord Arundel, were arrested and sent for trial at the Summer Assizes for the county of Surrey. And now follows, according to the reports, a state of things for which I am not able to account, as, unless for some explanation which is wanting, it would appear that, contrary to all precedent and to the well-recognised law of England, which the judges at this period were administering with scrupulous exactitude, the culprit would appear to have been tried twice for the same offence. The *Faithful Scout* of the 7th August, 1652, has the following paragraph : "The Lord Chandois is quitted at Kingston-on-Thames," (which, as the duel was fought in Surrey, would have been the proper assize town for this trial,) " by the jury, notwithstanding the Judge seemed very much his adversary ; but at last (for all the threatening of the Bench) the country found it no more than manslaughter, and there is no doubt but upon his Lordship's appearance he shall have his book by course of law," meaning that he could claim benefit of clergy and thus be released. Here the matter would have terminated according to our present conception of the law, but Lord Chandois was again imperilled for the crime, being tried a second time for the murder before the Lord Chief Justice and a jury in the Upper Bench. Whitelock, under date of 17th May, 1653, says, " Lord Chandois and Count Arundel were tried in the Upper Bench and found guilty of manslaughter by the jury."[1] And the *Perfect Diurnal* for 23rd May, 1653, is to the same effect: "The Lord Shandois and Count Arundel receiving their tryal in the Upper Bench Court, Westminster, about the killing of Mr. Henry Compton in a duel fought in Surrey about a year since, they were both by the jury found guilty of manslaughter." I cannot explain the second trial of Lord Chandois except upon the hypothesis that for some reason the first trial may have been set aside. The Bill, read twice and sent to a committee, in 1652, had not been further prosecuted, but the failure of justice in the case of Lord Chandois brought the subject of duelling again before Parliament. And in order authoritatively to declare the law and to lead public feeling against the practice of

---

[1] Vol. IV., p. 11.

avenging private injuries, whether real or supposed by a private inquisition of blood, the Protector, by one of his earliest ordinances, bearing date the 29th June, 1654, declared that if any person from and after the 1st July, 1654, should send or accept a challenge, or should receive a challenge and not disclose it within twenty-four hours, such person should be committed to prison without bail for six calendar months, and before his release enter into recognizances with two sureties to keep the peace for twelve calendar months. Any person fighting a duel from which death should ensue was declared guilty of wilful murder, and to suffer death accordingly. If death did not ensue, then both principals and seconds were to be banished the realm for life. And for preventing the occasions of duels, Justices of the Peace were empowered to fine persons giving provocation, and to require due reparation to be made to the offended party, "upon consideration had both to the quality of the person injured and of the offence committed." This enactment seems to have been in accord with popular feeling, for there is very little account of duels after this date, and except that in May, 1651, a soldier was shot under martial law for fighting a duel, I find no record of any capital conviction for that offence. The following are all the records of duelling that I have met with :

On 8th July, 1654, a written apology was published in the "Proceedings of Affairs, &c., No. 254," from John Willoughby, of Gumdon, Northampton, Esquire, stating that he had libelled Sir William Farmer, Bart., of Northampton, and had sent him a challenge, and acknowledging himself sorry for his offence, committed against the peace of the nation and against Sir W. Farmer. His apology is dated "Tower of London," and his signature attested by Colonel Barkstead, the Lieutenant of the Tower.

On the 28th March, 1656, a true bill was found by the Middlesex Grand Jury against one Chamberlain for a d   l.

He is described as being " at large,"[1] and there is no subsequent record of his trial.

On the 12th April, 1656, Sir John Chichester and Mr.
Seymer were arrested on information that they were about
to fight a duel,[2] and on 29th August of the same year a
Coroner's jury found one Giles Rawlings guilty of murder
for killing William Ashburnham in a duel,[3] but there is no
record of any further proceedings. The last of these
occurrences that I find referred to during this period is on
the 17th July, 1658, when the Middlesex magistrates
bound over the Earl of Chesterfield and William Whalley
on suspicion that they were about to fight a duel.[4]

This Act, amongst others of an excellent type, was
suppressed at the Restoration, and duelling again became
the fashion for many years, but what repressive legislation
failed to effect ridicule appears to have accomplished. For
the incidents of the trial of Lord Cardigan by the House of
Lords for fighting a duel with Captain Tucker in September,
1840, where their lordships failed to identify the
Captain Tucker of the indictment with the Captain
Tucker of whom the witnesses spoke, seem to have
thrown so much ridicule on the practice of duelling, that it
speedily ceased to be the fashion, and now appears to have
entirely died out.

Acts against immorality were by no means an exclusive
feature of the Commonwealth. There had been statutes
addressed to the punishment of these offences almost as
far back as we have any record of criminal law in this
country. Originally of purely spiritual cognizance, they
speedily became subject to the operation of the common
law, which was intermittently applied to them from time
to time. By a law of Canute, a woman was liable to lose

---

[1] Middlesex Records, Vol. II., p. 249.
[2] *Public Intelligencer*, No. 28.
[3] Middlesex Records, Vol. II., p. 254.
[4] Middlesex Records, Vol. III., p. 272.

her nose and her ears for this offence, and among barbarous nations, such as the North American Indians, mutilation is even at the present day the penalty commonly inflicted for a breach of marital duty. Under the Tudors the High Commission Court took cognizance of this class of offence, and inflicted fine and imprisonment, but entertained no case not within ten years of the trial.[1] Latterly, however, these laws had fallen into desuetude except for the punishment of women who had illegitimate children whose fathers were either unknown, or could not, for other reasons, be made responsible to the parish for their support. In Scotland adultery had always been a crime. In 1563 much scandal arose through one Paul Meffane, a pupil of Miles Coverdale, being so convicted[2]; and in the following year Mary Queen of Scots passed an Act inflicting pecuniary penalties on persons convicted of this offence. " A very pretty way," as Randolph says in a letter to Cecil, " to get money to the Queen's coffers.[3] On the advent of the Scotch Puritans to power the laws against immorality, which had for some years lain dormant, were again revived; and so ferocious were the people in the prosecution of their neighbours that the Commonwealth found it necessary to send specially commissioned judges from England to see that some approach to justice was done to the general population, it being officially reported to the Council of State that hundreds of people of the poorer classes were imprisoned or held to bail on charges of immorality committed some thirty or forty years before, since when they had married and borne children, and their early errors had been almost forgotten. All these persons the Commonwealth Commissioners held to bail and then discharged, together with some sixty old men and women accused of witchcraft, but with regard to whom the Commissioners could find nothing

---

[1] Stephen's History of the Criminal Law, Vol. II., p. 422.
[2] State Papers, Scotch, Elizabeth, 22nd January, 1563.
[3] State Papers, Scotch, Elizabeth, 15th December, 1564.

but the malice of their neighbours.[1] In England the laws
against immorality, though milder in effect, had been almost
forgotten. In the pressure of foreign and domestic trouble
they had been laid upon the shelf, and the dust of some
half a century had settled upon them. But when the
strong-minded Independents took them down it was not to
brush away the cobwebs of intolerance, but to forge anew
an engine of punishment framed on the doctrine of the old
dispensation, rather than on that of the new, and to give
a greater prominence to faults than to crimes in pursuance
of that almost immutable order of nature which decrees
that when power is given to the masses they shall ever be
governed by sentiment rather than by reason, and shall
find in the breaches of the moral law the highest crimes
against the peace of a nation.

An Act making adultery a capital offence without benefit
of clergy, and making other acts of immorality punishable
with three months' imprisonment, was passed on the
10th May, 1650.[2] It was provided, however, that the
Act should not extend to women whose husbands should
be remaining continually three years beyond sea, or reported
dead, nor to persons who were not indicted within
twelve months after the offence committed. It further
provided, and in this it was in advance of other
statutes of the period, that persons indicted might produce
witnesses at the trial, and the judges might examine those
witnesses on oath, and that the confession of one of the
parties should not be taken in evidence against the other,
nor should a husband be permitted to give evidence against
his wife or *vice versa*.[3] The provisions of the Act were,

---

[1] *Proceedings in Parliament*, 27th September, 1652.

[2] Statute, 1650, c. 10.

[3] This Act, together with one for the better observance of the Lord's
Day, was printed by order of Parliament at the charge of the State
and sent to every parish in England.—State Papers, 16th May, 1650.

It is very commonly stated that acts of immorality were punished
by imprisonment for the first offence and death for the second. No

however, too advanced for the public sentiment of that age,
which, then as now, rebelled against laws making crimes of
offences against morality, and Henry Martin (the regicide)
during the debate on the Bill used the argument, now
recognised as sound in reference to legislation of this
character, that the severity of the punishment, being death,
would probably increase the amount of the offence, as
persons would necessarily be far more careful and circum-
spect, and being undetected would become the more
emboldened.   And Henry Martin appears to have
had ground for his belief, for notwithstanding the
vigour of the preachers and the writers of that period,
I find few instances of persons being punished under
that statute, and it appears as if the juries by whom
these offences were tried took the only constitutional
means at their disposal of expressing their disapproval
of the law by, in all but very rare cases, refusing
to convict the accused.   The first in order of date
with which I am acquainted is a report from
the West, where it appears that a Court of Quarter
Sessions, under the chairmanship of Colonel Desborough,
Cromwell's brother-in-law, convicted a woman at Taunton
on the 19th July, 1650, of adultery *with a priest*,[1] and one
cannot avoid seeing that with the national hatred of priests
and seminaries, a woman·under suspicion of crime with
such a paramour would have but scant measure of justice.
On 7th November, 1651, a man was condemned at Chester
Assizes for adultery with a married woman,[2] having been
tried probably by Lord President Bradshaw, who, as
Chief Justice and Judge of Assize of Chester, would
have the cognizance of these cases.   These two cases,

such provision is to be found in the Act, which limits the punishment
to three months' imprisonment, with sureties for good behaviour for
twelve calendar months, but has no reference to repeated offences of
this nature.

[1] Whitelock, Vol. III., p. 220.

[2] *Proceedings in Parliament*, 13th November, 1651.

together with one at Exeter, are the only cases in which, as far as I can ascertain, there was in England a conviction for this offence followed by the extreme penalty of the law. I have carefully examined the newspapers for this period, and though there are numerous accounts of trials of importance, both in London and in the provinces, the above cases are all that I can find recorded as capital convictions under this law. With a view to arriving at some conclusion as to the extent to which this statute was enforced, and the feeling of the country upon the subject, I have taken two distinct and separate jurisdictions, first the Western Counties: Hants, Dorset, Devon, Somerset, Wilts, and Cornwall, a part of the country where the people have, or had, the reputation of a somewhat looser morality than in the Midlands or the North, and secondly the county of Middlesex, which may be said to have been under the direct influence of the Parliament, and of the preachers who made and expounded the law against sin and immorality. I will first take the records of the Western Circuit, which, however, for this period, consist solely of the recognizances of defendants and witnesses, sometimes taken in Court before the judge, and sometimes taken before a Justice of the Peace and continued by the Judge, and they date, so far as they are available, from February, 1653, to the summer, 1660.[1] There is also an order book containing various orders made from time to time by the judges in relation to various indictable offences, criminal and quasi-criminal, the latter being such as non-repair of bridges, nuisances, etc. The following is the result of the investigation: There were three charges only of the capital offence, viz., Nicholas Tyrett, and Joan, the wife of Henry Marks, in 1654; John Grouch in 1655; and John Ford and Joan, wife of Anthony Jollen in Summer, 1660, after the Restoration.

---

[1] The Gaol Books containing the names of prisoners, with their indictments and sentences, appear to have been destroyed.

The result of these three cases I have been unable to ascertain.

At the Lent Assizes, 1653, Edward Jenkins, gentleman, was bound over, himself in £40 and two sureties of £20 each, to appear at the next Assizes for marrying Maude, his brother's wife, and the said Maude had to find two sureties of £20 each for her appearance at the same time and place.

In the summer of 1654 Philip Blake, of Niton, in the Isle of Wight, was bound over by the judge, himself in £100 and two sureties in £50 each, *to appear at the next Assizes, and in the meantime to get himself married according to the new Act.*

There were twelve cases of the minor charge of incontinence, of these seven were women and five were men. In the result one woman was acquitted, in two cases there was no prosecutor ; in one case the Grand Jury found no true bill, but indorsed upon the indictment, " hee was an idle fellow." One woman was convicted and bound over, herself in £40 and two sureties in £20 each, *to be of the good behaviour for one year.* Three women and one man were bound over from time to time and then discharged, and of the remaining three cases there is no further record. The recognizances of the accused and of the witnesses were taken in a form which enables one to distinguish this class of case from the robberies, assaults, homicides, and other offences with which the books are filled. I give a few instances of the language in which they were bound over either to appear and take their trials or to appear and give evidence at the Assizes.

Nicholas Tyrett . . . to appear at the next to answer for being accused to live incontinently with Johan, wife of Henry Marks, and in the meantime to be of good behaviour. In the case of John Ford de Studland, the recognizance was drawn by the clerk in a style combining the Commonwealth and Monarchical form, and ran thus : *To appear at next, etc., and interim de bono gestu* [here his Latin apparently broke down, and he added] *and not to keep company with Johan, wife of Anthony Jollen.* In the other cases the recognizances ran in the following form: *To appear at the next, etc., and in the meantime to be of the good behaviour, for incontinence with, etc.* Mr. Hamilton, however, the Clerk of the Peace for the County of Devon, has kindly sent me the following extract from the Minutes of Quarter Sessions for the County of Devon, under date 4th April, 1654: "Whereas Susan Bounty, being lately delivered of a child and executed at the last Assizes for adultery, whose husband, as this Court is informed, lives in the parish of Biddeford, it is therefore ordered that the said child shall be sent unto Richard Bounty, the father, in Biddeford aforesaid, and by him to be provided for according to the law, and to be conveyed thither from tything to tything," which seems under the circumstances to be rather hard upon the said Richard.

The records of the County of Middlesex are, however, far more precise and instructive, giving not only the indictments, but in nearly every case the results of the trials. The diligence of Mr. Cordy Jeaffreson and the public spirit of the Lord Lieutenant and the Magistrates have resulted in a careful arrangement and index of the indictments and other criminal records of the County, thus enabling us to have a very interesting and accurate view of the procedure of the time. From an examination of these records I find that in London and the County of Middlesex, during the whole period from 1650 to 1660, one person only, *Ursula Powell*, was convicted of this crime and sentenced to death. This was on the 30th August, 1652. She was sentenced to be hanged, as appears from the letter S *(suspendatur)* against her conviction, but she was respited on the ground of pregnancy, and her ultimate fate is left in mystery. Mr. Jeaffreson concludes from the S that the woman was executed, but inasmuch as this letter only denotes the sentence, and

is consistent with the prisoner having been permanently
respited, as I do not find any star denoting that she was
left for execution, and as no reference is made in any of the
London newspapers to any woman having been executed
for such crime, a fact which would certainly have been
noted had it taken place, I come to the conclusion that
the capital sentence was never carried into effect. In
every other case in the county of Middlesex of which there
is any record the juries acquitted the prisoners. Of these
no less than eighteen were tried between April, 1651, and
December, 1657, and in nearly all the evidence of guilt was
conclusive. In the offences not made capital by the Act
the juries took the same course. Whatever may have been
the view taken by the public as to the policy of this legislation it must have been felt by all and by none less than
by the Parliament and the Council of State, that the
persistent and resolute setting at naught of the laws of the
realm by the juries who duty it was to enforce them, was
little less than a gross public scandal, and accordingly a
Committee was appointed in October, 1656, to consolidate
and revise the Acts against these offences with such
alteration as might be necessary. But public sentiment is
hardly affected by the consolidation or revision of unpopular
laws. Nothing came of the Committee. Trials under the
Act where it was impossible to obtain a conviction became
yearly more rare, and in 1657 died out altogether in the
metropolitan county.

There was one class of the community, however, on
whom the provisions of the Act were pressed with stern
severity. Those were the soldiers, and although I do not
find that any soldier suffered death for any offence of this
character, yet the punishments, especially in Scotland,
where the lassies appear to have given the Commanders
incessant trouble, were frequent and severe. One instance
out of many reported in the papers will suffice. On the
13th December, 1651, one Nathaniel Nash, a soldier, being

found drunk in the company of one Jennet Ferris, at Leith, they were both tried by court-martial, with the result that the said Nash was sentenced " to be duckt twice at a high tide, and then whipt at cart's tail and receive 39 stripes on the naked back from the main guard at Leith to Edin-burgh port. The woman to be whipt in like manner, to receive 39 stripes on the naked back, be twice duckt and then both turned forth of the town at several ports."[1]

This sentence was carried out, as were many others of a similar character, and there is no reason to doubt that whatever may have been the view of the civilians, the Army heartily concurred in these acts of discipline. From the fall of the Commonwealth to the present day there has been no serious attempt to revive this class of legislation. A proposal to do so was faintly suggested at the Restoration, and a similarly fruitless effort was made in 1857, when the Divorce Act was passing through Parlia-ment, and it was proposed that the guilty parties should be subject to fine and imprisonment. The only portion of the Queen's Dominions where this offence is now treated as a crime is the Indian Empire, where, in order to suppress the cruelties exercised by natives over women guilty of infidelity by providing an efficient substitute, it has been enacted, and the law applies alike equally to all subjects of the Queen in that country, that when a wife has been found guilty of adultery she may, on the prosecution of her husband, but of him only, be sentenced, at the discretion of the Judge, to imprisonment for a period not exceeding five years.[2] I understand, however, from persons conversant with the administration of the law in that Empire, that the experi-ment has been absolutely without effect, for there is hardly one recorded case where a native has taken advantage of the Act to inflict a punishment on his offending wife.

---

[1] *Proceedings in Parliament*, 24th December, 1651.
[2] Stephen's History of the Criminal Law, Vol. III., p. 318.

Before departing altogether from this subject, it is right
here to record the fact that the Commonwealth also
interfered in a manner hitherto unknown for the protection
of women from those forcible abductions and marriages
which were but too common under the former and later
reigns of the Stuarts. Fraudulent marriages, induced by
needy men or intriguing women, formed the common staple
of the plays and interludes which the Puritans so heartily
condemned. In these comedies, while the unhappy father
or deluded guardian was not infrequently the subject of
mirth or of contempt, the lucky intriguer was made
the hero of the play. From this species of offence,
carried from the play-house into private life, the
middle class peculiarly suffered, and while the wealthy
merchant or prosperous tradesman had to endure as best he
might the entrapping of his daughter or the abduction
of his ward, the gay cavalier or dashing spark who carried
her off was the lion of the hour. Of this phase of society
the Puritan party had long and loudly proclaimed their
horror and detestation, and the Commonwealth was not
long installed before an occasion arose which enabled them
to give practical effect to their expressed opinions. The
case was that of Mistress Jane Puckeringe or Pickering, for
the name is spelt indifferently either way. This young
lady, who was the only daughter and heiress of Sir Thomas
Pickering, knight and baronet, deceased, while walking in
Greenwich Park with her maids in October of 1649, was
seized by one Joseph Walsh and his companions, who
forcibly carried her on board a ship in the Thames
and thence transported her to Flanders. After which
Walsh asserted a marriage to have taken place between them and was prepared to claim his pecuniary
rights as her husband. The Council of State, hearing
of this "foul fact committed at Greenwich," at once
issued their warrant to Sir Thomas Walsingham and
others to take all means for recovering the young lady

and punishing the offenders.[1] They also, with the prompt-
ness habitual to the party, sent one Mrs. Magdalen Smith,
with a pass for Flanders and with recommendations to the
agent of the Parliament, to recover the young lady. Mr.
Frost, the Clerk of the Council, was ordered to ask for letters
from the Spanish Ambassador, and for his assistance, and
also for the surrender of all persons who had been parties to
the abduction. In November Colonel Popham, at the
Admiralty, was instructed as follows by the Council of
State : " You are to order a ship of considerable force (as
there is a party there that will endeavour to engage the
pickeroons thereabouts to rescue her) to go to Nieuport in
Flanders and there receive Mrs. Pickering and carefully
bring her over to England, and the captain must give her
and her company the best accommodation the ship will
afford."[2] The gentleman, however, not being willing to
give up his prize, the Council of State sent to their agent,
Peter Thelwell, at Brussels, to press for the delivery of
Mrs. Pickering, that she might be sent to England.
Having done which, they turned their attention to more
pressing matters, and apparently forgot all about her. On
the 21st March, 1649-50, however, her friends again brought
her case before the Council of State, who ordered the Clerk of
the Council to look up the papers and to draft a letter to
the Archduke on her behalf. In the meantime, Mr. Thelwell, thinking that a little persuasion from Prince Charles
would have more effect upon the Cavaliers than any
number of letters from the Commonwealth, had endeavoured to get hold of the lady through the Prince, an
attempt which brought upon his head a dispatch[3] from the
Council of State, who required to be informed whether he
had made any and what application on her behalf to the
King of Scots, and if so, why, and by whom he was

[1] State Papers, October, 1649.
[2] State Papers, 5th November, 1649.
[3] State Papers, 10th December, 1649.

authorized.[1] Whether through the mediation of the
Prince, or the threats of the Parliament, the lady was at last
given up, and a man-of-war sent over in June, 1650, took
the lady on board and brought her to England. At
the same time, Walsh and the others concerned in the plot
were surrendered to the English authorities. There was no
difficulty in dealing with the abduction, but the Ecclesiastical
Courts being for the moment suppressed there was no mode
of getting rid of the lady's marriage, which being valid in
form according to the law would have existed as a valid,
marriage until set aside by some competent tribunal. An
Act was accordingly passed[2] in January, 1650-51, which
after reciting the above facts, and that Parliament desired
the whole matter to be examined and justice done, enacted
that the Lords Commissioners of the Great Seal should
appoint delegates with power to inquire into and to annul
the marriage after taking proof, and further that any other
woman making a similar complaint might apply to the
Lords Commissioners, who should have power to grant
commissions to delegates to inquire and make such decree
as justice might require without prejudice to any criminal
proceedings that might be taken against any persons
concerned. On the 5th March, 1650-1, the delegates,
consisting of Chief Justice Rolle, Justice Ask, and other
Judges and Serjeants-at-Law, met at Serjeant's Inn and
admitted the libel[3] which alleged that the lady was
carried away by force and by threats of violence to her
and her maids while walking in Greenwich Park, that
she was forced on to a horse, and then put on board a
hoy and taken to Dunkirk. On the 7th March the case
was heard,[4] and it is to be presumed that she had judgment in her favour, and her marriage set aside, for we

[1] State Papers, 18th May, 1650.
[2] Statute 1651, c. 43.
[3] *Perfect Account, &c.* : 12th March, 1650.
[4] Whitelock, Vol. III., p. 293.

learn from Lord Commissioner Whitelock that on the 14th
July, 1651, an indictment of felony was found against
Walsh and his companions for forcibly carrying Mistress
Jane Pickering to Erith, and compelling her, contrary to
her will, to say words importing a marriage.[1] In April,
1654, the Council of State ordered the Commissioners of
the Great Seal to inquire into an alleged contract of
marriage between William Blunt, a recusant Papist, and
Lady Ann Blunt, not yet seventeen, living with her father,
Mountjoy, Earl of Newport. The order appears to have
issued on the complaint of the Lady Ann, who states to
the Council that one William Blount, a Papist, who has
been in arms against the Commonwealth, publishes that he
is contracted to her, and that he intends to marry her
whether she will or no, and begs for a Commission, as these
scandals prejudice her and trouble her father.[2] Mr. Blunt
was accordingly examined by the Council, and the lady's
scruples set at rest. This young lady seems, however, to have
had other reasons for wishing to get rid of Mr. Blunt, for
I find that on the 17th July of the following year, 1655, the
Court of Quarter Sessions for the County of Middlesex,[3] on
the application of the said Earl of Newport, set aside as
fraudulently contracted, a marriage between Lady Ann
Blunt, aged 18, daughter of the Earl of Newport, and
one Thomas Porter. The order was made upon proof, that
about 9 p.m. on the 24th February last, the said Lady
Ann ran away from her father's house in St. Martin's-in-the-
Fields, with Thomas Porter, gentleman, and, without the
knowledge or assent of her father the Earl, married Mr.
Porter at an Inn at Southwark, called the Katherine

---

[1] Ibid, Vol. III., p. 319. I know nothing more of this young lady, or
whether her fortune was captured by a cavalier or a roundhead.
Pepys, however, frequently mentions a Mistress Pickering, daughter
of a deceased baronet of that name, and describes her as " a very well
bred and comely lady, but very fat."

[2] State Papers, April, 1654, Vol. 69.

[3] Middlesex Records, Vol. III., p. 237.

Wheel, to the intent that a marriage might afterwards
be solemnized at the Church of St. George's, Southwark,
in which parish neither of the parties dwelt.

In the early part of the same year, viz., in January,
1654-5, judgment was given in another similar case which
is thus recorded in *Mercurius Politicus*, No. 241 : " Thursday, 18th January, at Doctors' Commons. The great case
of the pretended marriage between one Chamberlain (a
pretended nobleman's son, though indeed a vintner's son
of very inconsiderable fortune) and one Mrs. Joan Hele (a
rich heiress of great quality in the West), was finally
determined and adjudged and sentence signed by all the
Judges then present, *nem. con.*, impowered by a commission
under the Great Seal of England, directed to the
Judges both of Common and Civil Law and other gentlemen of known ability and integrity, which sentence
declared thê marriage null and void to all intents and
purposes whatsoever. And indeed the Judges gave their
judgment upon very great and mature deliberation, for it
was after (at least) forty hearings and adjournments from
the Rolls to Doctors' Commons and back again, the Master
of the Rolls[1] having (for the most part) had the chair till
he was divested by his attendance at the Parliament."

In October, 1657, the Quarter Sessions proceeded to deal
with one of those marriages which not infrequently occur
between very young gentlemen and the elderly daughters of
their preceptors, and set aside a marriage between Anthony
Lowther, son and heir of Robert Lowther, deceased, and
Bridgett, daughter of James Fleetwood, D.D., on evidence
that Anthony was not of an age to make a valid matrimonial contract.[2] The power thus exercised was vested in
Courts of Quarter Sessions by the Statute of the 24th

---

[1] Lenthall.

[2] Middlesex Records, Vol. III., p. 264. The necessary age for a man
was sixteen years, and for a woman fourteen, and any marriage had
before those respective ages was null and void.

August, 1653, which regulated the form of marriage,
provided for the due registrations of marriages, births, and
burials, and committed to Justices of the Peace at Courts
of General Quarter Sessions the hearing and determining of
all questions relating to the lawfulness of marriages, and
of marriage contracts.

In some respects, however, the attempts at legislative
interference with the rights or wrongs of women were not
so successful. The affectation of wearing patches, which
survived to a comparatively recent date, was adopted by
the ladies of England towards the later years of the Long
Parliament. It was believed to have had its origin in
imitation of a supposed attribute of Venus, whose
beauty was said to have been enhanced by a mole
on one of her cheeks. But although under Queen
Anne, as we learn from the *Spectator*, the Court ladies
demonstrated their Whig or Tory sympathies by patching
either on the right or the left side, the ladies of the
Commonwealth had not arrived at that pitch of political
fervour. Those of the Cavalier and of the Puritan party
patched alike, to the great grief of their brethren in
Parliament. And accordingly on 7th June, 1650,[1] a Bill
was introduced and read a first time to deal with the " vice
of painting,[2] wearing black patches, and immodest dresses
of women," but no one ever moved its second reading,
and paint, patches and low dresses still held the field
when the Stuart was restored to his kingdom. Another
attempt was made in 1656 to deal with indecent fashions,[3]
and to abate the abuse of wearing gold and silver lace, fine
linen and other excess in apparel, but the proposal was
referred to the Grand Committee on Trade, which had far
more weighty business to transact, and was there shelved.

---

[1] Parliamentary History, Vol. III., p. 1347.

[2] Painting, according to Evelyn, did not become fashionable among
respectable women before the spring of 1654. Diary, Vol. I., p. 288.

[3] *Mercurius Politicus*, No. 329.

But although the Commonwealth passed Acts for the constituting of civil marriages, requiring all marriages after a certain date to be celebrated before a Justice of the Peace, and Acts for the protection of women and for the punishment of conjugal offences, no steps whatever seem to have been taken towards formulating a system of divorce, or providing for a dissolution of the marriage tie except by the hands of the executioner. Thus, while on the one hand they treated marriage as a civil contract, on the other hand they gave to it all the inviolability of a sacrament, an inconsistency which is, however, to be found in many other Acts of this period. The Jewish law, to which they much adhered, provided for and regulated divorces. They were recognised by most Protestant communities, and Milton, oppressed by his own domestic difficulties, had written powerfully on the subject, but through all the Minutes of the various Parliaments and Councils of State I find, what I conceive to be somewhat surprising, no trace of any proposal to introduce into England any system of divorce. And, indeed, the prejudice against divorce appears to have been so strong that the laxity of the Jews in this respect was found in 1655 to be one of the strongest arguments against their proposed admission to the rights of citizenship. Nor was any attempt made to confer upon women the capacity of holding and dealing with personal property apart from their husbands which recent statutes have somewhat tardily accorded to them.

Profane cursing and swearing was also dealt with, and a scale of charges for oaths, to be assessed upon various classes of the community, was settled by Parliament. Thus, by the Act of 1650 for the first offence a Duke, Marquis, Earl, Viscount, or Baron forfeited 30s., a Baronet or Knight 20s., an Esquire 10s., a Gentleman 6s. 8d., and all inferior persons 3s. 4d.; double for the second offence, and so on to the ninth, and for the tenth offence to be bound over in sureties to be of good behaviour for the future. A wife or a widow indulging in oaths to pay according to the quality of her husband, and a single woman according to that of her father. The penalties to be recovered by distress, and in default the party to be put in the stocks if over twelve years of age, and to be whipped if under.[1]

Wherever a question of religion arises in England there comes up with it, as a natural pendant, the question of tithes. These two questions seem as inseparable as Damon and Pythias; and I doubt whether, in England at least, either will die so long as the other survives. The actual and precise origin of the compulsory payment of tithes is by no means clear, however much lay or ecclesiastical authors may dogmatize on the subject. Abraham, it is said, paid tithe or tribute to Melchisedec. Just so, argues Selden, and very praiseworthy of him, no doubt, to do so, but there is no more reason why I should, therefore, pay tithes than that I should marry my sister, or imitate any other action of Abraham's. That they are mentioned in Deuteronomy and Leviticus[2] is beyond a doubt, but the institution of tithes for the Levites was founded upon the reason that the Levite had no lot or inheritance in the land, which the other tribes occupied by annexation or conquest, and he was, therefore, entitled, if only in a fair spirit of justice, to some compensation for the material benefits of which he was thus deprived. A case which had been tried in the reign of King James, arising out of the vexed question of tithe on wood, shows the view taken of it at that time. The statement there was that tithe was payable by the Judicial Law of God (whatever that may mean), but that the King had power to appoint what quantity should be paid. That in fact it was not stated what amount or proportion of tithe was paid by Melchisedec or by anyone else, or when or how or under what ordinance,

---

[1] Parliamentary History, Vol. 1II., p. 1351, Statute, 28th June, 1650.
[2] Deuteronomy, c. xiv., v. 22; Leviticus, c. xxvii.

custom, or regulation. That although Edmund, Ethel-
stone, William the Conqueror, and the Council of Magans
provided that tithe should be paid, yet it was not decreed
to whom or when or of what amount. That before the
Council of Lateran everyone might pay his tithes to
whomsoever he pleased, and they were in fact paid to the
monasteries as oblations. And not till Edward I. appointed
a tenth to be paid as tithe was any legislative action
taken in reference to this subject.[1] Whatever may have
been the origin of this payment, and whether or not it can
rightly be regarded as a tax, tithe had long before the time
of the Commonwealth been paid to certain persons, religious
and lay, who claimed it by the highest of all titles, that of
prescriptive right. And it has in truth survived many
furious assaults, both before and since that period, because
the English being a practical people, find it a convenient
mode of providing for the payment of the clergy of the
Established Church. Apart from sectarian prejudice, there
is no difficulty in its collection. It is fairly even in its
assessment. It is not heavy enough to be severely felt, and
although it is weighted with many anomalies, and with
none more than in the claims of lay impropriators, who,
however, exist in other countries, and were in the first
instance created by the assent of the patron, the incumbent,
and the king, and afterwards by the will of the king alone,
the question of its discontinuance is neither more nor less
difficult in principle now than it was at the time of the
Reformation. But it is, and always has been, a source of
irritation and of friction between the Clergy and the Nonconformists, and its enforcement on the one hand, and its
repudiation on the other, frequently assume the aspect of
a case of conscience both to the payer and the receiver.
When, therefore, religious and sectarian differences had
become accentuated during the Civil War, the propriety of
paying tithes naturally became a burning question with

---

[1] Urrey v. Bowyer, Goldsborough's Reports, Part II., p. 24.

which it was necessary at once to deal. There had been,
in and before 1647, refusals to pay tithes on religious and
other grounds, but up to that date any ordinances that had
been made were that the payments should be made subject to
what might hereafter be decreed.[1] When, however, the
Commonwealth was established, and no one had the courage
to propose Selden's solution of obtaining peace and toleration by chaining up the Clergy of all denominations,[2] the
matter became one of practical and necessary politics. I
do not know that anyone would have objected then, nor that
they would object now, to the abolition of tithe *per se*,
provided its object could be attained by other means.
Certainly the landowner would not object that his acres
should be freed from a perpetual tax, the clergyman or the
lay-impropriator would care little whence his income proceeded provided it came in due course. And the Non-
conformist, whose objection lay to the application of the
money to religious purposes of which he disapproved,
would have his scruples removed by the cesser of
tithe once and for ever. The cry of the present day
that the landowner should still be mulcted of his tithe,
but that it should be applied to other purposes than
that of the Church, for whose support it is collected under statutory sanction, thus wounding at the
same time with a two-edged sword the landowner and the
Church, had not been raised, and formed no subject of
discussion during the period now under consideration.
And, indeed, the judgment of the Commonwealth undoubtedly was that in order to secure a worthy, educated,
and efficient ministry, means must be found for their payment other than the scanty stipend that might be obtained
from various congregations. The question was not, Are
our clergy to be paid? but, How are they to be paid? The

[1] See, for instance, Bill committed in 1647 for payment of tithes to
the Ministers in the City.—Whitelock, Vol. III., p. 270.
[2] Table Talk, "Clergy."

object, independently of this question, was quite as much to relieve the pockets of the landowners as the scruples of the religionists. Can we do away with tithes ? said they, and if so, how are we to make a provision for our ministers ? Why should landowners alone be called upon to support the clergy ? and how if we relieve them can we make all classes of the community equally bear the burthen ? This was the subject of one of the first Parliamentary Debates in 1649,[1] when proposals were made to abolish tithes and to pay the ministry by a general assessment and by the sale of lands held by various ecclesiastical bodies. The subject was started by the Council of State, who early in 1649[2] recommended Parliament to consider in the next session the issue of a Commission for valuing tithes throughout England, in order to take them away and settle in their room a competent means for preachers of the Gospel. The debates, however, upon this proposition, like many others in the Long Parliament, came to nothing beyond indicating the feeling of people on the subject. In 1653, the business of tithes was again under consideration by the Convention or Barebones Parliament, who debated the subject on the 13th, 14th, 16th, and 18th June. The difficulty was, as stated by Whitelock,[3] who took much interest in the subject, to find an expedient for satisfying impropriators and at the same time for providing some maintenance for the clergy. A motion that tithes should continue till the following November only was negatived, and it was then debated whether the property of tithe was in the nation or in particular persons. And as this was one of those difficulties which had exercised the minds of men for many generations, and was in effect an academical question, that might have been debated for many days without affecting anyone's views, the whole matter was referred to

---

[1] Whitelock, Vol. III., p. 6.
[2] State Papers, 1649.
[3] Vol. IV., pp. 22, 23.

a committee to consider of the claims of propriety (?) of all persons interested in tithes. This committee sat, and after much deliberation reported that preachers of the Gospel should retain the maintenance already settled by law, and that the payment of tithe should be capable of enforcement by Justices of the Peace. With this report of their own committee the Parliament in December, 1653, disagreed by a majority of two,[1] and immediately afterwards surrendered their powers to the Protector. Acting, as was said, like one of their own apparitors, who nails his citation on the Church door, and then runs away for fear of a beating. In his Parliament of 1656, Cromwell again raised the question of tithes. In his speech in opening that Parliament, he said, "For my part, I should think myself very treacherous if I took away tithes till I see the legislative power settle maintenance to ministers another way."[2] And while quoting from some ministers that it would be a far greater satisfaction to them to be maintained another way if the State would provide it, he repeated his strong opinion that any practices to take away tithes without also providing for a ministry should be altogether discountenanced. Nothing, however, came of the matter in this Parliament, which was mainly concerned with the frame of Government, and quarrels over the new House of Lords.[3] Tithes accordingly continued payable as before, and were as before enforced by distress and by sale, by order sometimes of Justices of the Peace and on more than one occasion of Justices of Assize. And thus the question appears to have slept for another three years, for the next we find of it is under Richard

---

[1] Journals of Parliament, December, 1653. Hallam's Constitutional History, Vol. I., p. 662.

[2] Carlyle Speech V.

[3] One of the grounds of the Anabaptists' enmity to Cromwell was that he had not done away with tithes. State Papers addressed to Oliver Cromwell, p. 141.

Cromwell's[1] Parliament in June, 1659. "Upon a petition against tithes, the House voted that for the encouragement of a godly, preaching, learned ministry throughout the nation the payment of the tithes shall continue as now they are, unless this Parliament shall find out some other more equal and comfortable maintenance both for the ministry and the satisfaction of the people." This Parliament, however, never did find out any such way, nor indeed did it concern itself any more with the subject. And accordingly the tithes that were paid under the various stages of the Commonwealth were so paid after the Restoration, the recipients being changed, but the payers and the proportions remaining the same.[2] The Tithe Commutation Act of 1838 has put the payments on a more equal and satisfactory footing, and some minor legislation since that date has dealt with anomalies to which attention has been drawn. But tithe still remains, and those who, thinking that the time has again arrived when, in the interests of religious and sectarian peace, it may be dealt with and disposed of once and for ever, have endeavoured to lead their countrymen to that conclusion, may recall with some satisfaction that if they have failed to persuade them of an expedient for satisfying impropriators and providing some maintenance for a godly ministry, they are at least in the same case as their ancestors, who, at a time when the whole country was in favour of abolition, discovered that their profoundest lawyers and staunchest republicans could not devise the mode of its accomplishment. Times, however, have altered in this respect; that whereas from 1648 to 1660 the Government knew not where to lay their hands on the supplies necessary for the protection of the kingdom's trade, and were accordingly unable, however willing, to

---

[1] Whitelock, Vol. IV., p. 353.

[2] On Richard's accession there were numerous Quakers in prison for nonpayment of tithe.

embark in any scheme for the extinction of tithe which involved a present expenditure of public money, under our own happy constitution and after a long era of peace, we are no longer terrified by the sword of impending insolvency, and are thus in a position, if we think fit, to deal successfully with any financial problem that may be submitted for our consideration. The scheme, however, which would seem to be most in accordance with a broad spirit of religious equality, and with a desire to secure some religious ministration for all people in the United Kingdom consistent with the retention of the tithe now collected, would be to provide (with a due regard to the vested interests of present incumbents) for a rateable division among the various recognised denominations of religious belief. Such a scheme in itself would be by no means impracticable; but the animosity of the various sects into which the country is divided would hold out but small hope of its ever being carried into effect.

CHAPTER II.

THE PEOPLE'S COMPENSATION FOR THE ABOLITION OF ROYALTY.

In wild and unfrequented parts of North Britain, are numerous subterranean dwellings, supposed to have been inhabited by the ancient denizens of these northern latitudes. Weird and uncanny in structure, covered by cairns, located in a region formerly a trackless forest, but now a broad moor, purple with heather and pastured by sheep, we may inspect the vaulted domes of these prehistoric habitations, and gaze at their mysterious monoliths. The mole-like owners of these stony caves are said to have been the ancient Picts, but their history, their customs, their government, their mode of life are wrapt in obscurity. We know little more of them than we do of the wild beasts that are believed to have roamed through the primeval forests. Does the average English citizen of the Nineteenth Century know much more of the habits, the sentiments, and the inner life of the people of the Seventeenth Century than he does of the ancient Picts? Books on this period are innumerable. Books on the Civil Wars; books on the lives of King Charles and of Cromwell, by friends and foes, by contemporary writers, and by modern compilers, partial and impartial; books treating the period scientifically, metaphysically, historically. Lives of all the prominent characters of the period. Memoirs, memorials, State Papers, accounts of great trials, drawn up, sometimes by the prisoners themselves, sometimes by their friends, seldom by any impartial hand. Carlyle, probing history after his manner, has collected and published the letters and speeches of Oliver Cromwell, and has afforded to the reader some rough sketches of Commonwealth heroes. Professor Thorold Rogers has written a History of Agriculture and Prices, a work of stupendous labour and research, which throws much light upon the general pecuniary condition of the country at this epoch. But I do not find in any of these works that which would be most interesting and invaluable to anyone in search of a lifelike picture of the times of the Commonwealth, an account of the middle and of the working classes, of the mode in which they made their living, and the laws and regulations by which they were governed.

There was nothing in Puritanism itself which would specially commend it to the English people. We are not, and never were, notwithstanding the jibes of foreign jealousy, a melancholy people, and the severity and asceticism of that section of the Puritans which appeared to spend one half of its time in finding out what the people liked and the other half in endeavouring to deprive them of it, could never in itself have been grateful to the great body of our countrymen. The dreariness of life under the Commonwealth must have been almost unendurable. The sports and pastimes canonized by James and Charles—the bear-baiting, the bull-baiting, the cock-fighting, the drama, dancing, boxing, quarter-staff — all those varieties and graduations of violent exercise, endeared to our people through generations of practice from youth to age, were gradually stayed. Horse-racing and wrestling were interdicted, nominally, for six months; in truth, altogether, under the pretext that they served as a cloak for the meeting and training of seditious cavaliers, while every sort of recreation on the Sunday, even to the harmless pastime of sliding on the ice, was not only forbidden but made penal, and the subject of presentment by grand juries.[1] In the place of these amusements, which, if some-

---

[1] The Grand Inquest of Rye, in the year 1654, presented three boys for sliding on the ice on the Sabbath Day.

times cruel, were at least physically healthy, the
country was indulged with a series of recitations
of which Davenant's " Rutland House Entertainment "
was an unusually favourable specimen; a very small
quantity of music, occasional hawking, a little coursing
for those who could afford it, and a good deal of
tobacco-smoking for all who liked it. For the rich, great
and sumptuous entertainments, dinners and processions,
and for the Protector, his family and his suite daily gallops
round and round Hyde Park, with the following of a
numerous and obsequious crowd. For all classes lectures
by qualified and unqualified persons,[1] sermons of intermin-
able length, and as they must often have been, of unspeakable dulness; and for the country people at least, the
hunting of Jesuits and malignants, varied with the occasional swimming of a witch. Once, indeed, the national
spirit broke out, when on the 1st May, 1654, a maypole
was erected by some enterprising persons in Hyde Park.
"This day," says the paper,[2] "was more observed by people
going a Maying than for divers years past, and, indeed,
much sin committed by wicked meetings with fiddlers,
drunkenness, ribaldry, and the like. Great resort came to
Hyde Park, many hundreds of rich coaches and gallants
in attire, but most shameful powdered-hair men and painted
and spotted women. Some men plaid with a silver ball,
and some took other recreation. But H. H. the Protector
went not thither, nor any of the Lords of the Council, but
were busied about the great affairs of the Commonwealth,
and, amongst other things, had under consideration how
to advance trade for the good of the people with all speed
that might be, and other great affairs for the good of the

---

[1] Selden says, "The lectures in Blackfriars performed by officers
of the army, tradesmen, and ministers, is as if a great lord should
make a feast and he would have his cook dress one dish, his coachman
another, his porter a third, &c."—" Table Talk " Lectures.

[2] *Proceedings in State Affairs*, 4th May, 1654.

Commonwealth." And so Maypoling also was not heard of
again for many years, and the gentlemen with powdered
wigs, and the ladies with paint and patches, had to find
their recreation elsewhere. And yet undoubtedly the
masses, as distinguished from what it is now the mischievous fashion to call the classes, supported the Puritans
to the end, and ultimately by their aid has been established
a government formed on the model for which the Puritan
leaders fought and died. Where, then, was the compensation to the country for the destruction of a monarchy to
which for centuries they had been attached, and for the
stoppage of those various forms of amusement to which
they had been habituated from childhood, and which they
loved, though they were contented to see them proscribed ?
A question much more easily put than answered, but to be
found I conceive in the belief instilled into the people
that the Puritan leaders, whether represented by the Long
Parliament, by the Council of State, or by the Protector,
had at heart the interests and the welfare of the necessi-
tous multitude as against the privileged few, and in the
fact brought home to them day by day that the party were
striving their utmost to carry their wishes into effect. How
otherwise can we account for the fact that from the death
of the King to that of the Protector no single plot or
attempt against the authority of Cromwell originated on
this side of the water? The Prince, as we know from
various sources, was time after time so much disheartened
and discouraged by the failure of his attempts through the
refusal of the country to rise on his behalf, that he almost
gave up in despair any hope of ever returning to England.
When he made his great effort and invaded this country at
the head of the army of the Scots, he marched through
England to the City of Worcester, observing, after the
fashion of the parliamentary troops, great order among his
soldiery, but obtaining the adherence of no great centre of
industry, and the country people through the whole line of

his route avoiding his standard and giving information to
his enemies. The Presbyterian plot found no supporters
in England. Penruddock and his allies had no
response to their call for a rising in the West.
Sexby, Sindercombe, Hewett, and Gerard, and others
found for their attempts no echo but indignation.
And even upon the death of Cromwell, when, if ever, the
Prince's opportunity arose, not a sword was drawn, not a
voice was raised on his behalf. The spirit of the Protector
even from his grave breathed peace over the accession of
his son, and it was not until the nation was convinced of
Richard's incapacity, and frightened by the prospect of
impending anarchy, that it consented to receive back the
heir of the former dynasty. From different classes of the
community two may be selected from opposite poles as
striking examples of the national feeling. The yeomen of
the various counties in England ,were Puritans to a man,
and the great City of London was ever loyal to Cromwell,
poured forth its thousands in money and in men whenever
his cause appeared to be in danger, and was the first
to welcome with enthusiasm the Proclamation of his
son. While the enthusiasm which Cromwell's states-
manship had aroused among the English youth burst
forth in the lines of Dryden, who, at the age of twenty-
eight, penned some of his most heroic stanzas on the recent
death of the Lord Protector.[1]

In order to appreciate the action of the Commonwealth
in their various projects of reform, and the hold they thus
obtained upon the people, it is necessary to consider the
position of various trades and manufactures, and the
position which the workmen employed in these several

---

[1] Dryden was at a later date, like many of his contemporaries,
satisfied that the only chance of peace, and of orderly government,
lay in the restoration of the Royal family. He became a zealous
adherent of and poet laureate to Charles II., but I am not aware that
he ever went back upon his published sentiments as to Oliver
Cromwell.

industries occupied towards the general body of the State.
Of these, I will give instances from which it will be
seen that, according to the old patriarchal system, the
Commonwealth interfered, more or less, with the exercise
of every trade and business, and that so far as the poor
were concerned they would appear to have been the gainers
thereby. The Government of the day had for many
generations set its stamp upon every transaction of human
life. It could not prevent births, but it would commonly
take security from immigrants into towns and corporations
that they should not have children chargeable to the parish.
It regulated the times, conditions and fees of marriage,
and unable to stay the hand of death, it nevertheless prescribed the material in which the dead should be coffined and
enshrouded. It could not prevent farming or grazing, but
it regulated the price of corn and bread, and the quantity
of cattle that a man should keep. It prescribed the dresses
of various grades of society and endeavoured from time to
time, but somewhat ineffectually, it must be admitted, to
regulate the fashions of the female sex. It fixed the rate
of wages at the same time that it fixed the price of food,
and although never able to define with absolute precision
the limits of either, kept them within a narrow margin from
year to year. It peremptorily dealt with the necessaries
of life, food, drink, clothing, and shelter, and the labour
necessary to produce them.[1] To effect this the price of
bread was fixed periodically, much after the present mode
of ascertaining the tithe rent-charge for the year, according

---

[1] I forbear to give references for all the various laws and provisions
incidentally referred to in this chapter, though I refer in a note to
those originating during the Commonwealth. For the rest I must
refer to the old Abridgments, especially one printed by Middleton, in
the time of Henry VIII., and to the Judges' Charges among the
pamphlets of the Commonwealth in the British Museum and in
various private collections. I have also consulted various order books
of the Judges of Assize, from Elizabeth to Charles II., and certain
presentments of Grand Juries in the Southern Counties.

to the price of corn in the market; and a printed assize
book from time to time set out the maximum price which
a baker, under certain penalties, was forbidden to exceed.
He was also bound, under penalties, to put his proper
mark on the bread; and to prevent the underselling of one
baker by another he was not to give more than thirteen
loaves to the dozen.[1] As a necessary corollary to this
regulation a miller, who was generally paid in kind,
was forbidden to charge for the grinding of corn more
than one twentieth or one twenty-fourth part according to the strength of the water required to work the
mill. He had to take out a license to grind corn at his
mill, and was bound to sell his meal only in open market
and directly as it came from the mill, without any mixture
or adulteration.[2]

Graziers and butchers were also under stringent rules.
The price of meat was not fixed by law, but to encourage
the production of beasts for food and to prevent the thinning
of herds, a butcher was forbidden, under a penalty of six
and eightpence for each sale, to kill and sell calves under
five weeks old or any "weanling" under two years old.
This killing of calves was always a subject of interest to
the Legislature. There had been numerous Acts of Parliament on the subject, the latest of which, and that actually
in operation during and after the Long Parliament, was the
28th Henry VIII., cap. 8, by which it was forbidden to kill
calves or "weyniynges" for sale under the age of two years.
It recited an Act of 21 Henry VIII. "which was devised
to the extent that calves once weyned shiulde not have been
kylled before they were mete for befes and at more meaner
pryces, yet nevertheless divers persons use syns the makynge
of the same Acte, to kyl yonge bestes called weyniynges,
called steres, bullocks, and hekters of one or two yere

---

[1] The origin of the term "a baker's dozen."
[2] Statute, 31st October, 1650.

olde, or lyttel more, by meanes whereof a great part
of the benefyte that ellys shiulde have followed the sayd
Acte hath been voyde," and declared a penalty on
on each sale of vi$^{th.}$ viii$^{d.}$ half to the king and half to the
informer. The half to the king was, however, under the
Commonweath applied not for Royal or Imperial purposes,
but towards the relief of the poor in the parish where the
offence was committed, a mode of relieving local burdens
which has found much favour in the present day.

The stock-grower was also for the good of the Commonwealth, and to discourage the practice of arable land being
converted into pasture, put under penalties unless he conducted his stockyard according to the prescribed system,
viz., if he failed to rear calves yearly in the proportion of
one calf for every two kine, or every sixty sheep that he kept.
If he kept more than two thousand sheep at one time he
was subjected to a penalty of 3s. 4d. for each sheep (not
including lambs) over that number, half to the Crown or
parish as the case might be, and half to the informer. This
regulation was, however, of a twofold import, for it tended not
only to the production of big beefs but also to the cultivation
of arable land, which then as now afforded more employment and consequent wages to the agricultural community.
The practice of restricting the operations of the landowner
in what was supposed to be the general interest of the
State has always been upheld in Ireland, and is now
attempted to be revived by Socialist reformers in England,
as a probable preliminary to a claim on behalf of the
Social Democracy for a return to the old system of the
raising of wages and prices by means of special Acts
of Protection. These ancient laws and customs, however, seem to be invoked as having during their time
added materially to the prosperity of the working-classes,
in unconscious forgetfulness of the fact that simultaneously
with the restriction on grazing and pastoral pursuits, there
was an absolute prohibition on the export or the import of

agricultural produce, with a periodical statutory fixture of labourers' wages, and of the prices of corn and of grain.

With a view also to make England, as far as possible, self-contained, and to meet the evils that would otherwise have arisen from this system of strict protection, it was a misdemeanour, under a statute of Philip and Mary, for anyone, without a license under the Great Seal, to transport butter, corn, cheese, or sheep beyond the sea,[1] and the offender who was so convicted of transporting sheep a second time was guilty of felony, which was, at that period, a capital offence.   Orders were also issued from time to time, especially during the foreign wars, prohibiting the export of horses, and an original system of game laws directed to prevent the extirpation of game, declared the fatal practice of tracing hares in the snow to be a misdemeanour, as also taking and killing pheasants or partridges " with engines, nets, or snares, or by shooting in guns," or killing red and fallow deer.   It was also, in accordance with the spirit of our own laws, a misdemeanour to destroy the fry of any fish, or to fish with nets less than $2\frac{1}{2}$ inches wide in the mesh ; to kill salmon under 16 inches long ; pickerel under 10 inches long ; " trowts " under 18 inches long ; barbel under 12 inches long ; and other fish in proportion.

So far with regard to common articles of food.   As to clothing, various punishments had been declared against tailors, clothiers, and others who dealt in bad material. Thus, if a clothmaker used any lime or undue mixture in whitening of linen cloth he was liable to certain penalties. These, however, seem to have been seldom if ever enforced, as the woollen trade had by the time of the Commonwealth almost entirely left our shores, owing chiefly to the badness of our material and the inferiority of our workmanship.   A shoemaker was also liable to be punished "if he did not make his wares of good leather, soale and upper leather,

---

Statute II., Philip and Mary.

well tanned and well sewed with thread, well waxed and. twisted, and hard drawn with hand leathers."

Other trades were put under similar regulations. Thus a brazier or pewterer committed a misdemeanour if he bought or sold any metal of his trade except in open shop, fair, or market, a regulation which, I fancy, did much to discourage the marine store dealer of the period. A tanner the like if he failed to conform to the published regulations for tanning leather, and "if he do not keep his soale leather twelve months and his upper leather nine months in the owze," and if he were a currier or a shoemaker as well as a tanner. A currier was also prohibited being a tanner or a shoemaker, and the latter being also a tanner or a currier. A tilemaker was bound to make no tile less than 10½ inches long and 6¼ inches broad, gutter tiles not less than 10 inches long, and ridge tiles not less than 14 inches long and 1¼ inches thick. A maltster was to make his malt of good sweet barley, to rub it, to dress it well, and to fan at least half a peck of dust out of every quarter.

Beer was, in the year 1649, fixed by law at not less than a quart a penny for the best and two quarts a penny for inferior sort, but not at the rate of more than 10s. per barrel above the Excise.[1] It was again assessed in January, 1654-5, the best quality at 8s. per barrel and not above ; the second quality at 6s. ; and the third quality at 4s.[2] But beer was in its various aspects one of the difficulties of the Commonwealth, and was dealt with by the Acts and Ordinances from year to year.

The prices of barley and malt were, during the Commonwealth, respectively, about 20s. the quarter, more or less, but hops were as fluctuating and as speculative a crop then as they are now, and no regulations or restrictions appear

---

[1] Statute, 26th September, 1649.
[2] *Perfect Diurnal*, 8th January, 1654-5.

to have materially affected their price. The quotations show the following fluctuations:—In 1600 they were 63s. per cwt.; in 1625, they were 37s. 2d.; in 1649, they were at 143s. 7d.; in 1650, 79s. 3d.; in 1651, 61s. 2d.; in 1652, 75s.; in 1653, 91s. 10d.; in 1654, 142s. 7d.; in 1655, 156s. 6d.; in 1656, 162s. 7d.; in 1657, 92s. 9d.; in 1658, 89s.; in 1659, 69s. 1d.; and in 1660, 71s. 6d. The decimal averages, as calculated by Rogers,[1] are :—

1633 to 1642	85s. 2d.	per cwt.
1643 to 1652	76s. 0d.	,,
1653 to 1662	101s. 5d.	,,

after which the prices steadily went back till after the revolution of 1688. With regard to these fluctuations in the value of hops it must be borne in mind that no foreign competition affected the prices, and it does not appear that the high prices of one year induced an over-cultivation in the year following. The hop is a three-years' crop. The first year it is not gathered, the second year it hardly bears sufficient to influence any market, and the third year it is in full fruit, and we should, under such circumstances, expect to find in the third year after a large price, that prices ruled low through a glut of the market. The figures, however, do not bear this out, and the fluctuations therefore depended, I conceive, upon a good or a bad season and the fulness or deficiency of the crop. When, however, the price got to 92s. in 1657, "petitions from thousands of planters and dealers in hops"[2] in Essex, Kent, Sussex, Suffolk, Surrey, Hertford, Hereford, Worcester, Salop, Monmouth, Gloster, Huntingdon, Somerset, Wilts, Oxford, Berks, Stafford, Notts, and Middlesex went up to the Council of State to devise some plan to keep up the price. Prices, however, persistently went down, and no action of the Council could operate to keep them up.

---

[1] Vol. V., p. 302.
[2] *Mercurius Politicus*, No. 336.

The price of wine was proclaimed in Chancery, which odd function had pertained to that Court for many generations, and accordingly one of the duties of Whitelock and the other Lords Commissioners of the Great Seal was to make a just declaration on this subject; which, after much consideration, they did in 1656. Their award was confirmed by the Council of State and by an Act of Parliament passed in March, 1657.[1] The prices were as follows : 1sh. 6d. per quart for Spanish wine ; 12d. per quart for Rhenish wine, and 7d. per quart for French wine. The importation of these wines was also hampered by the still existing navigation laws of Richard II., confirmed successively by Henry VII. and Henry VIII., which forbade the carriage of foreign wine in any but ships of British register. These Navigation Acts were, however, much opposed by the Dutch, and in the result a tacit arrangement appears to have been arrived at by which the Dutch were allowed to bring various goods to England in their own ships in consideration of English ships being given a free right of entry into Dutch ports with goods exported from England.[2]

Other prices of this period, which I have taken from Rogers, from entries in the Council of State, from the newspapers, and from other sources, were as follows :—

The labour of women was worth uniformly about 2s. 6d. per week, and it remained at that sum for many years.
Chickens in 1650 were about 6d. each.
Cheese about 4d. per lb.
Rabbits, 1s. 6d. per couple.
Sheep, 13s. each.
Oxen of the average weight of 580lbs. were about 144s. 10d. each.
Hay was 26s. 4d. per load.
Straw, 9s. 3d. per load.

---

[1] Statute, March, 1657.
[2] Thurloe, Vol. II., p. 605 (1653) ; *Ibid.*, Vol. VII., p. 848 (1660).

F

Sea-coal was fixed by order in January, 1652-3, at 12d. per bushel.

Ordinary table linen was 1s. 6d. per yard.

Sheets or shirts, 1s. 5d. per yard.

Saddle or coach horses are put by Rogers at £20 each. This price would, however, naturally vary with the quality. I find from an entry in the accounts of the Council of State that the horses purchased by them for Cromwell's dragoons before the battle of Worcester cost £6 each, and I fancy a £20 horse must have been a very superior and well-trained animal.

The cost of the equipment of the troops was as follows :—

In 1646, 500 suits for Portsmouth garrison, viz., jackets, breeches, caps, shirts, stockings, and shoes were purchased at 24s. a suit (£600).

100 saddles and furniture for Gloster were purchased at 16s. each (£80).

300 pairs of pistols and holsters cost 28s. per pair (£420).

1,000 swords, with scabbards, and hilts cost 3s. 4d. each sword.

5 tons of bullets at £18 10s. per ton (£92 10s.).

6 tons of round shot at £12 per ton (£72).

In October, 1649, a contract for 16,000 coats and breeches for the soldiers in Ireland provided that the coats were to be of Coventry or Gloster cloth, of Venice colour, red struck in cold water, all three-quarters and a nail length, with tape and strings, and bound about with the same. The breeches were to be made of grey or other good colours, of Reading or other good cloth, well lined and with hooks and buttons, at the price of 17s. for each coat and breeches.

The daily pay of the flag officers of the Fleet appears from the following memorandum[1] :

---

[1] State Papers, 3rd July, 1654.

Captain Richard Badiley, Rear Admiral of the Fleet, which
is to go to General Blake's Squadron, 30s.
Captain Jordan, Rear Admiral, 20s.
Captain Goodson, Vice-Admiral, to General Penn's
Squadron, 30s.
Captain Deakins, Rear Admiral, 20s.
Captain John Bourne, Commander of the Newfoundland
Squadron, 20s.
The Chief Clerk of each Squadron, who is also Deputy-
Treasurer, to have for himself and clerks (no fees to be
taken), £200 a year.

As against the benefits which the middle and the working
classes obtained by this indirect limitation of the price of
food, and of other necessaries, they were in turn also
subjected to penalties if they failed to do their duty to the
Commonwealth. Thus, for refusing to work from 5 a.m.
to 7 p.m. in summer, and to 5 p.m. in winter, or for refusing
to work whenever so required in haytime or harvest, they
were liable to be stocked by the parish constable ; and
labourers, artificers, or servants conspiring together not to
work under wages in excess of those prescribed by Quarter
Sessions were liable to the penalties of misdemeanour.
The master, on the other hand, had certain statutory
duties towards his workmen somewhat analogous to those
now imposed upon him by trades unions. To prevent his
getting his labour for nothing he was liable to penalties if
he did not for every three apprentices keep at least one
journeyman, and for every apprentice above three one
journeyman more. And the employer of agricultural labour
was compelled, if he built a cottage, to lay out four acres of
ground to be occupied with it, the neglect of which ordinance
in the neighbourhood of London was the subject of frequent
complaint in the early days of the Commonwealth. But,
as might have been expected, this hard-and-fast rule broke
down immediately it was applied to the large towns, for

when the necessity for increased accommodation overrode the stringency of the law, and when it was found that trade and other necessities of life rendered impracticable the enforcement of the rule, the ordinances of the Paternal Government had to give way to the general convenience.

A statute of Queen Elizabeth, passed mainly to give power and influence to the Guilds, and to regulate the Trade of London, worked to the detriment of the poor in the country districts. If a labourer, finding no work in the fields, came into a town and baked bread for his fellows, he was liable to the penalties of misdemeanour, on indictment at Quarter Sessions, for " setting up the Art, mistery or occupation of a Baker, never having been brought up in that art or mistery for the period of seven years as an apprentice, nor having been in business as a Baker in the twelfth year of the late Queen Elizabeth." Woollen drapers, linendrapers, shoemakers, and all trades in existence in the twelfth year of Queen Elizabeth were subject to the same restrictions, and thus all foreigners and many English subjects were debarred from working at trades not requiring any special knowledge or qualification, to the supposed advantage of the existing trader but to the undoubted injury of the Commonwealth. The peasant was thus subjected to buy at the prices of the trade, not always kept in reason by the orders of Quarter Sessions, and was precluded obtaining a living for himself and his family by the exercise of an industry for which he might have been sufficiently well qualified. In the later years of the Commonwealth these restrictions were very much relaxed, and among the hundreds of indictments to be met with in old municipal records the penalties were gradually reduced. One instance in particular I have found in the Corporation records of the Cinque Ports, in which one Claudius Gilliat, a French merchant, resident in Rye, was indicted and pleaded guilty of exercising the combined misteries of a haberdasher and a grocer without being duly qualified by apprenticeship.[1] He was fined £12, but £1 being given to the informer the rest was returned to the defendant.

These instances, and many more might be given, sufficiently indicate the position towards the law of the tradesman, the mechanic, and the peasant. But one great and substantial grievance of the time, affecting more or less, as was believed, the welfare of the lower middle classes, was the practical suspension by the Stuarts of the laws against *forestalling*, *regrating*, and *ingrossing*, in other words—the encouragement of the middleman to the detriment of the farmer and the mechanic.

A more or less complete system of legislation had resulted from the efforts of several reigns, and had for its object to prevent the capitalist overpowering the manufacturer and making enormous profits while the other starved. The justification for such legislation must be found in the great difficulties of locomotion, in the danger of travelling long distances without an escort, and in the extraordinary want and consequent high price of public conveyance either by land or water.[2] These combined impediments to trade gave undue power to the man with ready money who was able to pay for carriage to and from his market a sum which to the needy would have been a prohibitive tax. And the State, having in the interests of the public fixed the maximum prices of various necessary articles, was accordingly compelled to have recourse to such further protective legislation as would enable the producers to live upon the prices so ascertained. No sooner, therefore, was the Commonwealth in office than petitions from all parts of the country poured in upon them pleading for the interests of the farmers, and instancing numerous cases where the middlemen had made enormous

---

[1] Bundle, No. 48, A.D. 1658-9.

[2] Land carriage of goods during the first half of the XVII. Century may be taken very roughly at a shilling (equal to four shillings now) per ton per mile.

fortunes while the unhappy farmers were on the brink of ruin. Forestalling, regrating and ingrossing, it was said, were the frequent subjects of presentment by Grand Juries, the names of the offenders were given and particulars of their offences declared, but the same names were recorded time after time by the Clerk of the Peace, and no indictments were preferred and nothing was done towards abating the evil. In May, 1649, a petition was presented to the Council of State by numerous inhabitants of Ipswich complaining of one Robert Green, a merchant of that town, for ingrossing of corn. It was referred to the Attorney-General to prosecute and to take information from W. Hanby, the Town Clerk, " So that the poor people may see that care is taken of them in time of dearth."[1] A similar petition from Lancashire was dealt with in the same way, and the subject was entertained and discussed by the Council as a serious and crying evil.[2]

At this period and for many years afterwards, markets and fairs were held at statutory periods. Every little town and many a little hamlet had its own market and its own fair, so that from one end of the country to the other there was always within an easy reach some open market where vendor and purchaser could meet and barter their wares, and where by the system of tolls and of market clerks they could always have credible witnesses of the contracts into which they entered. The law, moreover, encouraged markets and fairs by restricting the operations of certain trades to sales in open market or fair, and by declaring that according to the old Saxon custom, stolen goods, if purchased *bonâ fide* in open market, could not afterwards be reclaimed by the owner. But the public object of these markets and fairs would have been entirely frustrated if a man with a few pounds of ready cash could waylay the small farmer or the industrious peasant on his way to the market town, and

[1] State Papers, 2nd May, 1649.
[2] *Ibid.*, 8th September, 1649.

purchasing his whole stock of butter, bread, or cheese, come into the market as the sole vendor and regulate the price according to his will. In like manner, if a man with capital purchased the whole of one article in the market, and thus compelled the peasant or the mechanic to buy at his price or go without, the peasant or mechanic similarly lost the benefit of an open market. Everything, therefore, in the nature of a ring or a combination to raise the price of the necessaries of life, was held to be contrary to the public good, and a fit subject for enquiry and reprobation. With a view, accordingly, to ensure the sale of these necessaries at a reasonable rate, every man was required by law to buy and sell all manner of victuals or food in open market, and to intercept such food on its way or to open a second market within reach of the first was a high crime against the general prosperity.[1] A man, therefore, who bought food on the way to a market or fair, whether the food was coming by land or by water, was guilty of *forestalling* the market. If he bought victuals in a market to sell again within four miles, or if he bought cattle and sold them again alive within five weeks, he was guilty of *regrating.* If he bought dead victuals or growing corn to sell again, he was guilty of *ingrossing.* Any such offender was liable, on conviction, to be "grievously amerced" for the first offence, to be put in the pillory for the second, to be imprisoned and fined for the third, and to be banished the town for the fourth. It was also declared to be a misdemeanour for a man to accumulate corn to the prejudice of the public, and if, therefore, he had corn sufficient for his house provision for one year and bought more, he was liable to penalties if he did not, the same day, bring so much other corn into market to be sold, that his remaining stock would not exceed his requirement for a single year. And more for the purpose, I fancy, of declaring the law than of

---

[1] Laws to this effect were passed by Edward III., by Henry VIII. and by Edward VI.

making any alteration in it, a Bill was read a second time
and committed,[1] but apparently went no farther, dealing
with persons who bought up many head of cattle and most
of the granaries of the nation to sell again at excessive
rates, and threatening with heavy penalties any such
combination as a "corner" in cattle or grain. These
various subjects were dealt with by the several judges on
their first circuits. Forestallers, regrators, and ingrossers
were "grievously amerced," and very general satisfaction
was given not only to the farmers but also to the squires
by the mode in which the judges dealt with these and
cognate matters. And although at the present day our
deep-rooted instincts of free trade lead us to condemn
this patriarchal system root and branch, yet if we re-
member that it was, and had been for years, the
recognised system of England, we shall then be able
to realize the feeling of satisfaction with which the
people saw once again the revival of the old laws of
which they had heard from their parents, and which were
associated in their own minds with the past and happy days
when peace and prosperity smiled upon England and her
people. And this contentment was further increased by
the reduction of the legal rate of interest in March, 1649,
from 10 per cent. to 8, to claim more than which was
treated as unlawful usury and extortion, and the further
reduction of the rate in 1651 from 8 per cent. to 6.[2]

The stability and equal administration of the law was one
of the strongest planks in the platform of the Commonwealth. But however much their leaders may have desired
—and we know that in very many respects they did desire
—to reform the law in accordance with modern ideas, they
could never have anticipated attracting the sympathies of
the people and inducing the nation to settle quietly down
into habits of business, if they had commenced by

[1] Whitelock, Vol. III., p. 9.
[2] Statute, 20th May, 1651.

making alterations in that system of taxation and of jurisprudence which the people had been for years accustomed
to regard as the perfection of wisdom. The storm and
tumult of war had abated, the tempest had passed over, the
waves had lulled, and the sea of politics was outwardly
smooth; but there yet remained the unquiet swell and the
working of the waters which follow a storm, and of which
a prudent mariner cannot fail but take account. All
changes were, therefore, for the time necessarily postponed;
the system of management and protection of the trades
and industries of the country was continued subject only to
such occasional relief as the circumstances of any particular trade required, and the law was administered in
the Courts, as laid down by Bacon, Littleton, and Coke.
Content for the moment with reforming the administration of the existing laws, Parliament left their repeal or
amendment to be dealt with as opportunity should arise.
But it hardly sufficed for the Council of State, who
had in hand all questions of trade and commerce, to content
itself with enforcing with strict impartiality the existing
laws or making small and necessary amendments. It was
their business to go farther, to restore, if possible, the
drooping energies of the country, to bring about a revival
of trade, and to improve, by such means as lay in their
power, the condition of the poorer classes.

It is difficult to say whether it entered into the views of
Cromwell or his Council at any period to adopt, either
wholly or in part, the principles of free trade. I think that
there was then growing up an indefinite idea, that, inasmuch as the complete system of protection had not
absolutely secured the trade of the country, and as the
control requisite to make it effective was irksome to the
citizen and operated frequently in restraint of trade, it
might be good policy to try a new or a modified system.
One instance of such proposal and perhaps the earliest
will be found in Milton's Areopagitica, published in 1643.

In that pamphlet, while contending against the licensing
of books, and pleading for a free press, he uses the
argument that the then existing practice involved the
logical consequence of regulating by law all the recreations
and pastimes of the people, their music and dancing, their
wearing of particular garments, and the cut of their clothes,
the conversation of men and women, and other minute
details of social and domestic life, a legitimate inference
from which would be that such domestic legislation was
even at that period contrary to the received opinions of
educated persons.   The protection and management of
various trades would logically fall under the same censure,
and would be subject to the same theory of leaving people
to manage their own affairs after their own fashion without
troubling the State with their prospective gains or losses.
When in 1650 an Act[1] was passed appointing a Commission

---

[1] Stat. 1, August, 1650. This Act is not printed in Scoble's Acts,
but I have transcribed the instructions to the Commissioners from a
copy of the Act issued in 1650 by the Printers to the Parliament of
England in the collection of Mr. Thorpe, F.S.A. These instructions
give clearly the views of the economists of the day, and show the care
that was taken to investigate the subject.

"First. They are to take notice of all the Native Commodities of
this Land, or what Time and Industry may hereafter make Native,
and advise how they may not only be fully Manufactured, but well
and truly wrought, to the Honor and Profit of The Commonwealth.

"Secondly. They are to consider how the Trades and Manufactures
of this Nation may most fitly and equally be distributed to every part
thereof; to the end that one part may not abound with Trade, and
another remain poor and desolate for the want of the same.

"Thirdly. They are to consult how the Trade may most conveniently
be driven from one part of this Land to another. To which purpose
they are to consider how the Rivers may be made more Navigable and
the Ports more capable of Shipping.

"Fourthly. They are to consider how the Commodities of this Land
may be vented, to the best advantage thereof, into Foraign Countreys,
and not undervalued by the evil management of Trade. And that they
advise how Obstructions of Trade into Foraign parts may be removed;
and devise by all means, how new ways and places may be found
out, for the better venting of the Native Commodities of this Land.

under the presidency of Sir Harry Vane, to inquire into
and report upon the State of Trade and how it could be
advanced and regulated, the Commissioners were required
among other matters to " take into their consideration
whether it be necessary to give way to a more open and

"Fifthly. They are to advise how free Ports or Landing-places for
Foreign Commodities imported (without paying of Custom, if again
exported) may be appointed in several parts of this Land, and in what
manner the same is best to be effected.

"Sixthly. They are to consider of some way, that a most exact
account be kept of all Commodities imported and exported through
the Land, to the end that a perfect Balance of Trade may be taken,
whereby the Commonwealth may not be impoverished, by receiving of
Commodities yearly from Foraign parts, of a greater value than what
was carried out.

"Seventhly. They are duly to consider the value of the *English*
Coyns, and the Par thereof, in relation to the intrinsic value which it
bears in weight and fineness with the Coyns of other Nations. Also
to consider of the state of the Exchange, and of the gain or loss that
comes to the Commonwealth by the Exchange now used by the
Merchants.

"Eighthly. They are (in order to the Regulating and Benefit of
Trade) seriously to consider what Customs, Imposts and Excise is fit
to be laid upon all Goods and Commodities, either Native or Imported,
and how the said Customs, Imports and Excise may be best ordered
and Regulated, and so equally laid and evenly managed, as neither
Trade may thereby be hindered, nor the State made incapable to
defray the Publique Charges of the Commonwealth.

"Ninthly. They are to take into their consideration whether it be
necessary to give way to a more open and free Trade than that of
Companies and Societies, and in what manner it is fittest to be done ;
wherein, notwithstanding, they are to take care that Government and
Order in Trade may be preserved, and Confusion avoided.

"Tenthly. They are to inform themselves of the particular
Ordinances, Orders, Grants, Patents, and Constitutions of the several
Companies of Merchants and Handicraftsmen, to the end that if any
of them tend to the hurt of the Publique, they may be laid down in
such manner as the Parliament shall think fit.

"Eleventhly. They are to consider the great Trade of Fishing, and
that not only upon the Coasts of *England* and *Ireland*, but likewise of
Iceland, *Greenland*, *Newfoundland*, and *New England*, or elsewhere,

free trade than that of companies and societies, and in what manner it is fittest to be done." This has somewhat the appearance of a leaning towards free trade, but I find that in an Act of 1656 sanctioning the export of numerous articles of food and other commodities, the preamble contains the recital detestable to freetraders and dear to protectionists, that the prosperity of the country, *as of all islands*, is dependent on the care that is taken that the exportation of native commodities overbalances the importation of foreign commodities,[1] a statement which shows that however enlightened Parliament may have been in many respects, it had not yet realized the true theory of the relative value of exports and imports. What, however, may have been the views of any individual members of the Council, in three respects only were steps taken even indirectly towards a system of free trade. The first was

and to take care that the Fishermen may be encouraged to go on in their Labors, to the encrease of Shipping and Mariners.

"Twelfthly. They are to take into their consideration the English Plantations in America or elsewhere, and to advise how those Plantations may be best managed, and made most useful for this Commonwealth ; and how the Commodities thereof may be so multiplied and improved, as (if it be possible) those Plantations alone may supply the *Commonwealth* of *England* with whatsoever it necessarily wants."

[1] The following is the text of the preamble : " Forasmuch as it is found by long experience that the prosperous estate of all islands is very much (under God) maintained and supported by a quick and flourishing trade, *and in a just endeavour and care that the exportation of the native commodities overbalance the importation of foreign commodities :* and forasmuch as it hath pleased Almighty God to bless the industry and endeavours of the People of this Nation in the great improvement of Fens, Forests, Chases, and other lands, with a great redundancy of Corn, Cattel, Butter, Cheese, and divers other considerable Commodities, much desired by and of great use to other Nations and the Plantations abroad : and if Liberty were granted freely to export the same and all restraints taken away and the Custom made easie, it would much encourage Manufacture and advance Trade, which H. H. and the Parliament duly considering, are pleased that it be enacted, etc."—Statute, 1656, c. 5.

the granting of greatly increased facilities for obtaining licenses to export various articles of English produce or manufacture ;[1] secondly, the positive refusal of Parliament and of the Council of State to give any sanction to proposals to regulate by law the dresses and demeanour of men and women ; and thirdly, the recognition and promotion of a system of free trading between the Northern ports of France and those of the Cinque ports, by which various articles of food, together with horses, the breeding of which was a great trade at that period, both in France and England, were freely interchanged between the two countries, and their carriage protected when necessary by an English man-of-war.[2] This international trade was carried on for many years. It survived the troubles and wars of the Commonwealth and even those of the Georgian Era. Mr. Holloway in his histories of Romney Marsh, and of Rye, of which town he was an inhabitant, refers to this commerce, and there are even now living in the ancient town of Rye some old people who recollect the French coming regularly in their boats from Tréport and Dieppe with vegetables and eggs for the fortnightly market.

In the multitude of industries claiming their assistance the Government, in the first instance, turned their attention to the wool trade and the manufacture of cloth, " the great staple commodity of this nation," as Cromwell called it when opening his first Parliament,[3] and complaining of

[1] This issuing of licenses became after a time so onerous upon the the Attorney-General, who appears to have had the duty, as well, I suppose, as the fees, of making the grants, that in 1655 he refused to issue any more, declaring that he had so much business and so little time to do it in, that licenses to export butter, etc., must be got elsewhere. They turned, he said, upon the Statute, II. Philip and Mary, and ought to pass under the Great Seal.—State Papers, 1655, A. G. Prideaux to the Council of State.

[2] An interesting correspondence between the Mayor and Jurats of Rye and Dover, and the Lieutenant of Dieppe is to be found among these records. A.D. 1656.

[3] Carlyle, Speech II., 4th Sept., 1654.

the incapacity and dilatoriness of former Parliaments in
that respect, he showed how the whole burthen of the
protection and advancement of the trade had fallen upon
him and upon the Council of State. Great cries and
lamentations had been heard from the wool-staplers and
the cloth-workers, whose trade had been gradually dying
away, and repeated appeals for assistance had been made to
the Government of the day. The Eastern Counties had for
generations been the centre of the wool and cloth trade, in
which great fortunes had been made under the Tudors and
in the early part of the century. It was recognised on all
hands that the climate of England, in respect of its cold-
ness and moisture, was especially adapted to the growth
and preparation of wool of a peculiarly strong and flexible
character, of which enormous quantities, being three
times as much as in the whole of France, were annually
worked up. The counties peculiarly addicted to this industry were those included in the Eastern Association, who
gave their undivided support to the cause of the Parliament
and afterwards to Cromwell, and who sought in return to
be rewarded by the protection of their trade. This had
during the Civil wars languished and sickened nearly unto
death, so that while the statesmen and soldiers of the Parliament were settling the kingdom by force of arms, the great
groundwork of their assessments, and of the sinews of war,
was gradually slipping away. Of these counties, Essex
was in 1646-7 in the foremost rank, and in the latter year,
in consequence of numerous petitions, the grievances of the
cloth-workers were entertained by the Long Parliament,
and Serjeant Thorpe, a distinguished lawyer of the Puritan
party and afterwards a great judge, was ordered by the
House of Commons to make enquiries and to report the
result to the House. He accordingly made a detailed
report, and seems to have been of opinion that the wool
trade in England had suffered and was still suffering, and
was likely to suffer more, but that the depression arose, not

from any neglect of Parliament, nor from any unpreventable
cause, but in great measure from the bad workmanship and
materials of the cloth-workers themselves. "Bad and
deceitful goods," otherwise shoddy, had been made
and sent abroad for sale to such an extent that the
English were in danger of losing the foreign market
altogether. And similarly with cloth, an instance was
given of one port in Spain, where they used to
sell 12,000 pieces, but then, in consequence of the dete-
rioration of their goods, they only sold 2,000 pieces, and
the Dutch, by their better manufacture, were getting a
monopoly.[1] But the wool-staplers and cloth-workers
continued to assert their grievances, which were doubtless
accentuated by the attempts made by the Dutch,. the
French, and the Spaniards to take advantage of the internal
dissensions of the English to filch away their trade. In the
result, after much discussion,[2] an Act was passed incor-
porating a company of worsted-weavers in the City of
Norwich for the making of *Norwich stuffs*, with all the
powers of a City company. And, subsequently, the Council
of State, in April, 1652, allowed the free import of the raw
material, took off the Excise duty formerly levied upon
foreign wool, and simultaneously issued orders that no
wool was to be exported from Scotland or from Berwick-
upon-Tweed.[3] The effect of these orders was to stimulate
the cloth trade, and when successful treaties of peace were ·
made, and some damages recovered to compensate the
English merchants for losses they had sustained from the
Portuguese, it gradually rose to its former standard. The
Norwich weavers in particular, in and after 1650, when the
Act was passed for their special protection, experienced a
great revival of trade[4], a matter of much concern to the

---

[1] State Papers, 1647 and 1651.
[2] Statute, 14th November, 1650.
[3] *Proceedigns in Parliament*, 22nd April, 1652.
[4] Rogers. Vol. V., p. 76.

country at large, as Norwich was then, and continued for years to be, the second City in the Empire for commerce and wealth.

The coal trade had also been carried on under serious disadvantages, for although coal was not declared contraband during the Civil War or during any of the foreign wars in which the Commonwealth engaged, yet the mariners sailed in constant dread of capture by some of the various hostile expeditions that infested the Eastern coasts. The advice of the Law Officers, who were called in upon this, as upon most other trading questions, only resulted in the obvious suggestion of a strong convoy, which being ordered by the Council of State, the colliers in fleets of three hundred vessels, with a convoy of fifty men-of-war, sailed periodically from Newcastle and arrived safely in London.[1]

The gold and silver thread-makers, a great trade at a time when tunics of gold and silver-cloth were worn by men and women alike, were several times before the Council of State. It appeared that great quantities of coin, plate, and bullion were daily employed in making gold and silver wire lace, thus causing the withdrawal of much bullion from the Mint. The difficulty arising from the absence of the precious metals was also accentuated by the conduct of the King of Spain. That Monarch, under the reigns of James I. and Charles I., had sent vast sums of bullion to be coined in our Mint for the use of the Low Countries, at least one-third of which, as was computed, was laid out in England on cloth and other commodities, and a substantial sum was paid to English shippers for carrying the coin to Flanders, thus filling our country with a great portion of the coin and plate which was afterwards melted down to supply the necessities of

[1] *Mercurius Politicus*, June, 1656 : Whitelock, Vol. IV., p. 2. Sea coal was fixed by order in 1652-3 at 12d. per bushel.—Middlesex Records, Vol. III., p. 212.

the ˙Civil War. This benefit was lost to England through the quarrels with Spain and the preference for a French rather than a Spanish alliance, causing, it is somewhat vaguely stated by Walker, a loss of ten per cent. on every man's income.[1] The industry had also suffered, like the cloth trade, from the frauds practised during the Civil War, when the gold and silver wire and lace-workers, not going in fear of their Guild, which, in those times of trouble, was unable to exercise any effectual control, adulterated their wares by mixing fifty per cent. of copper with their gold and silver, and sold the product as pure metal. This cheating was punishable by statute with pillory, fine, and imprisonment, and the sentence was, at least upon one occasion, carried out during the early part of King Charles reign.[2] But years of impunity had made the traders reckless, and their craft had consequently suffered from the intervention of foreigners. In 1649 skilled persons were called in to assist the Council of State, and in January, 1650-1, an Act[3] was passed at the instigation of the Council of State permitting the free import of bullion and foreign coin. Of the amount so imported by any merchant he might export two-thirds on payment of a custom-due of one per cent., and on taking the remaining one-third to the Mint to be coined into gold or silver coin. In 1656 an ordinance[4] was issued regulating the manufacture of gold and silver laces and wire, providing for the necessary supply of metal to the trade, and ordering prosecutions to be instituted against fraudulent dealers. Whether arising from the withdrawal of bullion for the manufacture of gold and silver lace and personal ornaments, or for that of gold and silver vessels and plate which the Civil Wars had seen melted down in voluntary gifts or enforced

[1] History of Independency, Part II., p. 197.
[2] Middlesex Records: Rex *v.* Gayer, Vol. III., p. 70.
[3] Statute, 9th January, 1650-1.
[4] *Mercurius Politicus*, No. 310.

requisition, or from the wars with Spain restricting the importation of the precious metals, it appears to be the fact that coinage under the twelve years of the Commonwealth was carried on to a far less extent than during any former or later reign. The coinage during the period 1648-1660 was, in gold, £154,511 ; in silver, £1,000,000 ; or an annual coinage of gold, £14,047, and of silver, £90,909.[1] As against this, Elizabeth coined annually of gold, £18,071, and of silver, £107,240. Under James the annual coinage was of gold, £138,320, and of silver, £74,582. In the reign of Charles I. the annual coinage was of gold, £138,320, of silver, £365,689, while under Charles II. the annual coinage was of gold, £167,090, and of silver, £148,887. The Mint, however, was reorganized under the supervision of the Attorney-General, and during the later years of the Protectorate a scheme was passed for an entirely new system of coinage, on patterns designed by Simon. The coin to be struck in a die and to be milled inside and outside the edges, with a legend on the larger coins, thus rendering more difficult the offence of clipping, which was supposed, though with very doubtful accuracy, to have accounted for the depreciation and defacement of the existing currency. Of this proposed coinage specimens, in very perfect condition, are to be found in the collections of most numismatists, but for reasons of State, and owing to the sudden death of the Protector, this very artistic and excellent coinage never found its way into general circulation.

One of the great industries of the sixteenth and seventeenth centuries was the manufacture of hats and hatbands. The latter went out of fashion towards the end of the seventeenth century, when the Prince of Orange introduced the three-cornered cocked hat, but up to that date men and women alike wore hats of various materials with hatbands,

---

[1] Rogers, Vol. V., p. 126, " Currency."

according to their rank or their wealth. Old prints and portraits give an infinite variety of these hats. They were made, according to Stubbs, of silk, of velvet, of wool, and sometimes of beaver, the latter being then of great price. They were furnished, by way of ornament, with jewels among the great, and in other classes by hatbands of gold or silver lace, by sashes of coloured silk, by feathers, and by any material or device which might suit the fancy or the purse of the wearer. Ben Jonson[1] describes Fastidious Brisk as having a gold cable hatband of massive goldsmiths' work, worn about a mulberry-coloured French hat, embroidered with gold twist and spangles. And he further refers to "a Naples hat with a Roman hatband." Mr. Planché[2] states that in the Lord Mayor's procession of 1644 one of the party wore a broad-brimmed hat with a large Cypress hatband, *i.e.*, a hatband of Cypress silk. Certain sections of the community also wore hats of special form and material, a particular description of which will be found in Mr. Planché's Cyclopædia, and will be interesting to the antiquary. It is sufficient here to say that the manufacture of hats and hatbands was a trade which, owing to the variety of costume in the seventeenth century, was of great importance to the country, and which for various reasons had, like the trade in wool and in cloth, gradually slipped from us and become monopolized by other countries. It was bound up, to some extent, with the trade of the gold and silver thread makers, and a similar course of protection was pursued in both cases. An Act was passed[3] prohibiting the importation of foreign hats and hatbands. Any goods so imported were to be forfeited and their value to be divided equally between the informer and the poor of the parish where the goods were seized. The execution of the

---

[1] *Every Man out of his Humour*, Act iv.
[2] Cyclopædia of Costume, p. 264.
[3] Statute, 5th September, 1649.

Act to be intrusted to the companies of hat makers and felt makers.

An Act was also passed, which appears to have given great satisfaction,[1] for preventing the growth of tobacco in England to the prejudice of the British plantations, and of the commerce and shipping of the nation. All tobacco, however, planted before the date of the Act, was excluded from its operation. No great injury, I take it, was done to anyone by this regulation. The climate of England, and particularly the absence of warm nights so necessary for the fructification of the tobacco plant, have always rendered abortive attempts to grow tobacco in this country, and the quality of such as was grown in 1650 was no better according to all accounts than that which is occasionally grown at the present day. The price of tobacco during this period was almost as fluctuating as that of hops.[2] Spanish tobacco of the best quality seems to have been from 7s. to 10s. per pound, and Virginia tobacco from our own plantations from 2s. 6d. to 4s. This regulation, combined with the repeal of all monopolies of the sale of tobacco, was followed by an import duty of 1s. per gallon on foreign salt, against which the pamphleteers of the Royalist party loudly protested, declaring that as home-made salt was inconsiderable in quantity this was to put a tax upon the greatest necessity of life.[3] The object, however, which was accepted generally as satisfactory, was to encourage the making of salt at home, so as to avoid the necessity of purchasing abroad in times of trouble. And for a similar reason Parliamentary powers were widely given to dig for saltpetre for the making of gunpowder.[4]

---

[1] Statute, 1st April, 1652; *Proceedings in Parliament*, 18th April, 1652.

[2] Rogers, Vol. V., p. 467. Some other prices are quoted of tobacco which the Professor thinks must have been smuggled.

[3] History of Independency, Part II., p. 197. The Excise is described as " that Dutch devil Excise."

[4] Statute, February, 1652.

It had also been enacted in the same interest that no whale oil or whalebone should be imported except from Greenland and in British ships.[1] This legislation, which, as I have suggested, was acceptable to the country, as encouraging British shipping and the British plantations, was adopted after the Restoration, and was the subject of an Act passed by Charles II. in the first year of his reign.[2]

The swarming of countrymen to London, notwithstanding the ordinances passed for their protection at home, with the consequent depopulation of the agricultural districts and inconvenience to Londoners, formed the subject of numerous Acts and ordinances, and amongst other petitioners to Parliament on the subject were the Benchers of Lincoln's Inn, who complained to the Council, without much effect, of various buildings being commenced in the fields in their immediate neighbourhood.[3] In March of 1652, the Master Warden and Commonalty of the Tilers and Bricklayers of London petitioned the Committee for Law, sitting at Westminster, for an increase of their powers, so as to enable them to reform the abuses of tile-makers, bricklayers, and lime-men, and that a Bill be drawn for regulating new buildings. According to their statutory powers the Company formerly inquired into and prosecuted abuses in these several trades, but since the distracted times the tilers, brickmakers, and lime-men had become stubborn and disobedient, and refused to submit to reasonable rules and regulations. "Building with brick," they say, " has been very graceful to the City of London, and is very beneficial in preserving the same from fire, also for the preservation of timber, for avoiding the many juttings and encroachments on ground, the darkening of lights, the straightening and stifling the streets and the infection of

---

[1] Statute, 6th May, 1645.
[2] 12 Charles II.., c. 34.
[3] *Public Intelligencer*, No. 45.

plague, and the excessive breeding of vermin which occurs in wood houses."[1]

In the result an Act was passed imposing a fine of one year's rent or annual value in respect of every house built since the 25th March, 1650, in the suburbs of London, *i.e.*, within ten miles of the walls of the City, not on an old foundation which had not four acres of land permanently occupied therewith. And in order to restrict building operations for the future, it was enacted that every person building in contravention of the enactment after 29th September, 1657, should pay a fine to the State of £100.[2] This was supplemented in the following year by an Act, providing for the inspection of the foundations of all new buildings in and near London, with a complete system of survey and of registration.[3]

A Bill was also printed about this time, and a Committee appointed to consider of the number and abuse of attorneys and solicitors,[4] but so far as is known the Bill went into the same waste-paper basket as the Bill against patches and low-necked dresses.

Some relief was also given to the poorer householders in the year 1651, when an order[5] was passed " for the ease of the Commonwealth," that after the 25th December, 1651, no ale or other beer should be exciseable but such as was brewed by common brewers, to be sold by vintners, inn-keepers, ale-house keepers, cooks, chandlers, or other persons brewing in their houses and selling again. The duty was thus taken off all beer home-brewed for the consumption of the household, and was an enormous boon to thousands of the poorer classes, who were thus not only relieved of the tax on their beer but also of the irritating visits of the gauger.

[1] State Papers, Vol. XXIII.
[2] Statute 1656, c. 24.
[3] *Mercurius Politicus*, No. 371.
[4] *Mercurius Politicus*, No. 331.
[5] This order was confirmed by statute, 12th December, 1651.

Orders were also made from time to time in accordance with statute to relax the prohibitions against the exportation of various articles of food, and from such orders we gather the prices of these commodities at the dates in question. In October, 1654,[1] the exportation of wheat was permitted (but only in British ships) when the price was not over 30 shillings the quarter, subject to an export duty of fourpence the quarter; rye, when the price was not over 24 shillings the quarter, subject to an export duty of threepence; barley or malt, when not over 20 shillings, with an export duty of twopence; peas and beans, when not over 24 shillings per quarter, with an export duty of threepence; and butter, when not over sixpence the pound, with no export duty.

In order to judge of the operation of this law, it is necessary to ascertain the prices of these various products at or about the time of the Act, viz., 1654. From the prices taken from " Rogers'," I find that from A.D. 1650 to A.D. 1660, both included, there were only two years when corn was not over 30s. per quarter, viz., in 1653, when it was 25s. 2½d. per quarter, and 1654, when it was 21s. 8d. per quarter.[2] During the same period there were only four years when barley was not over 20s., viz.: 1652, when it was 17s. 1d.; in 1653, when it was 15s. 4¾d.; in 1654, when it was 13s. 3¾d.; and in 1655, when it was 17s. 7¾d. per quarter. Peas in 1654 were at 16s. 4d. per quarter, and they remained liable to exportation, except in the years 1656 and 1658, when they were at 26s., till after the Restoration, when they rose to 31s. Beans were in 1653, 1654, and 1655 at 21s. 4d., after which they rose to 25s., 26s., 28s., etc. Butter in 1654 was at 6d. per lb., and it thus

---

[1] Whitelock, Vol. IV., p. 155.

[2] The following are the figures :—*Corn:* A.D. 1650, 55s. 4d.; 1651, 48s. 10d.; 1652, 33s. 10¾d.; 1653, 25s. 2½d.; 1654, 21s. 8d.; 1655, 33s. 2½d.; 1656, 37s. 1½d.; 1657, 46s. 5¾d.; 1658, 57s. 10¾d.; 1659, 52s. 1d.; 1660, 51s. 7¾d.

remained liable to exportation till long after the Restoration.
It will thus be seen that, although the removal of the embargo
on the exportation of corn was in operation, except for the
agricultural year, October, 1654 to October, 1655, yet that
there was a considerable relief to the producer in the power
to export freely and at a small duty, when the excess of
home produce over the requirements of the nation had
reduced prices below the standard generally accepted as
yielding a fair profit.

Before these Acts were passed, however, it had
become necessary in the interests of the public to rectify
the barbarous system of weights and measures which
in the disorders of the kingdom had crept into use. The
old Winchester and Westminster weights and measures
had become obsolete for the time, and their place had been
taken by stones and wedges, and indeed by any contrivance
that the ingenuity of the seller could impose upon the
purchaser. But while this eccentricity of weights and
measures enured to the prosperity of the wealthy trader,
the poorer dealers and shopkeepers in the small country
towns were visited periodically by jurors in grand inquisition, who presented them to their Quarter Sessions for
their "quart pots lacking a spoonful," and for their
"quartern loaf lacking an ounce," and thus the poor were
fined for their misfortunes, while the rich grew wealthy in
their frauds. But as this system had lasted for nearly a
generation it could hardly be reformed except by Act of
Parliament, and a Statute was accordingly passed[1] in March,
1650, declaring that "the weighing by stones, wedges,
bricks, and other unwarrantable weights of butter and cheese
are to be utterly left, nor in any sort to be used hereafter,"
but that such commodities and all others were to be weighed
only according to the standard weights, under penalties
to be divided between the poor of the parish where the
offence was committed and the informer who brought the

---

[1] Statute 12, March, 1649-50.

offender to justice. And here again came in the care for
the poor, inasmuch as penalties throughout this period,
instead of being divided as formerly, between the king and
the informer, were divided between the latter and the
needy, making thus a substantial though fluctuating
provision for the poor, and, at the same time, making it to
the pecuniary interest of each parish to see that the law
was strictly observed within its limits. And it undoubtedly
had that effect, for, in and after 1650, the grand juries who
assumed the duties of inspecting weights and measures
always kept a sheet of their presentments for complaints of
the deficiencies of tradesmen and others in this respect,
together with occasional reports of the abusive words used
towards them and their officers when discharging their
necessary but disagreeable office. And thus also was
initiated a system of finance giving aids to local burthens
by the appropriation for their relief of certain fines and
duties levied in the district, which is now finding great
favour in the eyes of both parties in the State.

There had also, about this time, arisen in England, but
chiefly in London, a comparatively new industry, that of
framework knitting and the making of silk and other
stockings. The process of stocking-making by machinery
and not by hand was invented by William Lee, of St.
John's College, Cambridge, actually, as was said, in
the year 1589. He had established, under Elizabeth,
a factory for making stockings, silk and worsted, by
framework knitting, but being refused assistance by James,
he emigrated with his family and his machines to France,
where he was received with enthusiasm by Henry IV.
At a later date, however, he was persecuted as a Protestant,
his trade was broken up, and he died in Paris of grief
and disappointment. Some of his workmen, however,
having escaped from persecution, returned to England, and
re-established the industry which the short-sightedness of
James had driven from our shores. It was stated in a very

numerously signed petition[1] of the inventors and promoters
of this branch of trade, that it was an entirely English
invention, no part of the world having it besides. That it
had been much coveted by strangers to be carried into
foreign parts, which, with much trouble and expense, had
hitherto been hindered. But that now by the insinuations
of foreigners with some ill-disposed persons of their own
trade, there was great danger of the secrets and exercise of
the trade being carried away, the effect of which
would be to reduce to beggary hundreds of families now
engaged in knitting and stocking making. The business
was at once referred for information to the Lord Mayor
and Aldermen, who reported that the trade being of
recent introduction was not within the Act of 5th
Elizabeth as to the City Corporations, and that steps
should, therefore, be taken to prevent the art with the
frame and instruments being taken abroad. The petition
and report were then sent to the Attorney-General for his
opinion, and from him to the Trade Committee to prepare
the necessary rules and Charter of Incorporation. Thus,
by a summary exercise of their powers, the Government
secured to the Londoners and others the exercise and
almost the monopoly of what was for many years a lucrative
and important trade. It rapidly increased, and the number
of the frames, each of which employed at least two persons,
quickly rose to hundreds and then to thousands. For some
reason, however, probably the stress of other affairs, the
Charter which had been prepared in 1656 was not issued
before the death of Cromwell, and King Charles II., in
1663, incorporated the Framework Knitters Company, and
reaped all the glory of resuscitating a trade which the folly
of his ancestors had driven from the country.

We are striving now by associations, by legislation, and
by wire-pulling in various directions to secure for the
agricultural labourer an interest in the land which he

---

[1] State Papers, 1655.

cultivates and on which he lives, assuming, in justification
of this procedure, that his natural ambition is to attach
himself and his family to his native soil. Our forefathers
struggled to the opposite extreme, and assuming, perhaps
rightly, that every peasant, unless otherwise restrained,
would naturally seek to improve his condition by migration,
made him, by their laws of settlement, almost inalienable
• from the soil of the parish in which he was born. If the
labourer became aged or infirm, or, if being young and
lusty, he married and had children, on the first symptom
of his being out of work, the parish officers would hunt out
the place of his birth, and send him and his family from
tything to tything to his place of settlement, lest by any
means he or his children might become chargeable to the
parish of his adoption. A code of settlement law was
gradually compiled, and every Assize and every Quarter
Session was occupied in the decision of cases where the one
parish had sent their poor to another, and the other
had endeavoured to repudiate the liability for their
support. The labourer thus, from his cradle to his grave,
carried with him the indelible stamp of his birth-place, to
which, from whatever clime he might affect, he was liable
at any moment of misfortune to be uninvitingly returned ;
women and children suffered the same treatment, and if
an unfortunate girl was known to be about to give birth
to a child she was at once sent or bribed to go into some
neighbouring parish, in order that the support of her child
might not be thrown upon the parish which had first discovered her condition. To alleviate the cruelties of this
state of things was one of the duties, as I conceive it was
one of the pleasures, of the Commonwealth Judges, and
their circuit books are full of orders restraining various
parish officers from the compulsory removal of poor and
aged people, of inoffensive life, from the spots where they
had passed their later years and from the comfort and
society of their children. This cruelty to the poor was a

subject of remonstrance by the Puritan party from the
early days of King James, and Dekkar in his " Seven
Deadly Sins,"[1] refers to this as one of the causes of the
Divine judgment upon the City of London, in visiting
it annually with the plague.   In one sense, indeed,
the poor were not unthought of, for every parish
had its stocks, every market town had its pillory,
and whipping-posts were as numerous as justices of the
peace.   Why, then, it was asked, if you have stocks to
confine your poor when they drink, and posts to whip them
to when they wander without your leave, have you not also
provided hospitals to cure them where they sicken in your
midst, and decent graves to receive them when they die of
the plague in your highways ?   But the whipping of vagabonds, which in many cases meant the torture of peasants
or artificers, male and female, seeking for employment
went gaily on till long after the Restoration, notwithstanding the attempted reforms of the Commonwealth.   How,
then, it may be asked, did the poor people of this period
ever travel about the country ?   They could only do so in
safety and without fear of being committed as rogues and
vagabonds by providing themselves with certificates from
their parish or their corporation that they were persons of
good conduct, that they had dwelt in a certain town or
parish for some years, and that it was necessary for
their business, and in order to assist them in providing
for themselves and their families, that they should be
permitted to pass and repass through other towns and
villages.   These passes or certificates concluded by praying
the favourable consideration of the bearer's case, and asking
churchwardens and municipalities to further their desires.
Papers in this form have been traced back by Dr. Sharpe
to the reign of Edward III. ; but whenever they may have
originated, they were in operation during the seventeenth
century, and often in regard to London contained threats of

---

[1] Published in 1606.

reprisals if their citizens were annoyed without reasonable redress. Without such passes the poor were apt to be fined, whipped, or imprisoned, and if the wanderer happened to be an Irishman, he was put in the stocks and whipped, and then sent back to his native country.[1]

A change had, however, during the sixteenth and seventeenth centuries, gradually and almost imperceptibly come over the tone of municipal life. As trades and manufactures had increased, the agricultural interest had diminished. Winchester, the ancient capital of the Empire, had long since given place to the supremacy of London, Norwich, and Bristol. The great trading centres of the Midlands were coming forward, the old historic cities were going back, and political power, which had formerly been almost exclusively centered in the counties, began now to be established in the towns. This change received its public recognition in Cromwell's Ordinance of December, 1653, when, for the first time in the history of our country, Manchester, Leeds, and Halifax were recognised as necessary factors in political life, and, at the same time, the Barons of the ancient Cinque Ports were reduced in number from sixteen to three, and many of the decayed and corrupt constituencies were deprived of the farce of electing national representatives.[2] Numerous petitions went up to the Council of State from the smaller towns complaining of their decaying trade, and praying for a consideration of their reduced condition, and the Council, ever willing to entertain, and, if possible, to redress municipal grievances, caused inquiries to be made into the causes of the alleged injury to their position and revenues. The reports from the various towns were long and argumentative, but they may fairly be summed up in the

---

[1] London, by Loftie, p. 179.

[2] Compare the list of the Long Parliament, *Parliamentary History*, Vol. II., p. 599, with the list for the Parliament under the Instrument of Government.—*Whitelock*, Vol. IV., p. 57.

sentence, "too much beer and too many strangers." All
these towns and large villages were more than amply
provided with licensed beerhouses, but in addition to these,
over which the Justices exercised some control, there were
at least as many unlicensed houses where beer was sold,
and to which the brewers supplied their beer with as much
freedom and impunity as to those that were licensed.
These unlicensed houses and the offending brewers were
frequently presented by grand juries, but as fines of very
moderate amounts were usually inflicted, the evil was not
abated but rather grew worse.   To check this unlimited
supply of beer, to which the citizens attributed the demorali-
zation of their apprentices, by the encouragement of idle and
thriftless habits, the Judges of Assize and Justices in
Sessions were called upon to reduce the number of licensed
houses, to suppress those standing " in blinde corners out of
view of towns or houses,"[1] and to punish with more than
nominal fines the unlicensed houses and the brewers who
supplied them.   Numerous orders of suppression were
accordingly made both at the Assizes and at Quarter
Sessions during the twelve years of the Commonwealth, the
fines on unlicensed house-keepers were increased to 20s.
for each offence, while those on the brewers laying in beer
to unlicensed premises were somewhat inadequately raised
from 3s. 4d. to 6s. 8d.   At the same time the fines leviable
by statute upon citizens who indulged in the then common
practice of letting their hogs, to the number of from ten to
twenty, run loose in the public streets, to the danger of
travellers and the pollution of the town, were increased from
12d. to 5s. per hog.[2]   The influx of strangers was, however,
that of which these townspeople mostly complained.   They
came in, it was said, not only from France and from
Holland, but from all parts of the United Kingdom, and

---

[1] Council Order, October 10th, 1649.
[2] The penalty on wandering hogs in London was 4d. each.—Middlesex
Records, Vol. III., p. 227.

bought and sold their wares without any regard to the time
or place of the market, or to the natural rights of the local
tradesmen to enjoy the commerce of their own town.   They
thus made friends among the inhabitants by underselling the
shopkeepers, sometimes married and remained among them,
and often in times of general distress became chargeable to
the town and a burthen on the local rates.   This last complaint, however, was one with which it was impossible for
any Government to deal, and we may fairly attribute the
decay of many of our old corporate towns to the injury
they unwittingly brought upon themselves by enforcing
their strict ordinances as to strangers and interlopers, and
thus driving into the open markets of the larger and more
modern towns much of the trade that they might otherwise
have secured for themselves.

The establishment of public works for the benefit of the
poor, which under the name of public workshops was
introduced with indifferent success under the French
Republic by Louis Blanc, and which has been resorted to
time after time by successive Governments for the relief of
distress in Ireland, was naturally a subject of experiment
with the Commonwealth.   The topic was introduced under
not very favourable auspices by Freeborn John,[1] in one of
his numerous pamphlets, who demanded that " provision
be made of work and comfortable maintenance for all sorts
of poor, aged, and impotent people."   But the claim on
behalf of the poor and needy was one which could not be
ignored, by reason of the character of its promoter.
Numerous pamphlets and letters, one among others by Sir
Mathew Hale,[2] pressed this favourite but Utopian scheme
upon the Government, who were compelled before long to
make a show of taking it in hand.   In the beginning of
1652, in consequence of representations from the City of

---

[1] Whitelock, Vol: II., p. 541.

[2] Burnet's Life of Hale.

London, it was referred to a committee[1] to consider and report how the poor might be set to work and relieved, and not suffered to beg ; to review all the Acts touching the poor and to report their defects ; and to receive proposals from the City of London and others touching the poor. From the terms of this order I gather that the City of London had made proposals for the provision of houses or money for the support of the poor ; but whether any practical steps were taken towards the institution of relief works or in other respects for the maintenance of the aged and impotent, I am not able to say. It is, however, most probable that the dire want of means from which the Commonwealth suffered from first to last, and their great difficulty in raising supplies, put it out of their power to do more than recommend the poor to the charity of others. They were not, however, without advice, for among other petitions presented to Cromwell on this subject, and included among the State Papers published from the collection of Mr. Milton, was one in July, 1652, suggesting that the poor should be provided for out of a public treasury to be supplied from tithes, from lawyers' fees, from parliamentary delinquents and unjust Courts and Judges brought in by the Conqueror.[2]

Other domestic matters were taken in hand at an early date, and among them were the regulation of the traffic in London and the circulation of news and of letters by the establishment of a General Post. London had always been badly served in the matter of public conveyance both by water and by land. The watermen were constant in their complaints that their trade was being supplanted by the increasing number and insolence of the hackney coachmen, and the ancient London coachmen complained that their trade was rendered dangerous,

---

[1] Whitelock, Vol. III., p. 418.
[2] State Papers addressed to Oliver Cromwell, p. 89.

their profits uncertain, and their reputation injured,[1]
by the frequent accession to their numbers of dis-
tressed soldiers of fortune from the Royalist camps, who,
their occupation being gone by the advent of peace, like
the unfrocked priests after the French revolution, either
took to the road as highwaymen or to the streets as hackney
coachmen. The public, with good reason, complained of
both, but, upon the balance of disadvantages, preferred
being robbed and bullied by the coachmen, to being soaked
and drowned in the wherries. The result of this general
discontent was that after many attempts an Act was
introduced in November, 1653, and passed in 1654, for the
convenience of the public in this matter.[2] And a consideration of its provisions will show how fully it was then
believed that the true interests of the public were best secured
by a well-regulated monopoly. By it the number of persons
keeping hackney carriages, within London and Westminster
and six miles round, was not to exceed two hundred at
any one time, the coaches so kept were not to exceed
three hundred, and the horses six hundred. It also
provided that the Aldermen of London should make
all necessary bye-laws and regulations, and select the two
hundred coachmen and their successors from time to time.
The admission to the "Fellowship of Coachmen," which
was then instituted, was put at 40s., with a quarterly
subscription of 2s. 6d. for each pair of horses kept for hire.
The regulations and prices fixed by the Aldermen, allowed
by the Council of State, and duly published, are given in
the subjoined note.[3]

---

[1] Whitelock, Vol. IV., p. 48.
[2] Statute, 23rd June, 1654.
[3] *Perfect Diurnal*, 2nd January, 1654-5.

For hire of a coach, caroach, or charret with four horses, 20s. a
day, and for a coach and two horses 10s. a day. Every coach with
four horses shall, at the rates aforesaid, travel upon the roads to and
from London, from the 25 day of March, until the 20 day of October,
thirty miles a day, within sixty miles compass of London every way

H

One of the remarkable features of the period was the appointment of a committee to look to the advancement of learning. It was nominated by the Little Parliament in August, 1653, and was composed of eighteen members, of

(excepting in Sussex roads, which being worst and hardest for journeying, shall be travelled as far only as is reasonable, or as shall be agreed or undertaken by the coachmen upon hire), and a coach with two horses at the rates before limited for two horses for the same season shall travel twenty miles a day; from and after the 20 day of October, until the 25 day of March, a coach with four horses shall travel 25 miles a day, and a coach with two horses shall travel 15 miles a day, within the like compass of sixty miles from London (excepting upon the said roads of Sussex). For the time a coach shall rest or lie still upon any journey, the hire shall be, viz., for a coach and four horses but 10s. a day, and for a coach with two horses, but 6s. 8d. a day. Also that none of the said coachmen (unless he be hired by the day) shall require, take, or have, for carrying any persons or person in his coach from any parts or places within the places and limits aforesaid, to any other place or places within the same limits (namely, six miles. compass of the late Lines of Communication, and back again) above 12d. a mile forward and backward, that is to say, 6d. a mile forward, and 6d. backward, if he be not put to above an hour's waiting and attendance for carrying back of such person or persons, and then to have 12d. an hour for every hour's attendance above the space of one hour. From the Old Exchange in Cornhill, London, unto Westminster, or to any other place of like distance of place or thereabouts, not above 18d., but if the persons carried exceed three persons, 2s., and from Old Exchange unto Temple Bar, Lincoln's Inn, or Gray's Inn, or to any other place of like distance of place or thereabouts, not above twelve pence; also from Guildhall to Temple Bar, or any part of Chancery-lane, Gray's Inn, or other place of like distance or thereabouts, not above 12d., and from Temple Bar, Lincoln's Inn, or Gray's Inn to Westminster, or to any place of like distance, or thereabouts, not above)12d., and from Westminster to White-Chappell, or the like distance of place or thereabouts, 2s. 6d., and from Temple Bar to White-Chappell, or the like distance or place, or thereabouts, eighteen pence and from the Old Exchange to White Chappell, or the like distance of place, 12d., and so after the same proportion from any place within the limits and places aforesaid. And if any person or persons admitted or that shall be admitted to keep coach and horses as aforesaid, shall deny to accept his pay

whom five to be a quorum, and they met in the Duchy Chamber at Whitehall.[1] Their secretary was William Thompson, at a salary of (apparently) £120 a year,[2] and among its members were to be found, Strickland, Ambassador to the Hague; Lawrence, afterwards President of the Council of State; Sir A. Astley Cooper, afterwards Lord Shaftesbury; Col. Sydenham, the Father of Medicine; Lockart, afterwards Ambassador to France; Col. Blunt, the great traveller; Sir Wm. Roberts, a Barrister; Dr. Goddard, and others. On the dissolution of this Parliament, the work of its various committees, and of this among the rest, necessarily came to an end, but the subject of their labours was still a matter of concern to the Council of State. And, indeed, the education of the people was not, at the era of the Commonwealth, of a very high standard. It had, I fancy, somewhat deteriorated even among the wealthy classes since the latter days of Queen Elizabeth. At Rye, a seaport town of considerable importance under Elizabeth, especially during the year of the Armada, and afterwards no less prominent during the naval engagements of the Commonwealth, out

according to the rates aforesaid, or shall wilfully refuse to be hired with his coach and horses at the rates aforesaid, and shall excuse himself, or pretend that he is hired before, whereas in truth he is not, or shall misbehave himself by uncivil carriage, or reproachful or railing words towards any person or persons who shall require or offer to hire his coach or horses, and offer to pay unto him for the same after the rates aforesaid, in such case such person or persons shall for the first offence, being proved before the overseers at their meetings who are hereby empowered to examine such abuses, forfeit and pay 10s.; for the second offence, being proved as aforesaid, 20s., and for the third offence, being complained of to the Court of Aldermen of the said City, and the thing there proved, shall, by order of the said Court, be dismissed, and put beside his keeping of coach and horses to work and hire out, within the limits aforesaid.

And, in the last place, it is provided: That such as shall hire any coach, and refuse to pay, may be carried before a Justice of the Peace, who shall cause payment to be made with reasonable damages.

[1] *Mercurius Politicus*, No. 166.
[2] State Papers, August, 1654.

of the one hundred and sixty-seven official persons who
took the engagement in March, 1649-50, at least fifty-nine,
or more than one-third, were unable to write their
names.[1] Under the influence of the times, however, education was slowly but surely progressing.
The subject of instituting free schools in every county
where they did not already exist, with a proper salary, to
be provided by such county, for the remuneration of
competent schoolmasters, was brought prominently before
Cromwell and his Council.[2] And had the Protector's life
been spared, and the financial position of the country
improved, such a scheme would doubtless have formed
one of those agenda hereafter to be classed with his proposed amendments of the law, as indicating an intelligence
and statesmanlike prevision far in advance of the age.
Meanwhile, the increasing demand for news engendered by
the stirring incidents of the Civil War, the enormous
number of speeches and pamphlets published by various
orators and authors, the natural desire of each party in turn
to lay its vindication before the country, and the necessity
for a more rapid and regular communication between
different parts of the kingdom than had hitherto been
practicable, owing to the disturbed condition of the country,
caused the Government to turn their early and serious
attention towards the establishment of some system by
which news, letters, and dispatches could be transmitted
safely and speedily throughout the community. It is
commonly said that Mr. Prideaux, the Attorney-General,
was also Postmaster-General under the Commonwealth.
This statement is not altogether accurate, although to him
especially belongs the credit of establishing the system of

[1] Many signed their initials, the names being written by the Clerk
of the Peace. The rest of the illiterates signed with a cross. Each
one, however, had a different cross, and the varieties of this simple
emblem are amazing.

[2] State Papers addressed, &c., p. 129.

postage on the plan since adopted. The scheme was under consideration for some years, and was dealt with by Acts of Parliament in September, 1654, and August, 1655. In the meantime the matter had been put very much into the hands of Mr. Prideaux. It was resolved in the first instance, by the Council of State, that the office of Postmaster should be at the sole disposal of Parliament. But Parliament not getting to business, the Council, on the 23rd of March, 1650-51, ordered that Mr. Prideaux do manage the business of the Inland Posts and be accountable to the Commonwealth quarterly for the profits. This arrangement was shortly afterwards altered, and Mr. Prideaux had a contract, under which he was to pay £10,000 a year, by equal quarterly payments, and to convey all letters at a tariff to be fixed. Under this order Prideaux organized the posts throughout the country. All requisitions for posts were by the Council transmitted to him, and he appears with much diligence and resolution to have founded the system which has since been brought to its present perfection. Having completed his organization for England, it became necessary in view of the trouble in Ireland to establish a post in that country; and we accordingly find that he appointed one Evan Vaughan postmaster for Munster, who hired two boats to convey the letters between the two countries, giving recognizance himself in £200 and two sureties in £100 each to make good the conveyance of all letters to and fro.[1] Serious difficulties, however, arose with local postmasters, and with certain persons who claimed to have a monopoly of the foreign posts. It appears from entries in the records of the Council of State, that Mr. Mathew Hale was constantly and confidentially consulted by them as to these claims and the mode of dealing with them. His view, acted upon by the Council, appears to have been that the Commonwealth could not justly revoke without com-

---

[1] State Papers, Warrants, 13th April, 1650.

pensation any patents granted by the late King before
the outbreak of hostilities, although as to any granted after
that date they had an absolute and uncontrolled discretion.
Among these patentees, the heirs of one Thomas Witherings claimed a monopoly of foreign posts under the following circumstances. It appears that during the reign of
King James there existed the offices of the Foreign and
of the Inland Posts, both of which were granted to
Thomas Witherings, the Inland for life only, the Foreign
for his life and that of Frizel, who was still living in 1654.
Before the Parliament of 1640 the King sequestered both
offices in favour of Burlomachi, on which Witherings
petitioned Parliament, the sequestration was voted illegal,
and he was restored to the Foreign, but not to the Inland
Office. After Witherings' death Sir David Watkins
enjoyed the Inland Office for Witherings' wife and
children till the Council of State put him out,
and in 1653 granted it to John Manley. Witherings' interest in the Inland Office ceased at his
death, but he had assigned it during his life to
the Earl of Warwick,[1] which was probably the reason for
his not being confirmed in it by Parliament. It appeared,
therefore, that the heirs of Thomas Witherings had some
claim for compensation in respect of their loss of the profits
of the foreign posts during the life of Frizel ; but that, on
the death of that person, the whole was at the disposal of
the Government. The claimants therefore probably had a
public faith bill for what Mr. Hale considered to be
reasonable.

In anticipation of some arrangement with these persons,
the Foreign and Inland Posts were both put up to tender,
and ultimately farmed to John Manley for two years at
£10,000 per annum, payable quarterly in advance. There

---

[1] See Report of Wm. Ellis (Solicitor-General) on reference from
His Highness as to settling the Post Office.—State Papers, Vol.
LXXIV., 13th August, 1654 ; also State Papers, Vol. XXXIX., fo. 8.

were various tenders[1] for this contract, the lowest being
£1,103 12s. 9d., and the highest £9,120 6s. 8d. John
Manley having tendered with an offer of *good security* at
£8,259 19s. 11¾d., he was accepted, and the sum ultimately
settled at £10,000. This contract was followed by a public
notice, dated 12th January, 1653-4,[2] appointing offices
where letters might be left for collection, and giving the
rates to be charged for postage. They were as follows :—

To any place within 80 miles of London, 2d. a single
letter, and 4d. a double letter.

To further distances, 3d. a single letter, and 6d. a double
letter.

To Scotland, a single letter 4d., and a double letter 8d.

To Ireland, a single letter 6d., and a double letter 12d.,
with a proportionate increase for treble or greater packets
of letters.

After Mr. Manley's time expired, a lease of the Post
Office was granted to Secretary Thurloe at the same rate,
viz., £10,000 per annum, he undertaking also to pay all
outgoings, and to charge only the authorized rates of
postage.[3] An Act of 1656,[4] under which the grant was
made to Thurloe, appears to have confirmed various
ordinances in 1654 and 1655, which provided for a *packet*
or *parcel* as well as a *letter* post. The packets, according
to the Act, were to be entered in a book, and to be
addressed on a label, and not as with letters, on the packet
itself. They were to be carried apart from the mail in big
leather bags, lined with cotton or baize, and the postman
was to blow his horn whenever he saw company, or at
least four times in each mile. Notwithstanding what
would appear to have been a low rate of postage considering the difficulties to be overcome, it is probable that

---

[1] State Papers, 29th June, 1653.
[2] *Proceedings in Parliament*, No. 225.
[3] State Papers, Domestic, Vol. 156.
[4] Statute, 1656, c. 30.

the Post Office as thus carried on, with a royalty of
£10,000 a year, was a sufficiently remunerative speculation
to the patentees; but the Government had too much
work on its hands to undertake a new branch of business,
and were content to see the general diffusion of intelligence
at a reasonable rate to the public. It was not, however,
until 1656 that the Post Office was actually established as
it exists at the present time. In the autumn of that year
an Act was passed establishing one office to be known as
"The General Post Office of England," and instituting
one officer, to be created by letters patent under the Great
Seal, and to be called "The Postmaster-General and
Comptroller of the Post Office," having exclusive jurisdiction over the management of the home and foreign posts,
the supplying of horses, the regulation of stages, and the
chartering of boats for foreign or colonial service.[1]

The business of the office was not carried on, however,
without serious danger and risk, not only to the letters but
to the letter-carriers themselves. The postman's horn,
which the poor fellow had to blow at the least every quarter
of a mile, not only warned pedestrians and others to avoid
his path, but gave a most inconvenient notice to the first
great enemy of the Post—the mounted highwayman. The
Dick Turpins of the period, most of whom were disestab-
lished Cavaliers, looked upon the new Post as their
legitimate prey, not only for the values to be found in the
letters and in the packets carried by the postman,
but also for the intelligence that might be gained and
turned to a profit from the investigation of the letters
and despatches passing between various Government
Officials. Thus, robbing the mail became, during the early
days of the Post Office, one of the institutions of the country.
It was certain death to a highwayman if he were caught,
and to facilitate his capture the Parliament, by an Act of

---

[1] Statute, 1656, c. 30.

1653,[1] decreed a reward of £10 to be paid out of the Exchequer, to any person who should take a highwayman or deliver him up to justice. Numerous reports were given in the papers of the robbery of the mails, but perhaps the most daring and the most successful of these exploits took place in March, 1654,[2] when the mail was stopped and robbed at 3 o'clock in the afternoon, within a mile of St. George's, Southwark, by a mounted band, who, having opened all the letters and found no money, broke open the packets and scattered the contents. Their courage was rewarded, for they all escaped.

Of the leaders of these bands two, according to the reports of the time, were especially noted. Captain Hynd, formerly a Royalist officer, had established himself on the Oxford Circuit, and was an occasion of great trouble to the Privy Council, who appear, amongst other multifarious duties, to have charged themselves with the protection of inland travellers. The Council, however, caught him at last, examined him in person, and sent his depositions to the Judges of Assize at Reading, with directions to proceed against him according to law.[8]

Another of these highwaymen was Captain Farmer, "the great robber of the North," who, with one Hewitt, his companion, rode the Northern Circuit. Farmer was, like Hynd, formerly an officer of Cavaliers, but the Council of State after a time caught these also. They were both apprehended at Lincoln, "after having performed," according to the papers, "as many and as notable exploits as ever Hynd did."[4] And they also, it is to be presumed, were proceeded against according to law. These robbers, however, still continued their exploits, and it was during an attack by highwaymen on the road

---

[1] Statute, 21st Oct., 1653.
[2] *Mercurius Politicus*, 25th March, 1654.
[8] State Paper, Vol. XXIV.
[4] *Mercurius Politicus*, 10th March, 1652-3.

between St. Albans and London, that Col. Pride (of the
Purge) was shot dead by one of the gang in August, 1657.[1]
There was also a gang of these gentry near Blackheath,
who, in the Spring of 1654, attacked Major Bourne and
some of his friends on Shooter's Hill.[2]   After a long fight,
during which one of Major Bourne's friends was shot,
the rogues were beaten off.   They escaped for the moment,
but were all taken within a week, some of them severely
wounded, through the captain of the band going to a
chemist in Shoe Lane to have his wounds dressed, and
being there identified by one of his victims, who was at the
chemist's shop for the same purpose.

It was strongly suspected at the time that the Post
Office was used by Thurloe as a means of obtaining
political information.   The instructions sent by John
Manley to the various deputy postmasters show that this
suspicion was well founded.   These directed them to be
careful in the selection of their riders, to report the names
of any of the King's party or any foreigners lodging at the
various inns, to keep a vigilant eye on the disaffected in
their various districts, to send up notice of their meetings
and conversations, and generally to keep the secretary well
informed of everything occurring throughout the country.[3]

This distribution of Posts led incidentally to a thorough
revision of the laws as to highways, and to an attempt,
successful in after years, to construct a general highway
system, under which the United Kingdom might be inter-
sected by sound, well-kept roads, and its various parts put
into easy communication with each other.   With a view to
this, Cromwell, in 1654, by a series of carefully-considered
Ordinances,[4] provided in much detail for a system of

---

[1] *Mercurius Politicus*, No. 375.

[2] *Mercurius Politicus*, 13th March, 1653-4.

[3] Private instructions to deputy postmasters. — State Papers,
Vol. XLII. (1653).

[4] Ordinances, 1654, Scoble. These highway Acts were drawn by Baron
Thorpe.

surveyors, overseers, and workers on the roads, with a scheme for their payment, and thus laid the first stone of the admirable highway system under which we are now governed.

It was not, however, by reason only of their exertions to further trade and to promote the general well-being of the people, that the Commonwealth commended itself to the sympathy and goodwill of the nation. I have mentioned the state of the gaols over-running with prisoners committed for debt, and unable to escape by reason of the accumulation of their liabilities. An inquiry was speedily instituted, and a Committee appointed to investigate the condition of the Upper Bench, the Marshalsea, and other prisons, the number of debtors, the length of their imprisonment, and the amount of their debts. The result of this inquiry was that in the Upper Bench Prison alone on the 2nd May, 1652, there were 399 prisoners[1] whose " actions and executions "—in other words, whose debts, together with accumulations of interest and costs, amounted in the total to £976,122. This prison was under the control of Sir John Lenthal, against whose management and rapacity very plain speaking was used, and who was, in consequence, much discredited during the later years of the Commonwealth. The Act for the relief of these and other poor prisoners in England[2] was founded on just, humane and statesmanlike considerations, and was, as nearly as may be, our own system of discharge by bankruptcy. By this enactment a prisoner in custody for breach of contract might require any Justice of the Peace to issue a writ calling upon the gaoler to bring him before a Justice of

---

[1] *Perfect Diurnal*, 16th May, 1652. Whitelock, Vol. IV., p. 19.

[2] Statute, 27th April, 1652, reciting Acts of 1649 and 1650, directed to the same object. This treatment of poor debtors kept in perpetual imprisonment, was one of the forms of cruelty denounced by Dekkar in his *Seven Deadly Sins*, in 1606.

the Peace, and if it appeared upon the return of the writ
that such prisoner was in custody for debt, and if he made
oath that he was not worth £5 in real or personal estate,
beyond his wearing apparel and bedding for himself, his
wife and children, and his tools of trade or business, the
magistrate was to return the writ into the Court which
issued the process of imprisonment.   Notice was then given
to the parties who issued process, and who could only show
as cause against his discharge, either that the prisoner had
more than £5, or that he had made away with his
estate to defeat or delay his creditors, or that he had
been in arms against the Parliament.   These questions the
prisoner was entitled to have tried by a jury, and if they
were answered in his favour he was at once released ; such
release not operating, however, as a dischage of the debt.
Power was given to debtors to sue *in formâ pauperis*, when
they were excused the payment of all fees, and applicants
were liable to an indictment for perjury if they falsely
stated their assets or their liabilities.   At the same time,
orders were made to prevent the extortions commonly
practised by bailiffs, and as a step in this direction they
were forbidden by the Middlesex magistrates to take their
prisoners to inns or alehouses kept by themselves or their
families.[1] Under this Act many hundreds of poor prisoners
were released from a lifelong captivity, and a general
chorus of gratitude must have resounded to the glory
of the Government from these victims of rapacity and
misfortune.   But to turn a pauper out of a gaol, where
at least he had food and shelter, into the cold world without a penny to commence life afresh, would hardly have
been a kind or a friendly action.   And accordingly an
assessment was made for the relief of such poor debtors as
these, and also, as a consequential duty, for the relief of such
equally poor creditors as had been ruined by the fraud or
the misfortune of their debtors. But the freeing of these poor

---

[1] *Mercurius Politicus*, No. 295.

debtors did not progress quickly enough for the Protector, who, in June, 1654, published a further ordinance commanding the judges to hold continuous sittings at Salters' Hall to consider the cases of the prisoners in the Upper Bench, the Fleet, the Gatehouse in Westminster, the Counter in Surrey, and the Prison in Whitechapel, and to discharge the debtors according to the requirements of the Acts.[1]

After attending to the captives at home the Commonwealth turned their attention to English captives abroad. The Grand Turk and the Moors of Algeria and of Morocco made a great part of their barbarous revenue from the capture of European men and women, selling them as slaves, or holding them as hostages for ransom.[2] Thus, in African dungeons or in Asiatic slavery these unhappy Christians wore out a life of misery, toil, and torture, rendered all the more sad by a long-deferred hope of release. The cry of these captives was from time to time heard in the land, and the sympathy of our people went out to them in their misery as day by day they invoked the pity of Heaven upon all prisoners and captives. But though an occasional prisoner obtained his release through the exertions or the wealth of his family,[3] no step was ever taken for a general release of captives; no Government, no Parliament and no great leader of the nation had oeen willing to declare in public that every Englishman had a Christian duty towards his fellow-subjects in foreign chains, till the great Puritan Chieftain and the great Puritan Party made it a part of their policy and a sacred duty to attempt the relief of these captives from their

[1] *Perfect Diurnal*, 19th June, 1654.

[2] Readers of *Romola* will recognise in Baldassare the counterpart of the Englishman sold into slavery.

[3] The collections for these captives were probably looked upon with suspicion, which may account for an entry in the accounts of All Souls' College, Oxford, showing that in 1659 the College subscribed *one shilling* for a Turkish captive with three crescents tattooed on his breast. See Rogers, Vol. VI., p. 667.

cruel servitude, and to seek the blessing of the Almighty
by exercising one of his attributes. Inquiries were made
as to the several captives abroad, and with a view to an
expedition for their relief an Act[1] was passed imposing a
duty on all exciseable imports to be levied for four years
to provide a fund for their redemption. By this means
sufficient money was collected, and the first cases attempted
were the victims of the pirates of Algiers. Of these there
were altogether one hundred and twelve, of whom twelve
were women, over whom there was much bargaining
between the Moors and the English agents. The captives
in Tripoli, who were attempted next, appear to have
consisted mostly of officers, and these were ransomed after
a time at a cost of 200 dollars each.[2] After which the
Speaker—not the Speaker of the House of Commons, for
poor Lenthal, with his various distractions, would have
cut but a sorry figure among the Turks—but the good
ship Speaker, a formidable man-of-war, mounting fifty-
eight guns, and carrying two hundred and sixty men,
was sent out by the Government with the sum of
£30,000 to redeem poor English captives from exile and
cruel slavery in Turkey.[3] Very little is said in the books
or in the papers about these captives, and it is not possible to give with any accuracy the numbers thus
released. They are not referred to either in the Parliamentary History or in Whitelock's Memorials. They
were regarded, I suppose, as the legitimate spoil of
the bow and the spear of the Mahomedan warrior, and
their release was regarded by the Commonwealth as merely
the exercise of a duty of mercy and charity imposed upon
all Christian men. But, one can well imagine that there
would not be one among these redeemed Englishmen, and

[1] Statute, 26th March, 1650.
[2] State Papers, 21st November and 8th December, 1653.
[3] *Faithful Scout*, No. 54, 30th January, 1651-2. A List of the Navy
of England. Parliamentary History, Vol. III, p. 1558.

probably not a man of his family, but would ever after
have had a good word and a stout heart for the Protector
and for the Government, which, under his good ordering,
had sent them their release.   Nor would it be easy to over-
estimate the effect on the public mind of the action of the
Protector with regard to the oppressed Protestants of
Piedmont.   It touched the heart of all the members of the
Reformed Church, it gratified the pride of those who
gloried in the power of their flag, and it showed a
sympathy with human suffering and a courage in its
declaration, which re-echoed the pulsation of every
English heart.   Nearly a century before, some thousands
of persecuted Protestants had fled from their native
country, and had landed penniless and homeless on our
shores.   During the latter half of the sixteenth century,
our southern ports were daily receiving cargoes of these
fugitives, who were received with open arms by their sym-
pathetic co-religionists, and were provided for at the
national cost, when private benevolence had failed to
relieve their wants.   But these unhappy Huguenots thus
thrown upon our generosity had brought an unexpected
blessing in their train.   They introduced into the land of
their adoption numerous industries of which our people
had heretofore been ignorant ;   and by the exercise
of weaving, cloth-making, glass-blowing, paper-making,
and various other crafts, they instilled a new life into our
country of farmers and graziers, and added many millions
of pounds to the national wealth.   No sooner, therefore,
had it become known in England that the Duke of Savoy,
imitating in a small way, but to the best of his ability, the
exploits of his late brother of France, on the Feast of
S. Bartholomew, had massacred and expatriated hundreds
of his poorer Protestant subjects in the Swiss valleys, than
Cromwell, representing the English nation, which had
taken upon itself, through him, the protection and cham-
pionship of Protestant Europe, constituted himself the

instrument of Divine mercy to obtain justice and redress for these unhappy persons. Not only did he interpose with the strong hand of his authority, with threats of armed intervention, and with pressure upon the King of France, who was not too willing to interfere with the proceedings of the Italian Guise, but he took a personal and direct interest in their helpless position in a manner which came home to every man, woman and child. He headed a subscription for their relief with a sum from his private purse equal to £10,000 of our present money, and he ordered a day to be observed as one of prayer and humiliation, with collections to be made in every church throughout the land. To these appeals great and munificent responses were made. In London alone the amount collected was fixed by some at £500,000.[1] It may be that the Metropolis contained the stouter-hearted and more wealthy Puritans. It may be that Milton, who, not content with putting into vigorous language the bold sentiments of the Protector, had endeavoured on his own behalf to raise the indignation of the people against the tyranny of the Italian, had successfully communicated his enthusiasm to the congregations.[2] However it may have been, the returns from the London churches, so far as we have them, show an amount collected far in excess of any sums we hear of at the present day.[3] St. Martin's-in-the-Fields paid over to the Council of State £325 4s. 6d. (equal to £1,300 of to-day); St. Margaret's, Westminster, £348 3s. 3d.; Hackney £214 7s. 11d.; Whitechapel, £110 18s. Two other churches collected over £300 each; three others over £200 each; sixteen collected over

---

[1] Nieuport, Dutch Ambassador, writing to the States-General from London, says the collection for the Waldenses amounts to £100,000. —Thurloe, Vol. II., p. 623.

[2] " Avenge, O Lord, Thy slaughtered saints, whose bones
    Lie scattered on the Alpine mountains cold," etc.

[3] State Papers, Vol. CXXXI., gives the results of various collections in addition to those mentioned in the text.

£100 each, and numerous other churches collected smaller
sums. In the country districts the parish church of Norwich
contributed£157 15s. 8d.,and that of Canterbury£149 1s. 11d.,
while All Souls', Oxford, debits itself with the sum of £20,
independently of a general assessment made on various
colleges and halls. The collections were not, however,
confined to the churches, but ministers visited their parishioners in their homes, and others aided them in their
efforts, so that a house-to-house collection was made through
the whole of London, and as far as practicable through
the country also. And all England knew and applauded
the conduct of the Government whose interest in these,
their fellow-religionists, did not cease with the first success
of their negotiations and the distribution of the large sums
collected for their relief. We learn now from a despatch
of Milton's to the King of France and a letter of Oliver's
to his Ambassador in Paris,[1] that not many months
before his death, and indeed as one of the last of his
public acts, Cromwell was still pleading with the French
King, and urging with all his vigour and determination the
cause of the people of Piedmont against the depopulators,
the robbers and the assassins by whom they were surrounded.

Many of the Acts of Parliament and Ordinances of the
Council and of the Protector, to which I have referred, are
habitually ignored or treated as of small importance and
somewhat beneath the dignity of history. But the comfort of
a nation, as of an individual, is as often secured by a careful attention to the small requirements of everyday life as
by a devotion to those of greater concern. And the interest
thus shown by the Commonwealth in the necessities of the
people must inevitably have tended to develop a good
feeling between the masses and the Government, or
perhaps more strictly between them and Cromwell, who
represented in their eyes not only the figurehead, but the

[1] Carlyle, Vol. IV., pp. 205-213.

sails and rudder of the vessel of State. Heavy assessments on Royalists' estates affected not them. The weight of ordinary taxation fell on their richer neighbours. The niceties of doctrine that convulsed Parliament and the preachers concerned them but little. The parliamentary soldier on his march despoiled no one and made good any horses or cattle requisitioned by the general. Free quarter was abolished, and the public faith was pledged for all supplies taken for the use of the Commonwealth. Equal justice was administered between rich and poor by fearless and independent judges, and the common people were put once more into enjoyment of those protective rights which the Tudors had conferred upon them. And more than all, their miserable and scanty wages, hardly, at the best of times, sufficing for a bare subsistence, fixed periodically at Quarter Sessions by employers whose interest combined with their instinct to keep wages at the lowest ebb, gradually but surely began to rise. This gradual raising of the wages of the working classes through all England began from the very moment that the Puritans took the field against the forces of the King. From the commencement of the century to 1642 wages had remained about the same, and from that time they began and continued steadily to rise. The common labourer and the artisan received 8d. a day during the reign of Queen Mary, and they were still receiving the same wages in 1633. Then came small modifications. In 1639 their wages had risen to 10d., in 1642 to 11d., in 1645 to 12d. per day, and from that sum they never receded. Similarly the carpenter, the mason, and the slater received 1s. 1d. per day, through a long series of years to 1640, when they got 1s. 2d., in 1642 they got 1s. 4d., and in 1644 their wages rose to 1s. 6d. per day, and there remained. Digging and hedging and ditching, for which the wages had stood variously at 8d., 9d., and 10d. per day during the previous fifty years, was permanently raised in 1645 from 10d. to 12d. per day.

Nor can it be said that the rise in wages was counter-
balanced by the rise in prices. Such was not the case.
Taking a comparison between wages and the price of wheat
which will be sufficient to illustrate this observation, we
find that whereas in 1625 the proportion between the.
price of a quarter of wheat and the weekly wages of
an artisan were as 1 to 9 : the same proportion in 1650
was as 1 to 7, and in 1655 as 1 to 4.[1] The effect of this
rise of wages, however satisfactory to the labourer, was
distinctly felt by the landowner and the manufacturer at
least as early as 1656, for in October of that year they
obtained the appointment of a Committee to consider of
"the excessive wages paid to labourers and artificers, to
the great prejudice of the Commonwealth," and also to
report upon the exorbitancy in the apparel and habits of
servants, "which is the ground of many mischiefs."[2]
Nothing came of this Committee at the time, but it bore
fruit during the first year after the Restoration, when the
proportion between the price of corn and weekly wages
went down nearly to 1 to 9.[3] So long as Cromwell lived,
however, the high rate of wages remained, and it thus
mattered little to these toilers in the cities and labourers in
the fields whether the laws of which they reaped the direct
and immediate benefit in their pockets and in their personal
freedom were passed by a Commonwealth without a King or
a House of Lords, whether they emanated from a supreme
authority composed of a Convention alone, or of a Lord
Protector and a Parliament, or whether they proceeded from
a Council of State with power to make and enforce its
orders. It was enough for them that they were the laws of an

[1] See a very careful comparison by Professor Rogers in his History
of Agriculture, &c., Vol. V., p. 826. In 1650 wheat was 55s. 4d. per
quarter ; wages were 8s. per week. In 1655 wheat was 33s. 2d. per
quarter ; wages were 8s. 11½d. per week.

[2] *Mercurius Politicus*, No. 330.

[3] In 1661 the price of wheat was 70s. 9d. per quarter; the rate of
wages was 8s. per week.

existing Government, that such Government was identified
with Cromwell, and that so long as he was in power their
interests and their happiness would be secured.   Such
were, in my judgment, in great part the reasons why the
English people, as a nation, stood by Cromwell and whatever form of Government he thought it right for the moment
to support;   and why there was, in fact, that contentment
among them which appears from their ready acceptance
of Cromwell's ordinances, and their abstention from any
schemes for his overthrow.

Other powerful reasons for the sympathy of the people
and the adhesion of the mercantile community were his
reforms in the administration of justice and his schemes
for improvement of the law; for it is a well-recognised
fact in European history that commerce is fostered by
liberal and equal legislation, and that the securities and the
public credit of a country rise or fall in value in proportion
to the confidence that is felt in the certain execution of its
laws and in the impartiality and independence of its judges.

CHAPTER III.

THE GERM OF RELIGIOUS TOLERATION.

To us who have been educated in the nineteenth century any declaration inconsistent with religious toleration would be abhorrent and inadmissible. But apart from early teaching and habits of life, a belief in, and a practice of, religious toleration would seem to be either the effort of a mind singularly imbued with noble and generous catholicity, or the concomitant of a calm indifference to every or any religion. To the ordinary layman or ecclesiastic of the seventeenth century, whose early training and habits of life were rather those of persecution than of fraternity in religion, a general toleration would have appeared more than the vain pursuit of a shadow—it would have seemed a direct negation of right and a distinct and unequivocal recognition and authorization of error. That oppressed religions, like oppressed nationalities, should clamour for a universal toleration would be natural enough, and we have from time to time witnessed combinations in which Presbyterians, Episcopalians, Catholics, and others have, in turns, taken part in order to obtain from the Government of the day such general toleration as would protect their own creed in common with others. But that the cry for religious toleration should come from the dominant, rather than from the servient, body betokened a new departure in religious thought. And it is with no idea of whitewashing damaged reputations or of painting the sepulchres of the Puritans to represent the temples of gods, but solely in the spirit of justice, that I desire to draw attention to certain qualities in which Cromwell and the leaders of the Commonwealth have been thought to be deficient,

and to the attempts made by the Protector during his
brief term of authority to establish the principle of religious
toleration. That bigotry and fanaticism were rife in the
first half of the seventeenth century ; that in the Parliamentary army there was a temper which, while dis-
tinguishing it in the matter of morality and discipline from
any army that ever existed, trod with an iron heel on the
sensibilities of thousands of their countrymen; that the
zeal and excesses of the Independents in the destruction of
so-called superstitious emblems brought discredit not only
upon their cause but upon their country ; that an outward
semblance of piety pervaded the party to an extent that
bordered on the ridiculous and led the opposition to
denounce as canting hypocrites all those who showed any
pretence to religion ; that the dress, the language, and the
demeanour of the extreme Puritans were offensive to many
even of their own sect, and that a strong vindictive and
bloodthirsty party-feeling raged on both sides of
the struggle, is no less deplorable than true.
But it is a no less incontrovertible fact that amid
all this fanaticism and violence was to be found
the germ of civil and religious toleration. It cannot be
said that very much came of it during the Interregnum,
but it was existent, and both the Protector and his various
Councils recognised it and attempted to foster it into life.
Cromwell himself stands in the unique position of having
never during his own times had a really friendly biographer.
His contemporary history is written by his enemies. There
are no memorials of his own. Some two hundred and fifty
letters on various subjects, extending over a life of nearly
sixty years, with some eighteen speeches delivered in Parliament, are all the materials that Cromwell has left for his
biographer. He cannot fairly be judged from the pages of
Whitelock. That painstaking and voluminous author posted
up his diary in many instances long after the events which
he recorded had taken place; he copied page after page

literatim from the newspapers of the day, he formulated his opinion of the Protector from time to time as the orders of the latter jumped with the good or ill fortune of the Lord Commissioner, and his memorials were not published till twenty years after the Restoration, when the writer had been five years in his grave. Under these circumstances they cannot fail to have been coloured by the influence which the Restoration must necessarily have had upon the fortunes and the views of the memorialist and his family. Ludlow was an enemy of the Protector from the moment that the supremacy of a single person with a Parliament became inevitable. Clarendon, though unable to withhold from Cromwell in many respects a tribute of praise, was the life and soul of the Restoration. Burnet, though liberal in his views even more than in his words, and by no means friendly to either Charles or his sons, wrote and published under a monarchy. Clement Walker, in his history of Independency (if indeed he is responsible for more than the first part of the work published under his name), accepts all the scandalous gossip about the Protector, and even permits himself to say that it was belie*v*ed, *and not without good cause*, that Cromwell, after the battle of Worcester, made a seven years' compact with the Devil, who, at the end of that period, carried him off in a gale of wind.[1] Heath, Harris, Oldmixon, and many other writers

---

[1] " It was believed, and that not without good cause, that Cromwell the same morning that he defeated the King's Army at Worcester Fight, had conferen*c*e personally with the Divell, with whom he made a contract that to have his will then, and in all things else for *s*even years after from that time (being the 3rd September, 1651), he should at the expiration of the said years have him at his command, to do all his pleasure both with his soul and body. Now, if anyone will please to reckon from the 3rd September, 1651, till the 3rd September, 1658, he shall find it to a day just seven years, and no more, at the end of which he dyed, but with such extremity of tempestuous weather, that was by all men judged to be prodigious, neither indeed, was his end more miserable (for he dyed mad and despairing), than he hath

of the Restoration seem almost to have joined in a conspiracy
of inaccuracy to prevent succeeding generations having a true
and clear conception of the Protector's character. This
must therefore be gathered as best it may from the scanty
materials to hand. As a soldier and as a director of our
foreign affairs, it may be held as established by universal
acclamation that he has no rival in our history; but as to
his possession of the other qualities or requirements of a
ruler or a man, hopeless discord reigns. A difficulty which
is accentuated by the wholesale destruction of Commonwealth records on the one hand, and by the preservation
on the other of every scurrilous pamphlet and paper
published during the Interregnum, which threw dirt and
discredit day by day upon the then ruler of the country.
Many of the most popular and best known libels upon
Cromwell are even now stored up in the Record Office, and
may be read in the intercepted correspondence between the
Royalist agents in England and their friends and employers abroad—agents who earned their pay by trans-
mitting in a cypher legible to Thurloe and his secretaries
scurrilous gossip and untrustworthy rumours for the gratification of the exiled princes in Paris or Amsterdam. We
know from the general history of his time that Cromwell
was capable of many acts of clemency to his enemies, and
that having once successfully asserted the supremacy of
his Government or of the law as the case might be, he was
unwilling unnecessarily to punish offenders. He was also
possessed of a quality which, although Clarendon debits it
to him as a weakness, others may credit it as a virtue—a
great love for his children and his family, and a sincere
sympathy for their afflictions. These traits in his character
give some ground for the consideration of how far a system
of civil and religious toleration, founded on a spirit of

left his name infamous." Part IV., p. 31. See, however, Carlyle's
account of the death of Cromwell, as described in Letters and
Speeches, Vol. IV., p. 214.

clemency, was regarded by him and his adherents as
a desirable element in English rule. Whitelock, on
more than one occasion, gives him credit for a sincere
appreciation of this great doctrine, and Burnet[1] mentions
with approbation the lively gratification experienced by
Cromwell upon hearing that Blake, while refusing to permit
English sailors to be dealt with by Spanish priests,
punished them himself for insulting, while on shore, the
Catholic population in the exercise of the established
religion of their country. And in the petitions presented
to Cromwell for his support in Parliament, "liberty of
conscience to all provided they lived quietly under the
Commonwealth" was a common form.[2] "The Independent
Junto," says Clement Walker, "bottomed all their hope
and interest to establish that chimera called *Liberty of
Conscience.*"[3] And he adds his opinion that it probably was
also Cromwell's ambition at that time, as it certainly
appeared to be afterwards from what subsequently
happened. In this ambition he was both supported by,
and he supported, the Council of War, who, meeting
together solemnly on Christmas Day, 1648, animated by
sentiments of peace and goodwill, voted for a toleration of
all religions,[4] and, so far as I am aware, never receded from
that position. In 1654 the Protector, much troubled by
the dissentions of various sects, and feeling how incapable
an uncontrolled popular assembly is of real toleration, was
anxious to inaugurate his rule by carrying out, as far as
possible, a scheme of general religious freedom. He accordingly convened a meeting, not, it is said, as a synod, but
as "a loving and Christian-like reception," where schemes
might be propounded for a mutual religious toleration. To

---

[1] Burnet, p. 52.
[2] State Papers addressed to Oliver Cromwell, from the collection of
Mr. Milton, p. 99.
[3] History of Independence, Part I , p. 31.
[4] Ibid, Part II., p. 50.

this reception were called representatives of all sections of
religious thought, bishops and Anabaptists, Independents
and Presbyterians. Their meeting, which took place at
Whitehall, was conducted, according to the Protector's
orders, without any discussion as to each other's religious
principles ; but they were all to labour in common to find
some basis upon which they could agree in union. [1] Several
meetings appear to have taken place, the attendance numbering about twenty, and the deliberations and resolutions were
kept as secret as the times would permit, so as not to
raise a factious opposition to any scheme for peace and
toleration upon which these various divines might agree.
Dr. Gauden (the author of Εικων Βασιλικη), writing to a friend
in the autumn of 1656, says that Episcopalians, Presbyterians, and Independents were in a fair way to become reconciled, and were " upon a very calme temper."[2]
In February, 1644-5, the Book of Common Prayer had
been abolished by Statute,[3] and the " Directory for the
Public Worship of God " established in its place. This
provided for various forms of prayer, of singing psalms, of
reading the Scriptures, and of preaching, for the administration of the Sacraments of Baptism and of the Lord's
Supper, for the solemnization of marriage, for the visita-
tion of the sick, for the burial of the dead, and for days of
public fasting and thanksgiving. And except that under
certain limitations it left a discretion to the minister as to
the order of the service, it was nearly as strict a formula
as was contained in the liturgy of Edward VI. Neither
was there any question of disestablishment and disendow-
ment, for the Presbyterians were as fully established and
protected by the State as had been the Episcopalians, the
endowment of the Clergy, in some form or other, was a recog-

---

[1] Beverning to the States-General. Thurloe, Vol. II., p. 67, 3rd February, 1653-4.

[2] Thurloe, Vol. IV., pp. 598-601.

[3] Statutes 1644, c 51. Scoble, p. 75.

nised necessity, and the Directory was at least as much a Parliamentary form of service as the Book of Common Prayer.[1] There was therefore no insuperable objection to the construction of a form of public worship to which all might agree, and the association of different divines in the same Christian brotherhood would not have been more incongruous than the position of the present day when under one and the same Sovereign Episcopalians are Conformists in England, Dissenters in Scotland, and in Ireland neither the one nor the other.

The assembly did, in fact, agree upon certain matters which ought to be believed by all Christian people, and a belief in which should entitle them to full religious toleration. But this promising agreement among the divines no sooner became known than the Royalist presses were again at work; pamphlets attacking the *chimera of religious toleration* were spread abroad and an illustrated broadsheet picturing the members of the committee, presided over by an Adamite, clad in the costume of the garden of Eden, sitting next to a bishop in full canonicals, threw ridicule as well as distrust upon the scheme. The action of Cromwell and the divines was not, however, altogether without effect, for although many of the members of his Council of State were by no means enthusiastic in their desire for religious toleration, and the Councils themselves were sometimes turbulent and self-asserting, yet they sat at Whitehall in immediate proximity to the Protector's residence, and the knowledge that his personal intervention in their debates might at any moment be expected, probably acted upon them after the manner of Peter van Stuyvesant's stick, and composed any unruly member who was disposed to vote against the well-understood wishes of the Lord Protector. And the Parliament of 1657, in an article to which the Protector gave his willing assent, declared that those who acknowledged the Trinity and the Scriptures,

---

[1] See 5 and 6, Edward VI., c. 1.

but differed in doctrine, should be convinced if possible, but should not suffer penalties, and should be protected in the exercise of their religion unless they disturbed the peace—not, however, extending to Popery or the countenancing of blasphemy or licentiousness : and further, that ministers who differed should be capable of civil offices, but not entitled to receive the maintenance appointed for the ministry.[1] Before, however, dealing with some few instances in which effect was given to the wishes of the Protector and the Council of Officers, let me say a word on the subject of that Book whose volume was always in the hands and whose language was ever on the lips of the great leaders of the army of Independents, and whose text was habitually appealed to indifferently by the partisans of bigotry and the lovers of freedom.

It has been said that much of the mischief of the seventeenth century arose from too much Bible reading in the sixteenth. This proposition, which has a certain tone of irreverence, has nevertheless a substantial foundation of fact. The translation of the Bible into the vulgar tongue, its free circulation through the country, and the encouragement given to its being read by all classes gave rise to difficulties and dangers not originally contemplated. Hobbes suggests that the great differences as to doctrine and ritual in the church arose from the printing and circulating of the new Bible in King James's time, as everyone who had read the book through once or twice felt himself competent to form his own views on the subject, set the old teachers at defiance, cast off all reverence for the bishops and pastors of the churches, and thus brought about a strange variety of sects. Henry VIII. had endeavoured to provide against the unlimited and unreasoning discussion of the Scriptures by persons incompetent to

---

[1] Petition of knights, citizens and burgesses assembled in Parliament, Art. 11. Consented to by the Protector on 25th May; passed 26th June, 1657.

understand or form opinions on the sacred writings, by procuring an Act of Parliament to declare that all men might read the Scriptures *except servants* (a very large exception in those days), but no women, except ladies and gentlewomen who had leisure, and who might ask somebody about the meaning.[1] After, however, some few years, all restriction was removed, and by the time of Edward VI. the Bible became the common property of all classes of society. This was followed by the natural result that inasmuch as the Bible contains as much good reading as any profane work ever published, persons commonly read for themselves those portions that afforded them recreation as well as instruction, and that the Old Testament being composed mainly of histories and of prophecies attracted more attention than the new, which, apart from the life of the Saviour, is chiefly concerned with doctrine and rules for moral guidance. There were also peculiar circumstances in relation to the production of the Bible which commended it to the people, and specially, perhaps, to the middle and lower classes, who, more than others, are susceptible to sentiment and romance. The English translation was effected in a way which distinguishes it from every other book that has been offered to the world, for while the words of the translation are English words, the thoughts, the expressions, and the phrases are Hebrew, so that in every page of the book, more especially in the Old Testament, we have the old warrior, king, or lawgiver speaking the sentiments 'of ancient Judæa in the language of modern England. But yet another danger hereupon arose. As the Protestant Bible was put into the hands of all classes of the laity, they were invited and indeed enjoined to search the Scriptures and to find eternal life within their pages. And accordingly the Bibles multiplied exceedingly. They were printed openly in England, in Holland, in Scotland, and in Switzerland, sur-

---

[1] Selden's Table Talk, "Bible Scriptures."

reptitiously in France, in Italy, and elsewhere, some in
Latin and some in English, some with illustrations and
comments, some without, so that by the beginning of
the seventeenth century every householder in the country
had his copy of the Bible, and proceeded to put his own
construction for his own guidance on his favourite
passages. And "Good Lord! what a mess they made
of it," said Selden, writing at the time and appreciating
at its true value the eccentricity of private judgment
applied to isolated passages of this marvellous work. The
evils of this course of reading were forcibly pointed out by
the Bishops of the Church of Rome, who went so far as to
have a book specially printed and illustrated, containing
all the more objectionable passages of the Bible carefully
collected with a view to warn parents, husbands and guardians
of the dangers they were incurring by placing such a book,
without proper supervision, in the hands of the young, the
giddy, or the thoughtless. But no such supervision would
have been tolerated in England, where the mere suggestion
of a mutilated Bible would have been met with roars of
indignation. To remedy the many errors that had crept
into the text since its first publication in English, King
James's Bible was published in 1611, and gave to the people,
as was believed and intended, the Word pure and undefiled
and without the guidance of the marginal and explanatory
notes to be found in generous profusion in the Bibles of
earlier date. Every Bible-reader in the country thus became himself the beacon of his own ship, with the inevitable
result that there were almost as many commentators as
there were readers, and that the multiplication of sects
became an incalculable evil. Some of these chose a solitary
passage, and, regardless of the context, made it the confession of their faith, and the greater the ignorance and
superstition the greater the devotion to their own particular views. That these texts should have been drawn
from the Old rather than the New Testament was

the natural outcome of their reading, and was, moreover, consistent with the state of society and the
troubles of the seventeenth century. The language of
Eastern hyperbole, of imagery, and of poetry in which the
ancient chronicles are couched attracted the half-educated
and the sentimental, and led them to garnish their
language of everyday life with the phrases and the
sentiments of the Hebrew fathers. From the adoption of
their language, their nomenclature, and their sentiments, it
was but a short step to the adoption of their principles,
and we accordingly find in the seventeenth century that
people were beginning to discuss from analogy with the
history of the ancient Jews what were the reciprocal obligations of a ruler and his subjects, and to mould themselves and their lives on the model of the blood-stained
hero of the Old Covenant rather than on that of the more
peaceful disciple of the new dispensation. This position
was in time accentuated by the threatened outbreak of
hostilities when the Bible reading supporters of Parliament naturally looked for guidance to the gospel of war
and of prosperous rebellion rather than to that of mutual
reconciliation and peace. All the winds of doctrine were
thus let loose upon the waters of our country without an
aroused Neptune to raise his trident and quell the storm.
Churchmen, Presbyterians, Independents, Anabaptists,
Brownists, Quakers, Levellers, Fifth Monarchymen,
Adamites, claimed not only a share but a monopoly of
the religion of the country, while the so-called saints
of the New Covenant, men and women,[1] preaching and
praying, regardless of time, place, or occasion, studying
Numbers and Leviticus rather than the Sermon on
the Mount, called for extreme and eccentric punishments,
and attempted in their ignorance and superstition to

[1] See Thurloe, Vol. I., pp. 368-398. One woman preaching in the
pulpit at Somerset House had to be carried away by the soldiers to
prevent the people stoning her.

adapt the code and manners of the East to the complex system of Western civilization. The tone of thought, the customs and the laws of the Hebrews were expounded and discussed by the greatest writers and thinkers of the age, among whom were Selden, Milton, and Hale; and courts-martial, not then in subjection to the Common Law, tried their prisoners by the laws of the Sanhedrim.[1]

---

[1] The following are some of the punishments inflicted by courts-martial, extracted from Whitelock and the weekly papers:—

In June, 1650, a soldier of Colonel Pride's regiment was tied neck and heels together, and left thus trussed while the regiment marched past him, and then cashiered, for stealing a hen and putting it under his coat in his march; "which justice pleased the country." —(Whitelock, Vol. III., p. 202).

27th July, 1650, a dragooner was sentenced by court-martial to be bored through the tongue with a hot iron for blaspheming the name of God in a drunken humour.

26th August, 1650, a serjeant was hanged on Portland Hills for plundering a countryman's house—three privates with him being pardoned by Cromwell.

10th September, 1650, Jasper Collins was hanged at Clay Cross for extorting money from the country as he marched with recruits towards Ireland.

12th November, 1650, four soldiers of Colonel Barkstead's rode the wooden horse in Smithfield one hour each. Two were whipped at a cart's tail, and one branded R for attempting to rob in the streets, and three were cashiered. (*Mercurius Politicus*, November, 1650.)

3rd January, 1650-1, a corporal was hanged for taking a man from a constable, and beating him, etc. Another ran the gauntellope for drunkenness and being found in bed with a woman not his wife.

23rd January, 1650-1, one Story, a soldier, was hanged for killing a countryman, and another soldier, accessory to the murder, was hanged on the same gibbet, while one walked ten paces and then cut down and recovered to life again.

By a court-martial held on 23rd January, 1651-2, a soldier that killed another, being first struck by him and highly provoked, was, according to Numbers xxxv., 22, adjudged only to be imprisoned for two years and to pay £20 to the wife of him that was killed. (Whitelock, Vol. III., p. 386).

12th March, 1651, a suttler, for having two wives, was whipped at the gallows and turned out of the army.

Meanwhile the increased and increasing demand for the Bible soon overran the power of its production by the licensed printers. Cheap copies were consequently circulated, bad in print and fragile in paper, ill-revised, and full of inaccuracies and misprints. On the outbreak of the Civil War, when every soldier carried his Bible and mostly his commentary in his kit, and every civilian had a Bible in his homestead, these bad and erroneous editions increased and multiplied. In one edition not less than six thousand errors were said to have been ascertained, in others upwards of three thousand five hundred; in 1632 the King's printers were fined £3,000 for omitting the word " not " in the seventh commandment, an omission supposed to have been due not so much to inadvertence as to design. Bishop Usher at St. Paul's Cross was astonished to find that the text upon which his sermon was founded was absent from the Bible from which he was preaching. Rebellion and religion were found in some parts to be used as convertible terms, and day by day as time crept on inaccuracies and misprints became more numerous. To deal with this distressing state of things was a duty which the Long Parliament and the Commonwealth felt was owing not only to themselves as religious leaders, but to the nation as a God-fearing and law-abiding people. A commission was accordingly appointed by the Long Parliament of which the Lord Commissioner Whitelock was constituted President, with instructions to consider and report upon the existing editions of the Bible, so as to get back as close as possible, and with such modifications, if any, as might be deemed necessary, to the famous Bible of 1611. The Committee was appointed in 1652, and an order was made on the 3rd March, 1652-3,[1]

February, 1653-4, a man, who had smuggled powder at Windsor, was sentenced " to ride on a 'saker' when it is shot off with half a charge." (Proceedings in Parliament, February, 1653-4.)

[1] *Mercurius Politicus.*

K

that the business of the New Bible was to be considered
and reported on the following Friday. In July, 1653, an
order was made by the Council of State, *on the request of
Mr. Milton,*[1] that all paper required for the translation
of the Bible should be imported free of duty, and a further
order was made at the same date that seven thousand
reams should be admitted free for the translation of the
Bible into Oriental and foreign languages.[2] By the end
of 1656 the work was complete and the new edition
was produced. The advertisement, published by authority of the Council of State (on the 5th March, 1656),
stated that, whereas for the space of twelve years and
more the printing of the Bible being in common so
that every man presumed to print it at pleasure,
with the result that many hundreds of very grave errors
had found their way into the common impression then
abroad, to the great scandal of religion and abuse of the
people, a Bible had now been finished by his Highness's
command free from those errata, and "notwithstanding
that the corrected MSS. cost £1,200, the printers were to
sell it at no more than 12 shillings the book in quires,
being the common *twelves*, without notes."[3]

This general study of the Bible did not, however, apparently diminish the superstitious beliefs of the people.
King Charles was himself perhaps among the most superstitious of men. Merlin's ancient prophecies as to the
White King,[4] which he understood as referring to himself,
troubled him at all times; he consulted astrologers, and in
his last hours was much harassed by vain fears. The loss
of his diamond seal at Windsor, the falling of the silver

---

[1] One of the very few occasions upon which John Milton appeared
before the Council of State.
[2] State Papers, 9th July, 1653.
[3] *Public Intelligencer,* No. 56.
[4] *Perfect Passages in Parliament,* 18th November, 1650.

head of his staff at the trial,[1] the narration of Herbert's dream,[2] were all subjects of concern to him ; and his last injunction to Bishop Juxon has always been somewhat shrouded in mystery. " Your young men shall see visions, and your old men shall dream dreams," was promised to the Jews as a sign of the advent of their restoration, and through the whole of the seventeenth century, more especially perhaps during the period of the Commonwealth, the seeing of visions and the dreaming of dreams were matters to which an inordinate importance was attached. The early life of Cromwell appears to have been much troubled by visions and by religious speculation, and that august body, the Council of State, was not above seeing and considering reports of extraordinary visions seen by numbers of people in different parts of the country. Whitelock chronicles as matter of deep concern, reported to the Council, the visions of armies of horse and foot rising from the sea, visionary fleets contending in the heavens, now clear and distinct with streaming pennants, now clouded with ·the smoke of battle and then again clear as after action, with a mighty great ship sinking by the head ; a vision of a great lion in the north, together with ghostly communications to various officers and soldiers of the line.[3]

But though they recognised, as sanctioned by Scriptural authority, the seeing of visions, and accepted to some extent the doctrine of witchcraft as involving the direct communication of evil persons with evil spirits, for which also there was Divine authority, they did their best to warn the masses against what they conceived to be superstition pure and simple. In 1647, finding that a great concourse of people sought out the King in order to be relieved by his touch of their various ailments, the Parliament issued a proclamation warning the people

[1] Sidelights on the Stuarts, p. 227.
[2] Herbert's Memoirs, p. 104.
[3] See Vol. III., p. 387 ; Vol. IV., p. 86.

against the superstition of being touched for the evil,[1] and having arrested a " Stroaker," who also professed as being the seventh son of a seventh son to have the same miraculous power, he was sent to Bedlam.[2]

The 29th March, 1652, was celebrated for a great eclipse of the sun, about which there was much deliverance by the astrologers.[3] To counteract this evil a paper[4] was published by the Council of State showing how " that ungodly race of judiciall astrologers have constantly done two things: (1) Stand in flat opposition to the hand of God; (2) amuse the people and bugbear the minds of the ignorant with the strange and dreadful things which they pretend to see in the stars." It then proceeded at length and in detail to explain that eclipses, blazing stars, conjunction of planets, and other scarecrows of astrologers are natural events, proceeding from natural and intelligible causes, and the natural motions of the heavenly bodies.

The Council had also before them on several occasions the celebrated prophet, astrologer, and almanack-maker, Mr. Lilly, in reference to his various visions and prophecies,[5] after one of which at a later date he inserted an advertisement in the paper of the day[6] declaring

---

[1] Whitelock, Vol. II., p. 134.

[2] *Proceedings of State Affairs*, No. 252, 27th July, 1654.

[3] Evelyn says that the astrologers had so exceedingly alarmed the whole nation that hardly any would work or dare stir out of their houses, " so ridiculously were they abused by knavish and ignorant stargazers."—Diary, Vol. I., p. 278 ; Vol. II., p. 354.

[4] *Perfect Diurnal*, 1st April, 1652.

[5] *Proceedings in Parliament*, 4th November, 1652.

[6] *Perfect Diurnal*, 11th April, 1655, No. 269. He was one of the most unlucky of prophets, for he lived to see most of his prophecies falsified, and this among the rest. He also read the prophecy of Merlin as to the white eagle's chicken, that Charles II. would never reign except over the hills of Scotland.—*Perfect Passages in Parliament*, 18th November, 1650. He also had a revelation as to the executioner of Charles I., which might have got him hanged.—Sidelights on the Stuarts, p. 261.

that it was false and malicious to say that he had ever prophesied that there would be a great fire in London burning the Exchange and the City, for that he had never thought of any such a thing. They also ordered the prosecution of certain quacks and alchemists, and with a view, perhaps as much to the interests of religion as to the restraint of superstition, they prohibited the circulation of the Koran, either in the original or in English.[1] It is possible that this prohibition of the Koran may not have been altogether without reference to the fall of Mahomet's Coffin, a remarkable and miraculous event which is alleged to have occurred, or at all events to have been reported, towards the end of the year 1653. It was recorded as follows in the paper, which approached most nearly to the position of a Government organ, *Mercurius Politicus*, for January 1653-4[2] : " By letters from Madrid of 16th December, 1653, there is to be seen in this city a copy of a letter, in print, from the Jesuits in Armenia, to those in this city, wherein they express a very strange thing happened in that country, which is thus briefly : That there being, about five months since, many Turks and Moors met together at a town called *Medinataloi* (but commonly known as Mecca), in the Mosque or Chappell where the body of their false prophet hath lain for many years; on a sudden about 10 o'clock in the forenoon this iron chest (which for many years hath been suspended in the roof of that house by virtue of the loadstone fastened there) did fall to the ground, which immediately opened and swallowed up both the chest and what was therein, the ground remaining open about one quarter of an hour, and in that space came forth of that abyss a great flame and smoke, which rendered a great stench, and so the ground closed up as formerly; that thereupon all the spectators fell on the ground, being struck with deadly fear at so dreadful a spectacle, and some of them are since

[1] Whitelock, Vol. II., p. 557.
[2] No. 188.

become Christians, leaving their superstitious service."
I find no contemporaneous refutation or condemnation of
this legend of the Jesuits. It may, however, have been
thought that the parable of the gorgeous coffin of the False
Prophet being swallowed up in the pit like Korah and his
company, was likely to stimulate the people in their energy
against the Moslems and the Moors of Asia and Africa.

One result, perhaps the most remarkable of the independent construction of passages of Scripture, was the
rise of Quakerism which took place during this period.
"A number of people called Quakers," says Whitelock
(under the date of November, 1653,)[1] "were apprehended
in the north." This is his first mention of the sect, and
he further relates in the following year that some of these
people at Haslington, in Northumberland, coming to the
minister on the Sabbath day and speaking to him, the
country people fell upon the Quakers and almost killed one
or two of them, who, going out, fell on their knees and
prayed God to pardon the people, who knew not what they
did, and afterwards speaking to the people so convinced
them of the evil they had done in beating of them that the
country people fell quarrelling among themselves with
those who had occasioned it, and beat one another more
than they had before beaten the Quakers. This state of
things, which occurred at Haslington, was afterwards repeated
at Bristol and at various other places, and the Quakers
might have obtained a considerable hold upon the people
and done much good in quieting their minds and softening
their manners but for the wild eccentricities of some of
their self-elected leaders. Looking at the Quakers of the
present day, one would naturally imagine that their simple
faith, the absence of all formality in their prayers and
meditations, their services, even their burials, devoid of
ritual, their refusal to bow the knee to any earthly power,

---

[1] Vol. IV., p. 46, 82-103.

together with their unobtrusive habits and doctrine of passive resistance, would naturally have commended them to the Puritans, as they commend them now to the sober and serious portion of the community. Other considerations, however, affected the administrators of the Commonwealth; and it must be admitted that peace and quietness did not distinguish the Quakers during the Interregnum. They appeared then as levellers and blasphemers, as persistent brawlers in churches and contemners of authority, as confirmed opponents of whatever Government might be in office, and as irreverent imitators of the most sacred incidents in Holy Writ. The Commonwealth, like every Government of whatever type, recognised only the hard flints and the pestilent miasma that lay upon the surface of the Quaker creed, leaving it for succeeding generations to exploit the soil, and to gather the priceless minerals that lay beneath.

The Quakers, especially their women, were largely occupied with visions and dreams, and habitually enhanced the difficulties of their position by insisting upon narrating their visions, with comments of their own, to persons and bodies high in authority, who naturally resented this unwelcome interference. One of the first of these disturbers of the public peace was Hannah Thrapnell, the Prophetess of Whitehall, whose insistence upon interviewing Cromwell and the Council of State led to her being forcibly turned out of London and sent to her own country.[1] She professed to have eaten and drunk nothing, but to have spent her time in songs and prayers, and yet when the order came for her removal she rose up and went away speedily and lustily for her home in the West. She was not long there, however, before she was brought before the justices at Truro as a vagrant, speaking openly against the Government, and was bound over to the assizes in sureties of £300 to take her trial

---

[1] *Mercurius Politicus*, April, 1654.

for vagrancy and sedition. In the following year
another Quaker woman was for three days clamouring
at the gates of Whitehall with messages from the Lord to
be delivered immediately to the Lord Protector,[1] and a
certain Mrs. Beckwith gave them much trouble in the same
direction. In April, 1656, one Parnell, a Quaker, having a
mission from on high, starved himself to death at
Colchester.[2] At Edgehill a disorderly meeting of Quakers
to protest against the existing Government, consisting of
nearly eight hundred women, was with difficulty dispersed,[3]
and the proceedings of a small community of the body was
likely to have brought upon them the summary vengeance
of the district.[4] A considerable number of male and
female Quakers, having a presentiment that one of their
brethren, though buried at the junction of four cross-roads
after a verdict of *felo de se*, was due again upon earth,
proceeded to his grave and attempted to raise him from the
dead. They dug up the body, and some of the
party lay upon him face to face, calling upon him
in God's name to rise again. As the corpse, after
much time and adjuration, showed no sign of returning
animation, and the country people were crowding
round with superstitious curiosity, the Quakers excused
themselves for their failure by saying to the spectators that
" their brother was not yet four days dead." These
instances might be multiplied through many pages. The
disorderly Quakers were excited to mischief by the cavaliers,
and were joined by many of the firebrands of the age,
notably by John Lilburn, whom they afterwards buried
according to their peculiar fashion, as if he were a hero or
a martyr. But of all the remarkable Quakers of the
period James Naylor was the most remarkable, and his

---

[1] *Perfect Diurnal*, February, 1654-5.
[2] *Perfect Intelligencer*, No. 31.
[3] *Mercurius Politicus*, No. 312.
[4] *Mercurius Politicus*, No. 351.

name is, perhaps, familiar to us more by reason of the punishments he underwent than of any other claim he has established to a niche in the history of his country.

James Naylor, who seems to have drawn his original inspiration from some German source, was formerly a corporal in Lambert's regiment, where he became a disciple of this new faith. He made his great appearance at Bristol, in the autumn of 1656,[1] when, accompanied by hundreds of male and female Quakers, he rode into the city seated on an ass, supported on each side by women described as two new Magdalenes, while the more enthusiastic of his adherents threw branches in his road. He believed, or assumed to believe, that he was a new incarnation of Christ born again to redeem the world. Whether this was in effect a more pernicious creed than that of Harrison and others who looked forward to the immediate reappearance of Christ on earth to establish a fifth monarchy, would perhaps be doubtful to determine, although it might fairly be argued that Naylor's creed as being associated with overt acts of a blasphemous type was the more damaging to religion and morals. However that may be, the fifth monarchy men, under the iron heel of Cromwell and his Council, were treated with every clemency consistent with the prevention of further ill-doing, while the unhappy Naylor, being in the hands of an irresponsible Parliament, was treated with a savage brutality which was never extended to their most implacable foes.[2] By their order he was driven with his face to the tail of a horse through the streets of London; he was whipped, he was branded on the forehead with the letter B, he was imprisoned, he was pilloried, he was bored through the tongue with a hot iron, and in the following month he was pilloried, whipped, insulted, and degraded

[1] *Mercurius Politicus*, 5th November, 1656.
[2] *Mercurius Politicus*, No. 343.

through the city of Bristol.[1]   And yet so staunch were
his friends, and so credulous his disciples, that one Rich,
    merchant of the City of London, took his place by
Naylor's side on the pillory and stood by him through all
the details of his punishment.[2]   His tortures ceased for
the moment on the 17th January, 1656-7, and yet on
Sunday, in the following month of February, he and eight
other Quakers, as if totally oblivious of the troubles through
which they had passed, attended the service at Westminster
Abbey, behaving with quiet and civil attention.[3]   This
extremity of punishment for matters of religious opinion,
however extravagant, was not to the taste of the Lord
Protector.   On notice of the punishment awarded to
Naylor by the House, Cromwell sent them a message
through the Speaker Widdrington desiring to know the
grounds and reasons on which they had proceeded.[4]
This, except as a message of censure, was somewhat
uncalled for, as the Parliament had spent three months
in almost daily debates upon the heresies of Naylor
and the mode in which they were to be met.   A
division had been taken in Parliament as to whether
or not Naylor should be put to death for blasphemy;
the majority against that punishment, which, however,
was only fourteen,[5] was mainly procured by the energy
of Whitelock, who, doubtless, with the entire concurrence
of the Protector, argued powerfully and at great length
against the infliction of any such penalty for any such
offence.   The desired information was doubtless forwarded
to the Lord Protector, but the sentence being an order of
Parliament, he was helpless to cancel it or to mitigate its
severity.

---

[1] *Mercurius Politicus*, No. 345.
[2] *Public Intelligencer*, No. 63.
[3] Carlyle's Letters and Speeches, Letter CCXVII.
[4] Carlyle's Letters and Speeches, Vol. IV., p. 20.
[5] Parliamentary History, Vol. III., p. 1458.   Ayes, 82; noes, 96.

In regard to this punishment of Naylor and of other
Quakers a distinction must, in justice, be drawn between
Cromwell (or the Government) and the masses of the
people on the one hand, and the Parliament and the local
Justices of the Peace on the other, some of the latter,
probably religious enthusiasts, many of them doubtless
Royalists in disguise, who exercised a summary jurisdiction over these unfortunate people. That any interference
with their accepted minister by these Quakers would
be strongly resented by the congregation, one can well
understand; that their various antics, approaching
if not reaching the height of blasphemy, would be considered
by all as an outrage on decency may be readily granted;
but I cannot believe that the great multitude of the
country would regard the opposition to the payment of
tithes that they hated, or irreverence towards magistrates
whom they feared, as being acts either sinful or deserving
of punishment. That this feeling was reciprocated by
Cromwell and his Council we have, as I have shown,
undoubted authority for alleging, and entertaining this
sentiment in favour of the Quakers, not as brawlers in
church, not as disrespectful to the judges, not as
recalcitrant payers of tithe, but as in many respects men of
good life, of peaceful habits and of proved loyalty to the
Commonwealth, they did their best to impress upon the
local administrators of the law that these persons should
be treated as mistaken and misguided enthusiasts, and not
as hardened breakers of the law.

In January, 1656-7, various persons had been in gaol at
Horsham, some for twenty-four weeks, others for a less period,
for not taking off their hats at Quarter Sessions and other
similar offences. They petitioned the Council, who, after
examination of the prisoners, the gaolers, the justices, and
the committals reported: (1) That the evidence did not
prove any crime; (2) That the committals were not in due
form; (3) That the defendants had not been brought to

trial in due course of law ; (4) That the whole process was for matter of opinion in worship. And thereupon it was ordered that the Quakers be discharged from custody.[1] On 6th March, 1656-7, Anne Blacklyn, a Quakeress, was ordered at the Gaol Delivery at Bury St. Edmunds, to pay twenty nobles for disturbing the minister at Haverhill Church, calling him a hireling priest and deceiver, and to remain in prison till the fine was paid.[2] But this being an order of a Judge of Assize, no interference with it was permitted. In the meantime, however, the Quakers became increasingly unpopular by reason of certain of their number, both in the Army and the Navy, refusing to serve the guns " lest blood be shed thereby," and causing much trouble to the officers, who had to find them employment as non-combatants or to get them quietly out of the service. These causes, perhaps, combined to bring about the great personal interest always taken by Cromwell in the Quakers and their misfortunes, and we know from the general history of the time that somewhere in the year 1655 George Fox had a long interview with the Protector, who received him with kindness and attention, and assured him he wished no more harm to him than he did to his own soul.[3] In October, 1656, Cromwell appeared in person at the Council Board, and ordered the release of many Quakers in prison at Exeter, at Dorchester, at Colchester, and at Edmondsbury in Suffolk, that their fines be taken off and they be sent back to their homes.[4] Among the papers before the Council on that day there is preserved a list of the names and addresses of Justices of the Peace in the county of Dorset who had persecuted Quakers. It was sent up from the county apparently at the request of the Quakers, and contains some remarkable facts. It appears that one John Fitzjames, J.P.,

---

[1] State Papers, 6th January, 1656-7.
[2] State Papers, 1657.
[3] See Carlyle, Vol. III., p. 343.
[4] State Papers, 2nd October, 1656, and 3rd February, 1656-7.

had sent many Quakers to prison for not taking off their hats ; that he had encouraged the rude people, mostly cavaliers, to rise against them and stone them while holding their meetings, and that he had imprisoned and stocked many others for refusing to go to church. Walter Fox of Milberry Bibb, another Justice, had cast many into prison and had them whipped as rogues and vagabonds for attending meetings. Many other magistrates whose names are given had stocked and whipped men and women till the blood ran and their backs were raw, and amongst them, one George Fulford, a cavalier J.P., had taken the horse of a Quaker who had come eight miles to a meeting, and had the rider whipped and threatened with prison. A long list of cruelties and imprisonments culminated in the action of Thomas Hollis, of Martin's Town, who, with a brother Justice, invented the process of calling upon all the Quakers in his district, though never once suspected of Popery, to appear before him and to take the oath of abjuration. Believing in the strict and literal application of the text, " Swear not at all," they refused to take this oath, though offering to give any guarantees of loyal allegiance to the Protestant faith, and they were forthwith committed to gaol for unlimited periods. This was considered so admirable a device by many of the more violent Justices of the Peace, that it was commonly acted upon throughout the country, and the gaols became rapidly filled with non-juring Friends.

In November, 1657, the Quakers, as a body, presented their grievances in the form of a remonstrance to the Council of State.[1] " We suffer," said they, " under the cruelty of men in authority, who, disregarding the laws of God and of the land, imprison us and release us at their pleasure, and inflict cruel things on our brethren, the people of God." They then gave a list of members of their body who had been so misused. Captain Thomas

---

[1] State Papers, Vol. CLVII.

Curtis, woollen draper, of Reading, and John Martindale, of Plymouth, were taken out of their beds and consigned to prison as vagrants, though accused of no evil. The Justices in Quarter Sessions refused to deliver them, and the Judge (Justice Nicholas), though no charge was brought against them at the Assizes, remanded them to prison, where they still remained, and fined them £40 for refusing to remove their hats. Ellen Roberts, a sickly maid, for attending a Friends' meeting, was left for nights without straw to lie on, her friends not being allowed to visit her, and was whipped cruelly in Exeter Bride-well, where she still remained. Another woman, for a similar cause, suffered seven months' hard labour and many stripes. Of the rest, some had been liberated after being committed to prison, and others had been stocked and whipped and subjected to heavy fines. On the receipt of this remonstrance orders were issued forthwith to the Justices and Clerks of Assize for a return of full particulars of these cases, with an instruction that if nothing appeared against these persons beyond that which was stated in their remonstrance, they should be liberated and their fines remitted. The following memorandum was also sent by the President of the Council of State by order of the Protector to all Justices of the Peace in England and Wales. It breathes the spirit of charity and toleration, and I give it in full.[1] "His Highness and the Council have received several addresses on behalf of Quakers imprisoned for not finding sureties for good behaviour. Some have long lain in prison, and are not likely to get out by conformity. Though His Highness and the Council are far from countenancing their mistaken principles or practices, especially in disturbing godly ministers and affronting magistrates, yet, as they mostly proceed rather from a spirit of error than a

---

[1] President Laurence to Justices of the Peace. State Papers, Vol. CLVII.

malicious opposition to authority, they are to be pitied
and dealt with as persons under a strong delusion,
who will rather suffer and perish than do anything contrary
to their ungrounded and corrupt principles. Therefore His
Highness and the Council recommend them to your prudence,
to discharge such as are in prison in your county (though
discountenancing their miscarriages), so that their lives may
be preserved, divers having died in prison. From tenderness to them you are, by causing their hats to be pulled off,
to prevent their running into contempt by the not giving
respect to magistrates, as those whose miscarriages arise from
defect of understanding should not be treated too severely."

In September, 1658, the Quakers again brought their
troubles before the Council.[1] Nearly one hundred and
fifty of them were in the various gaols in the
country on charges of interrupting the minister in the
parish church, refusing to remove their hats in Courts of
Justice (construed as a wilful contempt of Court), nonpayment of tithes, of which there were no less than sixty in
prison at the same time, holding meetings, refusing to take an
oath, and the general and far reaching charge of being vagrants
or vagabonds. "What have we done?" said they. "What
laws have we broken? What plots have we engaged in?
Have we not patiently borne the greatest sufferings ever
since Queen Mary's days? And yet we have been persecuted, beaten, stoned, stocked, dragged from our meetings, cast into noisome dungeons and vaults, denied food
for days together, not allowed pen, ink and paper, and a
trial refused or postponed for months or years, during
which many of us have died. And all for conscience sake,
for which you and all of us have fought." Again the
Council interposed. From every gaol in the country came
a return of the Quakers in custody and of the offences with
which they were charged, fully bearing out the terms of

---

[1] State Papers, Vol. CLXXXI.

their petition, and again the Council addressed the magistrates, ordering the discharge of the captives and counselling moderation in the exercise of their functions for the future. But by this time Oliver, the Protector, had passed away, and with him the spirit of clemency and toleration that had alleviated the Quakers' position. Their history under succeeding reigns is one of continued and unmerited suffering.

For another class of people also Cromwell and his Council endeavoured to enact some rules of justice and toleration. It is a saying of Lord Beaconsfield that no country has more Jews than its sins have justly brought upon it. And although England was at this period exercising its profoundest theological minds and its greatest lawyers on the discovery and exposition of Hebrew law, legends, and observances, with a view to form its own laws and customs on that ancient model, yet the respect and veneration bestowed upon the Jewish fathers was not extended to the Jews themselves. And this ancient race, whose presence in the midst of any people is marked not only by wealth, but by the cultivation of literature, of music, of painting, and of all those artistic tastes which enliven and refine society, were as much outcasts from the England of the seventeenth century as they are from the Russia of to-day.[1]

[1] The following note of an order at the Middlesex Quarter Sessions under date 13th January, 1647-8, will show the position of the Jews at this period and the turn of the political tide somewhat in their favour : " Whereas, by an order of Sessions dated the first day of September last, it appears that Anne Curtyn stood then committed to the New Prison at Clerkenwell by warrant of Law : Whitaker, Esq., one of the Justices of the Peace of this County, for that she denied Jesus Christ to be a profitt and his prophetical office, for being a professed Jew and causing children to be circumsided, and that the keeper of the said prison was thereby ordered (with the said Curtyn) to attend the Assembly of Divines, who were thereby desired to examine her and to endeavour to reclaym her from her said errors, and if they find her obstinate, that they certifie the same, etc. Now for that Dr. Adoniram Byfeild, scribe to the Assembly of Divines, did attend

But the fame of England's power and a belief in her zeal for religious toleration was greater abroad than perhaps at home, and it attracted to our shores a great Rabbi named Manasseh Ben Israel, who, in 1655, approached Cromwell and induced him to take the first step towards Jewish emancipation. He was a Portuguese-Jew, resident at Amsterdam,[1] a man of much learning, zeal, and force of character, who was not altogether unknown in England, having previously endeavoured to persuade the Long Parliament to consider his proposals, or, at least, to give them a hearing. Cromwell's more open mind realized the position and claims of the Jews, and gave their chosen representative the hearing which the Parliament had refused.

The question was not now for the first time brought before the country, for the Jews, in 1648, had, according to Clement Walker[2] (who was at that time a member of the Long Parliament) petitioned the Council of War for leave to have the Acts of Banishment against them repealed, and to be permitted to build synagogues and to trade in England. For this concession they offered to provide a sum of £500,000 to be divided between St. Paul's and the Library at

the Court and did certifie in the name of the Assembly that as they were an Assembly they were only to consider and debate of such matters as are referred to them from one or both Houses of Parliament, and that, therefore, though not as an Assembly, yet as private Christians, they have had conference with the said Anne Curtyn about her opinions, and for what cause her opinion of Christ being no profite, etc., they found she differed only in terms but not in substance ; but as to her profession and practice of a Jew, they found her obstinate. Upon which this court, conceiving they have no conuzance of the fact, being merely ecclesiasticall, order the sayd Anne Curtyn to be discharged from prison."—Middlesex Records, Vol. III. p. 186.

[1] Archbishop Laud consulted Manasseh Ben Israel as to some disputed passages in the Bible.—See Thorndike to Williamson (Secretary to Charles II.), State Papers, Vol. CXXVIII., p. 48.

[2] History of Independency, Part II., pp. 60, 61, 83.

L

Oxford. In reply to this petition, the Council of Officers sent up a petition of their own to Parliament in January 1648-9, praying for the repeal of the Acts of Banishment against the Jews. Nothing, however, was done by Parliament, who were doubtless much disturbed by pamphlets[1] and tracts, declaring that the Army had resolved to sell the City of London to the Jews, who would plunder it, and steal the women and children in order to sell them as slaves to the Turks, Moors, or other Mahometans, with whom it was said they kept a constant traffic for this purpose. To meet these objections, the Rabbi published a book dedicated to Cromwell, and presented to the Council of State, and thenceforward the objections took the form of anticipated derogation of religion and injury to trade. Their cause, however, made some way, for in the petitions to which I have already referred, one of the items was that the Jews should be called into the Commonwealth, and have places allotted to them to inhabit, and to exercise their liberty. One of these is qualified by the words "for their tyme is neer at hand,"[2] which shows that the desire for their emancipation arose, in some cases at least, from a somewhat mixed sentiment of freedom and superstition.

Manasseh Ben Israel accordingly pleaded once more on behalf of his nation that they might be admitted to a freedom of living, of trading, and of worshipping in the Commonwealth. Numerous meetings on this subject were held at Whitehall, at which the Protector, the Chief Justices Glyn and St. John, the Lord Chief Baron Steel, various ministers and others, numbering altogether twenty-eight persons, representing the interests of law, trade, and religion, were present, and the doors were thrown open that the public might, if they chose, hear all the discussion. The Chief Rabbi was fully heard, and

---

[1] History of Independency, Part II., p. 61.
[2] State Papers addressed to Oliver Cromwell, etc.. p. 100, 4th August, 1653.

the Protector in fine declared himself in favour of the admission of the Jews.[1] Their proposals were in substance seven[2] : (1) To be admitted and received into the Common-wealth of England ; (2) To be allowed to build synagogues and to observe their religion ; (3) To have cemeteries in which to bury their dead ; (4) To traffic freely in merchandise ; (5) To have passports granted them to come into the country on their taking the oath of fealty on arrival ; (6) To have their disputes decided by the head of the Synagogue and two almoners, with appeal to the Civil Judges ; (7) To have the laws against their nation revoked. His Highness, it is said, expressed himself at these conferences impartially and with moderation, as one that desired to have the fullest knowledge of a matter of so high and religious concernment. And he consulted, as we learn, with many of his most trusted advisers, and amongst others with Mr. Justice Hale, who, so far as I can form an opinion, unlike his great master Selden, classed the Jews with the witches in the evil influence they were likely to exercise over the land. Of the same way of thinking were most of the learned divines, who would therefore require much argu-ment and persuasion before they would be induced to preach the toleration of the Jews from the pulpits of the country. Many of the naval officers were opposed to the admission of the Jews,[3] but the military were generally in their favour.[4] While on the one hand it was said that as we pray for and believe in their ultimate conversion, we should in the meantime treat them as fellow-citizens, it was, on the other hand, urged against them that they would endeavour to convert all England to Judaism, would ruin trade, and would set a bad example by their laxity in regard to marriage and divorce. The subject, therefore, was one

---

[1] *Mercurius Politicus*, No. 286 ; Carlyle, Vol. III., p. 360.
[2] *Public Intelligencer*, No. 12.
[3] Letters of Captain Willoughby. State Papers, December, 1655.
[4] Commissary-General Whalley to Thurloe, Vol. III., p. 308.

which required delicate handling and time to allow natural prejudice to subside and to bring public feeling into accord with the dictates of civil and religious freedom. It was therefore necessarily slow of progress. Manasseh Ben Israel received, however, in the meantime an annuity of £100 per annum for his support during the discussion of his proposals, and the Jews obtained as an instalment of their demands leave, by an order of the Council, to meet together for private devotion in their own houses, and to bury those of their nation who died in London, in such place beyond the City walls as the proprietors of the land might sanction.[1] This, however, was one of those many projected reforms which Cromwell's early death postponed for many years. The hopes that beat high for the Jews under the Protectorate of Oliver, were crushed by his demise ; and as Richard was unwilling or unable to pay Manasseh's allowance, he was reduced to a state of penury. Bigotry and intolerance once more raised their heads after Richard's deposition, the condition of the Jews was remitted to its former severity, and the old Rabbi, worn out with anxiety, unable to live in England or to return to his home, having failed in the moment of apparent success to remove any of the disabilities of his race, gave up the struggle and died of a broken heart.[2]

To deal with the Roman Catholics in the same spirit was a matter of far greater difficulty. The persecution of Papists and Seminary priests was by no means the invention of the Commonwealth or even of the Long Parliament. An Act of Queen Elizabeth[3] banished all Jesuits and Seminaries, and pronounced the penalty of death as traitors upon all that were hereafter found within the realm. Ever since those days the penalties against recusancy, hearing mass, and harbouring Seminaries had been severe and

---

[1] State Papers, 24th March, 1655-6.
[2] Sadler to Richard Cromwell, State Paper, 1659.
[3] 27 Elizabeth, Cap. 2.

rigidly enforced. And during the reigns of Elizabeth and James, trials, convictions and executions of Seminaries were of almost monthly occurrence. The form of thanksgiving for the happy deliverance of King James and the Three Estates of the Realm " from the most traitorous and bloody intended massacre by gunpowder," which referred to the " secret contrivances and hellish malice of Popish conspirators," reflected, no doubt, the feeling of the time, which showed itself again in the monumental inscription attributing the fire of London to the treachery and malice of Popish incendiaries. Cromwell, therefore, and the leaders of the Puritans had been born and brought up in the belief that the extirpation of Popery by the removal of the insidious promoters of that faith was a matter of high political as well as of religious concernment. The natural tendency, however, of a steady and thoughtful mind is to ripen with the sun, and to grow moderate and generous with age, and Cromwell in his later years seems to have abandoned to a great extent the circumscribed errors of his youth, to have become reconciled to a steady and gradual progress, and to have been convinced of the propriety, and, indeed, the necessity of the toleration and protection of the Catholics in common with other classes of the religious community. The nation, however, was not yet ripe for this consummation, although the numerous acquittals of persons charged with being Seminary priests from 1640 to 1660 show that the tide had begun to turn somewhat in their favour. Two instances, however, are on record of the execution of Seminary priests in London during this period, one under the Parliament and one under the Protector. In May, 1651, Peter Wright was convicted at a General Gaol Delivery at the Old Bailey for being a Seminary priest, and was sentenced to death as a traitor.[1] And in June, 1654,

---

[1] Middlesex Records, Vol. III., p. 286.

at the same place, John Southworth was also convicted as
a Seminary priest and sentenced to be " drawne, hanged,
and quartered."[1] The description of this priest's execution,
as given by Monsieur de Bordeaux, the French Ambassador,
in a dispatch to the Governor of Calais,[2] shows how
popular sentiment, at all events in London, was declaring
itself against these acts of intolerance. "We had here
yesterday," says the Ambassador, "a martyr, being a
priest, who was executed notwithstanding my interposing,
and that likewise of other Ambassadors to get him
reprieved. He was attended to the place of execution
by two hundred coaches and a great many people on
horseback, who all admired his constancy." Such a spectacle as this, a Seminary priest publicly treated as a
martyr and followed by crowds in private and public
coaches (for three hundred was the extreme limit of
the number of the latter provided for London), by horse-
men and pedestrians, was an indication of public feeling to
which the Protector would gladly have given effect. But
there was little to encourage him either in Parliament or
the Council of State, and indeed the latter body in the
beginning of 1655 advised him to issue a proclamation for
putting in force the laws against Popish priests, Jesuits,
and Popish recusants."[3] There was, however, no more
executing of Seminary priests, and Cromwell's own views
and wishes upon the subject are clearly set out in a letter
to Cardinal Mazarin in December, 1656.[4] "I may not,"
he says, "(shall I tell you I cannot?) at this junc-
ture of time, and as the face of my affairs now
stands, answer to your call for toleration. I say I cannot,
as to a public Declaration of my sense in that point;

[1] *Ibid*, p. 390. Whitelock says he had been previously condemned,
pardoned, and banished, and had returned again, Vol. IV., p. 113.
[2] Thurloe, Vol. II., p. 406, 29th June, 1654.
[3] Thurloe, Vol. III., p. 405.
[4] Carlyle Letter, CCXVI.

although I believe that under my Government your
Eminency, in the behalf of Catholics, has less reason for
complaint as to rigour upon men's consciences than under
the Parliament. For I have of some, and those very many,
had compassion, making a difference. Truly I have (and
I may speak it with cheerfulness in the presence of God,
who is a witness within me to the truth of what I affirm)
made a difference, and, as Jude speaks, 'plucked many out
of the fire'—the raging fire of persecution, which did
tyrannize over their consciences and encroach by an
arbitrariness of power over their estates. And herein it is
my purpose, as soon as I can remove impediments and
some weights that press me down, to make a further progress and discharge my promise to your Eminency in
relation to that." The promise in this letter may perhaps
be said to have been prompted by the desire for some
reciprocal advantage, but the reference to what he had
done for the Catholics was written to the Cardinal, who
was in intimate relations with the Catholics of England,
and who knew well all the facts to which the
Protector referred. The Cardinal would hardly, under
these circumstances, have been made the recipient of a lie,
as the writer and the receiver of the letter must equally
well have known its falsehood or its truth. It was at all
events satisfactory to the Cardinal, who, in April, 1657,
instructed the French Ambassador in London not to press
for open declarations in favour of the Catholics, as assur-
ances had been received from Lockhart, the English
Ambassador, that the Lord Protector would not suffer the
rigour of the law to be executed against ¡them.¹ I cannot,
therefore, doubt that Cromwell had, as far as circumstances
would permit, shown consideration and relief to many persecuted Catholics, and that he was anxious as time rolled

---

¹ De Brienne to M. de Bordeaux, Paris, 28th April, 1657.—Thurloe,
Vol. VI., p. 214.

on to give them, subject to their loyalty being guaranteed, further relief from their oppression.   And it must be put to his credit in this respect, that in the several pamphlets successively composing the History of Independency, Cromwell is denounced as a Papist in disguise, and charged with a secret resolution to do away with the penal laws and to remove the disabilities under which the Catholics were then suffering.

The course pursued in these three instances of the Jews, the Quakers, and the Catholics shows the mind of the Protector and his Council to have been imbued with a definite anxiety on the subject of religious toleration.   His speeches to his Parliaments breathed that same spirit and indicated the reform which was looming in the future. But the future was farther off than was then anticipated, for it was not till this nineteenth century that the Jews were admitted to equal rights of citizenship, that the scruples of the Quakers were respected, and Catholic disabilities removed.

CHAPTER IV.

THE ADMINISTRATION OF JUSTICE AND REFORMS OF THE LAW.

I.

THE ADMINISTRATION OF JUSTICE.

THE due administration of justice had always been a great feature of the Puritan programme, and the first business apart from legislation to which the Commonwealth turned its attention after the fatal 30th of January, 1648-9, was to constitute the Courts of Law, and to provide for the due administration of justice. The army had for some six years been seen in all parts of the United Kingdom. Its conduct had been remarkable for its submission to law and to the orders of the commanders, and it was now for the new Government to show that in peace or in war law would be respected, and its behest enforced. *Inter arma silent leges* was not, perhaps, actually or literally true for the six years of that war, but there had been great confusion and uncertainty; the King holding his courts, so far as he could, at Oxford and elsewhere, and other judges sitting at Westminster, actually nominees of the Parliament, but technically administering justice in the name of the King. From the autumn of 1642 to the autumn of 1646 no judges went the circuits, although Sir Robert Heath, the King's Chief Justice, sat at Oxford, and justice was administered as best might be by county magistrates in Petty or in Quarter Sessions. In the autumn of 1646, some judges were appointed by

Parliament and some went their circuits; amongst others, Justice Rolle, Justice Godbolt, and several Serjeants, but they sat as Justices of His Majesty the King; and writs were issued and judgments given in the name of the King. In the autumn of 1648, more Judges were appointed. Rolle was made Chief Justice of the King's Bench; St. John, Chief Justice of the Common Pleas, and Serjeant Wilde, Chief Baron of the Exchequer. Matters thus continued till the end of the year 1648, writs and judgments still being issued and delivered in the name of the King, and legal proceedings being dated as of the actual year of his reign. From the falling of the axe, however, this was no longer possible, and a new state of things had at once to be constituted. The courts in January, 1648-9, were fully constituted as follows :—

THE KING'S BENCH.—Lord Chief Justice Rolle, Justices Bacon, Jermyn, and Brown.

THE COMMON PLEAS.—Lord Chief Justice St. John, Justices Pheasant, Bedingfield, and Cresswell.

THE EXCHEQUER.—Lord Chief Baron Wilde, Barons Gates, Trevor, and Atkins, with Serjeant Tomlins as Cursitor Baron.[1]

---

[1] When in the time of James I. the Barons of the Exchequer were put on the same footing as other judges in Westminster Hall, tried civil causes in London, and were sent on circuit, an extra baron called a Cursitor Baron was appointed, whose special duty it was to guard the revenue and keep the Court informed on all matters touching the Royal prerogative. The first of these barons was Nowell Sotherton, a member of Gray's Inn, but not a serjeant-at-law. He exercised no judicial functions and held altogether a lower rank than the other members of the Court. He was appointed in July, 1606. Baron Tomlins is said by Mr. Foss to have been a garrulous and jocose old gentleman, and to have cracked jokes with the Lord Mayor and Sheriffs when they came into court to invite the judges to their dinner. Bacon would probably have described him as "no well-tuned cymbal." His only other distinction that I can find is that he frequently petitioned the Council of State for payment of his arrears of salary, and that in March 1657-8 he actually succeeded in obtaining

THE INTERREGNUM. 155

Of these the three chiefs, Rolle, St. John, and Wilde, agreed to remain together with one puisne Judge from each Court, viz., Justice Jermyn, of the King's Bench, Justice Pheasant, of the Common Pleas, and Baron Gates, of the Exchequer. The rest, Atkins, Bacon, Bedingfield, Brown, Cresswell, and Trevor, declined to retain their posts. There must have been much searching of heart among the various judges, though with regard to some the reason of their retirement is not very apparent. They had all acted as judges holding their offices actually from Parliament. Some had gone their Circuits and tried causes and prisoners with the support of Parliamentary officers and the guard of Parliamentary troops, and Justice Bacon, who had been appointed in 1642, had ever since sat in the King's Bench, and under the direction of Parliament had tried and convicted Lord Macquire for the Irish massacre, a rising undoubtedly undertaken in the nterest of the King. Atkins had been made a Baron of the Exchequer in 1645, Justices Brown, Bedingfield, and Cresswell had been made Serjeants and Judges by order of Parliament on the 12th October, 1648,[1] when the King was in confinement at Carisbrooke, and they had sat regularly during the six months of their appointment, though the last-named judges had not, as judges, been yet on circuit. There was, however, no want of efficient lawyers to supply their places, and one, indeed, of the old judges, Baron Atkins, not long afterwards repented of his retirement and became in 1650 a zealous and efficient

something on account. He pleaded at that time that his salary of £163 6s. 8d. a year was in arrear over £500, for which he had a warrant that he could not get cashed, and that he had "six children yet undisposed of for want of his salary," and he begged that he might be paid from the Exchequer like the other barons and judges.— See Foss's Judges, p. 624 ; State Papers, Vol. CLXXX., 16th March, 1657-8.

[1] Whitelock, Vol. II., p. 420.

judge of the Commonwealth as a Justice of the Upper
Bench.   The new judges were Mr. Aske, a Bencher of the
Inner Temple, who, with Mr. Steel, the Attorney-General,
Mr. Cook, the Solicitor-General, and Dr. Dorislaus, a
civilian, had been of counsel for the Commonwealth at the
trial of the King,[1] and who, with Serjeant Nicholas, were
appointed to the Upper Bench ; Serjeant Puleston, of the
Middle Temple, who with Mr. Peter Warburton, formerly
Judge at Chester, were appointed to the Common Pleas,
and Serjeants Thorpe, of Gray's Inn, and Rigby, who were
appointed to the Exchequer, Baron Tomlins continuing
until the restoration to hold the post of Cursitor Baron.
Of these Serjeant Thorpe, who was made a Serjeant with
Whitelock, Bradshaw, Glyn, Keble, and Widdrington, in
1648, was a man of much distinction in Parliament.   He
had been a member successively for Richmond, Beverley,
and the West Riding of Yorkshire, and had acted as Chief
Commissioner and as Chairman of Committees on various
questions of trade and finance.   He had reported
elaborately and successfully on the woollen and cloth
trade, and had a thorough knowledge of all branches
of the law.   Before, however, the old judges would accept
their re-appointments, they insisted on what Clement
Walker calls a "fig-leaf to cover their consciences," but
what was in fact a most necessary precaution and one
eminently qualified to secure their position and to render
their services acceptable to the country.   The chiefs with
their puisnes refused to go into Court and open Hilary
Term until the House had duly read and passed a declaration settled by themselves that the fundamental laws of
the country should be continued, and that the judges should
administer justice accordingly.[2]   This declaration was
accordingly passed, the six judges took their seats in their
respective Courts and the Commissioners of the Great Seal

---

[1] Sidelights on the Stuarts, p. 217.

[2] Whitelock, Vol. II., p. 528.   Scoble's Acts, etc., 9 Feby., 1648-9.

sat in the Court of Chancery. The declaration was read aloud in each Court, and on and after the 9th February, 1649, the Judges of the Commonwealth of England, with their successors, administered justice throughout the land. .

The Great Seal was put into Commission, the Commissioners being Serjeant Bulstrode Whitelock (the historian of those times, a successful Chancery lawyer), Mr. Lisle, one of the assistants to Serjeant Bradshaw at the King's trial, and Serjeant Keble, a common lawyer, of much learning and of firmness and courtesy in the conduct of his cases. Judging from what history has left us of these men, they were as well qualified to fill their offices as any men that could then have been appointed. Of Whitelock we can judge from a perusal of his Memorials and from the eminently satisfactory manner in which he conducted the various matters of State that were committed to his care. His embassy to Sweden was peculiarly successful, and his schemes for the amendment of the procedure of the law were sound, liberal, and well-conceived. He was an intimate personal friend of Selden, on whose recommendation he was appointed librarian of St. James's, and had the care and arrangement of the King's library and works of art. He was president of a commission, in which he took much interest, for the reprinting of the Bible and the expurgation from the editions commonly in use of all such errors and misprints as, from the carelessness or wilfulness of the printers, had found their way into the text. He was a friend equally of Milton on the one hand and of Davenant on the other, and if his Memorials show some traces of egoism and of personal vanity, they were only those defects which were perhaps inseparable from the times, while his surrender of his post as Commissioner of the Great Seal in the year 1655, rather than administer what he considered to be an emasculated equity, was not devoid of courage and patriotism. Serjeant Keble is chiefly known from certain reports and abridgments that bear his name. Of Mr. Lisle we know less, but the fact that he was named assistant at the trial of King Charles is in itself some guarantee of his legal reputation.

The Commissionership of the Great Seal had in the first instance been offered to Sir Thomas Widdrington, who had been made a King's Serjeant in 1648. He, however, declined, first, on the ground of ill health, which was not accepted, and secondly, on the ground of some scruples of conscience he had about the business, not being quite clear where his authority would come from and how far it would go; and, as he evidently meant declining, he was excused. He was treated, however, in the same spirit as those of the King's Judges who had refused to sit at the trial, and, in consideration of his former services, had a patent to practise within the Bar and a quarter's wages more than was due to him as Lord Commissioner up to that date.[1] Whitelock being then selected, made a long series of excuses, occupying three pages of his book, of the usual *nolo episcopari* order, which, being at once recognised as of that type, were incontinently overruled and his appointment made out. We are compelled to estimate the character of these Commissioners from the scanty materials left to us by history, but it may be as well to learn what one of the party, the Lord Whitelock, says of the other two. That he had no very high opinion of them appears from the following entry under date 12th February, 1648-9: "The burthen of the business of chancery lay heavy upon me, being ancient in commission, and my brother Keble of little experience in practice, my brother Lisle of less, but very opiniative."[2] Their salary. was £1,000 a year, which Whitelock says was less than he made at the Bar on account of the extra cost of living imposed upon him by his title of Lord Commissioner. They wore handsome velvet gowns, similar, I suppose, to

[1] Whitelock, Vol. II., p. 523. See Sidelights on the Stuarts, p. 263.
[2] Whitelock, Vol. II., p. 532.

that worn by Lord Bacon in the celebrated portrait in
Lord Verulam's collection, and they lived in the Duke of
Buckingham's house. But they fully occupied their time,
for they sat in their Court at seven every morning,[1] and
did their best to deal with the mass of undetermined
causes, hearing as many as forty-five demurrers one afternoon.[2] They sent back into the several counties causes
that had been improperly transferred to London, and they
succeeded by means of their own intervention and by
orders of the Council of State, of which they were
members, in allaying the jealousies between the Courts
of Chancery, Admiralty and Common Law. They issued
orders[3] to the judges at Westminster and at the Admiralty,
directing the former to consult with the latter before issuing
prohibitions, of which in any case they were to be sparing,
and warning the latter to be more careful of exceeding
their jurisdiction by entertaining matters within the sole
jurisdiction of the Common Law. They were not, however,
very successful in their own mode of delivering justice, for
Whitelock himself complains that in Michaelmas Term,
1652,[4] " Chancery was full of trouble, no man's cause being
determined how just soever without the clamour of the
party against whom it was given ; they being all stark
blind in their own causes, and not to be convinced by
reason or law." Whether this arose from the obstinacy of
the litigants, from the peculiar temper of the times, or from
the questionableness of their decisions, must be left an
open question, but it may also have arisen from the fact
that the Chief Commissioner, though a sound lawyer and a
resolute and honest judge, had not that faculty of conducting causes and delivering judgments which in a far

---

[1] Whitelock, Vol. III., p. 20.
[2] *Ibid*, Vol. III., p. 9.
[3] State Papers, Vol. CXXVI.
[4] Vol. III., p. 468.

inferior judge would satisfy the litigants, that at least they had received a fair hearing and an impartial decision.

From the Common Law Judges a different duty was expected. Term began on the 9th February, but in the first week of March the judges were due to ride the Spring, or what was then called the Hiemal or Winter Circuit. And, above all things, it was necessary in the interests of the new Government, that the judges should at once appear in every ancient Assize town, read to all the citizens the declaration they had obtained from Parliament and clear away, as far as they could, the arrears of work that had been left by their predecessors. The Government, accordingly, having selected the counsel whom they proposed to make judges, sent them after the fashion of the time to ride a circuit as serjeants, and to try their prentice hands on the cause lists and the prisoners. I have endeavoured to make a calendar of the different circuits and the judges who rode them from 1648 to 1660. The result, which will be found on a later page, is not, I fear, very satisfactory. During the early period it is only, as will be observed, by scant references in the newspapers, or in the State Papers of the period, that any information can be obtained, for although the dates and places of the circuits are regularly given, the names of the judges do not appear to have been published until the year 1654. In this, their first circuit, therefore, there went the three Chiefs, Justice Jermyn, one of the old Judges (Justice Pheasant[1] and Baron Gates being ill and unable to attend), the six expectant judges, a serjeant in place of one of the sick judges, and Mr. Swanton, a West Country Chairman of Quarter Sessions, in place of the other.

Of the judges who went that circuit as Commissioners of Assize for and on behalf of the Keepers of the Liberties of England, no greater judge, no sounder lawyer, no more steadfast politician or honest man ever sat upon the

---

[1] He died 1st October, 1649.—Foss's Judges, Vol. V., p. 469.

judgment seat of England than the Lord Chief Justice of the Upper Bench. As a judge he was in those troublous times but was nòt of them. Like the precious metals in the golden angels he passed through the fire and emerged with a brilliant lustre, and it is, I think, mainly to Chief Justice Rolle and the good influence he exercised over Cromwell, whose inclination was always towards a firm and loyal administration of the law, that we owe the preservation of our old laws which some persons, as Burke asserts, were only too anxious to erase from our Statute Book as relics of feudalism and barbarity. That he was no great politician would go far to have made him a great judge, for the qualities necessary to the one are detrimental to the other. The capacity for bold expedients necessary in a statesman is out of place and incongruous in a judge, while the deep veneration for existing laws, and the profound, if not sacred reverence for vested rights, which are the natural instinct of a judge, would be fatal to the career of a politician. Constructive and administrative powers, which are indispensable to a statesman, are almost thrown away upon a judge, while the refined abstruse and technical constituents of a judge's mind would be useless and impedimental to the advance of a politician. The wave of popular opinion, the expression of popular sentiment, and the fluctuation of public affairs, while they are the pole-star of the politician, are the rocks and shoals of the channel through which the judge has carefully to steer. Stability is the motto of the judge, progress is that of the politician.

Serjeant Rolle was born in the year of the Spanish Armada. He was a member of a good family in Devonshire, the names of whose descendants are still to be found in the peerage, and who still hold their estates in their native county. He was a man of good classical attainments, having been educated at Exeter College, Oxford, and, from his earliest days to his latest, was a firm

M

and consistent member of the Puritan party. He sat in Parliament for the boroughs of Callington and Truro, was made a Serjeant in 1640 and a Justice of the King's Bench in 1645, of which he, with Justices Bacon and Godbolt, were the sole occupants until November, 1648, when he was made Lord Chief Justice and the other vacancy was filled up. There is an excellent portrait of him which has been frequently engraved. It represents him in his old age, and is that of a firm, but kindly old man, rather disfigured, however, by the close fitting coif of large dimensions which was the " black cap" of the judges of that time. He was also a man with the courage of his opinions : for, objecting to trials for treason by High Courts of Justice constituted for the occasion, he never sat in any High Court during his term of office. For his mental and legal qualifications I make no apology for giving the following extract from the preface to his Abridgment (although it has been partially extracted by Lord Campbell in his " Lives of the Chief Justices "[1]), as it paints the old chief and his character in lines we are unable now to draw :—

" He was a man of very great Natural Abilities, and of a ready and clear Understanding, strong memory, sound, deliberate and steady judgment, of a fixed attention of Minde to all business that came before him ; of great freedom from Passions and Perturbation, of great Temperance and Moderations, of a strong and healthy constitution of Body, which rendered him fit for Study and Business and Indefatigable in it.

" He spent his time under the Barr and for some years after in diligent study of the Common Law, neglecting no opportunity to improve his knowledge therein ; and he had this happiness in relation thereunto, that from his first Admission to the Society of the Inner Temple, which was 1st February, 6 Jac.[2] [1st February, 1609,] and till his call to be a Serjeant [10th May, 1640], he had Contemporaries of the same Society of great Parts, Learning and Eminence ; as namely, *Sir Edward Littleton*, afterwards Chief Justice of the Common-Pleas,

---

[1] Vol. I., p. 434.
[2] According to the Records of the Inner Temple, he was admitted, *November, 1608.*

and Lord Keeper of the Great Seale of *England;* Sir Edward Herbert,
afterwards Attorney-General ; Sir Thomas Gardyner, afterwards Recorder of *London ;* and that Treasury of all kind of learning Mr.
John Selden ; with these[1] he kept a long, constant and familiar
converse, and thereby greatly improved both his own learning and
theirs, especially in the Common Law, which he principally intended ;
for it was the constant and almost daily course for many years
together of these great traders in learning, to bring their several
acquests therein, as it were into a Common Stock by mutual communication, whereby each of them became in a great measure
the participant and common possessor of the other's learning and
knowledge.

" He did not undertake the practice of the Law till he was sufficiently
fitted for it, and then he fixed himself unto one Court, namely, the
King's Bench, where was the greatest variety of business; by this
means he grew Master of the Experience of that Court, whereby his
clients were never disappointed for want of his Experience or Attendance. He argued frequently and pertinently; his arguments were
fitted to prove and evince, not for ostentation; plain yet learned;
short (if the nature of the business permitted) yet perspicuous; his
words few but significant and weighty ; his skill, judgment and advice
in points of Law and Pleading was sound and excellent.

"Although when he was at the Barre he exceeded most others, yet
when he came to the exercise of Judicature, his parts, learning, prudence, dexterity and judgment were more conspicuous. He was a
patient, attentive, and observing hearer, and was content to bear with
some impertinences rather than lose anything that might discover the
truth or justice of any Cause. He was a strict searcher and examiner
of businesses, and a wise discerner of the weight and stress of them
wherein it lay, and what was material to it. He ever carryed on as
well his search and examination as his directions and decisions with
admirable steddiness, evenness and clearness : great Experience
rendered business easie and familiar unto him, so that he gave convenient despatch, yet without precipitancy or surprise. In short he
was a person of great learning and experience in the Common Law,
profound judgment, singular prudence, great moderation, justice and
integrity."

[1] It was not, perhaps, convenient to add that amongst his other
colleagues on the Bench were Edmond Prideaux, for ten years Attorney-
General to the Commonwealth, a man of learning and experience.
Mr. Aske, a Judge of the Upper Bench, and Serjeant Wilde Lord Chief
Baron of the Exchequer, and among his cotemporaries at the Inn
was the regicide Ludlow.

I can hardly conceive a more accurate description of a perfect judge. It is moreover the verdict of his contemporaries, of men who were conversant with his public and his private life, of whom some were his comrades in the Temple and some his colleagues on the Bench; some had practised before him during the times of trouble, and some having learned the law under his Republican administration were now dispensing it under a Monarchical Government. This panegyric of Chief Justice Rolle, written as is believed by his pupil, Sir Mathew Hale, was published in 1668, and the book was authorized and adopted by nearly every judge then on the Bench.[1] It is also expressed to have been published by the " condescension of his worthy son (the Inheritor of his Father's virtues as well as of his Possessions), who, at the request of some that honored his Father, was content to permit this work to be published for the common good." Of the judges who licensed the book, let it also be borne in mind that Sir Mathew Hale was not only his pupil but his colleague, as also was Baron Atkins. That Justice Archer had been refused audience before him through not having taken the engagement, and that Justices Twisden and Wadham Wyndham had been committed to the Tower for words spoken before him in the Upper Bench.

Early, therefore, in March, 1648-9, the judges, with their clerks of assize, their associates, their marshals, and their staff, left Westminster for their various circuits. They went in all the pomp and with all the cere-

---

[1] The printing and publishing of the book was allowed by: Orl. Bridgeman, C.S. (the Lord Keeper); John Kelynge (Lord Chief Justice); Matthew Hale (Lord Chief Baron); Edw. Atkyns (formerly Judge of the Upper Bench); Thos. Twisden (Justice of the King's Bench); Thos. Tyrrill (Justice of the Common Pleas); Chr. Turner (Baron of the Exchequer); Wadham Wnydham (Justice of the King's Bench); Jo. Archer (Justice of Common Pleas, one of Richard Cromwell's Judges); Ri. Raynsforde (Baron of the Exchequer, afterwards Lord Chief Justice); Will. Morton (Justice of King's Bench).

monies attaching of old to the Judges of the King; for the Commonwealth, while it well knew the necessity for a firm and impartial administration of the law, did not fail to recognise the effect which a show of authority and dignity in a judge lends to the transaction of judicial business, and the salutary effect thereby produced on the minds of the ignorant, the timid, and the wicked.[1] This riding of circuits had existed from time immemorial. As tithes date back to Father Abraham, so the yearly circuit to judge the nation dated back to the time of Samuel and the Prophets.[2] And upon the moral effect produced by these judges, more than upon the presence of troops, depended the future of the Commonwealth in the eyes of the nation. Of this first circuit of the judges, we know that Serjeant Thorpe and Serjeant Puleston went to the north, and that Lord Chief Baron Wilde and Mr. Swanton were in the west. Of the distribution of the others, I have no information. This going of circuits by the judges is still a familiar spectacle, but shorn of all that dignity and appearance of power which was calculated to affect the minds of the people. The appearance of an elderly gentleman stepping from an express train with some hundreds of other passengers does not appeal to the imagination, even though he may afterwards be conducted to his lodgings in a coach guarded by a score of county police armed with wands. Nor is the sheriff's circuit dinner comparable with the profuse hospitality formerly showered on the judges by the gentry of the county. The advance of civilization and increased facilities for the transaction of business render such changes

[1] It did not, however, give universal satisfaction, for I find among the petitions for amendment of the law in 1653, one in which it is prayed that every county should have its own natural privilege in deciding all differences between parties, " soe that there will need no lordly judges to ride circuits to frighten people with their bloody robes, state and pomp."—Papers addressed, etc., p. 99.

[2] 1 Samuel vii. 16.

necessary, and a growing spirit of centralization has brought up to the Courts at Westminster a great part of the business formerly transacted by the Commissioners of Assize. But the old system had many advantages. It rendered the judges personally acquainted with the various habits, prejudices, tones of thought and country customs in different parts of England ; for before the institution of railways and the diffusion of cheap literature welded our people more or less into a compact mass, there was as much difference of sentiment between north and south, east and west, as there was between inhabitants of different countries, a difference which is even now to be found in the varying customs of tenant right, and as to the descent of land in adjoining counties in the south of England. With regard to the personality of the judge himself, his progress through the country with his numerous staff, his retinue and his guards of yeomanry or of dragoons, was a matter of state and dignity, each county being held accountable through its High Sheriff for the safety and honour of the chief representative of the law, while the outlay necessary on the part of the judges, of the barristers riding the circuit, and of the gentlemen of the county, distributed among the country people an amount of money which was to them an important consideration. And it had also this inestimable advantage, which, to a great extent, still continues, that it brought all classes of the community into touch with the law, and made them as jurors actual participators in the administration of justice. For juries then as now not only tried all criminal cases on circuit, but also, subject to certain property qualifications, were judges of fact in issues between party and party.

Of the judges' charges to the grand juries, a matter of most vital interest, and which, as it is said, gave great satisfaction and comfort to the people, we have no record, except in the instance of Serjeant Thorpe, Justice of

Assize at York, whose charge, carefully prepared and containing a brief summary of the law under various heads,
was published by authority, and is still to be found in many
an old library among the pamphlets of the Commonwealth.
It would have been, however, to the chiefs of the
several courts, to the great Puritan Chief Justice
Rolle, even then known through Europe for his deep
learning, to Chief Justice St. John, of the Common
Pleas, "the Common Shop for Justice," as Sir Orlando
Bridgman called it at a later period,[1] or the
Chief Baron of the Exchequer, who had retained their
seats after the King's death, and were now riding their first
circuits as judges of a Commonwealth without a King or
a House of Lords, that people would have naturally looked
for some exposition of the laws under which they were for
the future to be governed, and under which the judges
themselves held their commissions. Disguise their position as they might, wrap up their judicial platitudes as
they would in folds of Scripture or of doctrine, verbiage,
metaphor and rhetoric, could not obliterate the fact that
they sat by the power of the sword, which, invoked on
behalf of the Commonwealth of England, had dissolved the
old union between a King and his people. And though
they might well agree with Selden and most other people
that as between a monarch and his subjects there is no
other measure of justice left upon earth, but by the final
arbitrament of arms, yet they doubtless thought it right
and convenient, on their first introduction to the country in
their new capacity, to say some comfortable and healing
words. That they did so we cannot doubt, and one may
imagine that one or other of the chiefs would justify his
position by a more or less lengthy reference to the history of
his own country. The theory that the sword is the greatest

---

[1] Charge to the Grand Jury on the Trials of the Regicides. State
Trials, Vol. V., p. 993.

and the most powerful civilizer of the world was hardly recognised at that period, and would not have been acceptable to a people just beginning to realize the cessation of a long period of domestic strife. They might, however, have pleaded, taking their first illustrations from the Old Testament, that as the flaming sword was the first emblem of God's displeasure in the garden of Eden, so also was it the engine of His right hand in establishing the kingdom of the Jews, and in punishing them for their disobediences. The King after God's heart was a man of war from his youth up, and the instances in which he offended against the Divine authority were mostly those in which, having the power of the sword, he had refrained from using it against his enemies. King after king and ruler after ruler had been deposed by the sword under the Jewish Dispensation, in pursuance of what was assumed to be a warrant from the Almighty; and even in the country in which we live the laws by which we are governed were the product of the sword. " You call us lawyers," they may have said, " Norman intruders, because our laws are written in a language you do not understand. But that very Norman intruder, whom you aptly term the Conqueror, from his wielding the sword with fatal effect against the Saxon King, is the very man to whom your late King succeeded through a record of blood and through the terror of the sword. The Conqueror died in a foreign land, and before his funeral-lights were dim the sword was invoked to settle his succession. William, the Red King, under whose roof we sit to deal out impartial justice at Westminster, wrenched the Kingdom by the power of the sword from his elder brother Robert, the rightful heir of his father,.and his still younger brother, Henry I., reigned by the same title of the sword. On the death of this Henry, the sword was again invoked, and Stephen secured the Crown as against the rightful claim of Matilda, heiress of Henry I., and Stephen in his turn was compelled by the sword to disinherit his own children

in favor of Henry II., the first Plantaganet. Henry II. took
the Kingdom of Ireland by the sword, even as Edward I.
annexed the Principality of Wales after condemning its
native princes to slaughter. And these provinces so ac-
quired by the sword we hold and govern as part of the
Kingdom, and we shall so continue to hold and to
govern until we also lose them by the sword.
The second Edward, a bad King and an incompetent
ruler, after appealing to arms against his subjects, was, by
the sword, driven from the Throne and sent to a violent
death in Berkeley Castle. He was followed by Edward III.,
whose grandson, Richard II., son of that great warrior, the
Black Prince, was deposed by force of arms by Henry of
Lancaster, who thus brought to an ignoble end the great
House of Plantaganet. Henry V. carved out by the
sword a title to the Crown of France, and his son, Henry
VI., was crowned in Paris King of France, and quartered
the arms of France with our own. But he lost his king-
ship of France, as he lost the Crown of England, by the
sword, and thus brought to an end the fortunes of the
House of Lancaster. Edward V. again was driven from
the Throne by Richard III., who, in his turn, was put to
the sword by Henry VII., who thus destroyed the House
of York and founded the House of Tudor. Henry VII., but
remotely allied to the Royal stock, after a civil war of thirty
years' duration, made his title to the Crown of England by
the sword, and from him in direct line does this
Charles Stuart, the King of Scots, now claim to be your
king. Let him, therefore, follow his ancestors and
get the kingdom by the sword if he can, and let
him be your king if you will have him. But even his
title is not free from blood, for the Eighth Henry, who was
empowered by Parliament to dispose of the Crown, had
declared against the succession of his Scotch relations.
And had it not been for the power of the sword in the
hands of Elizabeth, who saved us from the possible

succession of the Queen of Scots, perchance the people of this country would not have received King James of Scotland, of unhappy memory, to reign over them. Seeing, therefore," they may have continued, " that these various monarchies and dynasties in unnatural succession, were created, upheld, and removed by the sword, and yet during the period of their power were accepted, obeyed, and reverenced by the people, why are not the same reverence and obedience to be paid to us ? What greater title had they than have we, who have also successfully appealed to the sword not to establish an unjust succession, but to free us from tyranny and arbitrary government, and to secure to you and to all the citizens of this Commonwealth the free and impartial exercise of those ancient laws that were passed for your welfare in happier times ? But the sword, under whose shadow we sit," they might have added, pointing to the sword of justice, which had replaced the Lion and the Unicorn of the Royal Arms, " is not only a sword of execution but of justice, and though its edge is set for the punishment of the malefactor, yet is it anointed with the oil of mercy for the penitent and for all who supplicate its grace."

Some such sentiments as these, but couched in the powerful language of the time, which I could in vain attempt to imitate, delivered with all the energy of sincere conviction, we may conceive to have been addressed to the grand juries of this Hiemal Circuit. And probably the judges themselves would have been the first to admit that the one great justification of their position was their success. For the future they may well have added that now for the first time the judges hold their offices during good behaviour and not during the good pleasure of the Crown, and that they had one and all refused to accept any office until Parliament and the Council of State had solemnly pledged themselves in the face of Heaven and of the nation, that the old laws of England were to be main-

tained and to be impartially administered, that the circuits
would be regularly held, that legal abuses would one by
one be sifted out and done away with, and that so far as
events would permit justice should be done to every citizen
within the limits of his own county.

The judges, both old and new, produced a
most salutary effect by their charges to the grand
juries, and by their dispatch of business. Their
first reception would necessarily have been cold and doubtful, but their declaration of adherence to existing laws,
of the removal of abuses, and of their own irremovability
except for misconduct in their office, quieted peoples'
minds, and prepared them to give a fair trial to the new
order of things. In the result, we find that when the
judges went their circuits in the autumn, by which time all
the vacant seats had been filled by duly appointed judges,
the magistrates and county gentlemen attended in considerable numbers. We find also from the papers that favourable reports were to hand of the charges of Judge Nicholas
at New Sarum, of Chief Justice Rolle on the Western
Circuit, and of Baron Thorpe on the North ; that peoples'
minds were much settled, and that in the County of
Wilts there was as great an appearance of gentlemen and
freeholders as ever was seen at the assizes for the county.[1]
In the following year we hear from Hereford that Chief
Baron Wilde had given excellent information and instruction to the county, and "we thanked God to see the day
when justice and judgment is executed in the land."[2] In
this tone the judges are spoken of in the newspapers, in
the memorials, and in the contemporary histories ; and,
with the exception of Mr. Justice Hale having at Warwick,
in the Spring Circuit of 1655, referred a cause which he
ought to have tried,[3] I do not find a note of trouble or dis-

---

[1] See Whitelock, Vol. III., pp. 167-174, 294.
[2] *Proceedings in Parliament*, 31st July, 1651.
[3] State Papers, May, 1655.

content in regard to the judges during the whole of this
period. Nor is independent testimony wanting in their
favour. Coke says Westminster Hall was never replenished
with more learned and upright judges than by Cromwell,
and Clarendon affirms that in matters which did not
concern the life of his jurisdiction he had great reverence
for the law. Harris says that the Protector filled his
benches with able and honest judges ; and " Cromwell,"
says Burnet,[1] " showed his good understanding in
nothing more than in seeking out capable and worthy men
for all employments, but most particularly for the Courts
of Law, which gave a general satisfaction " ; and referring
to the administration of law in Scotland, which formed part
of his general scheme for the management of the two Kingdoms, he further says, " There was good justice done, and
vice was suppressed and punished, so that we always
reckon those eight years of usurpation a time of great
peace and prosperity."[2] And the judges, be it remembered,
differing in this respect from the military courts, which
ruled the Army, adminstered the laws of England and not
of Judæa. Although they freely took their language and their
illustrations from the Old Testament, which had become
for the moment the language of the people, yet the law of
Moses, as expounded in Leviticus, was as foreign to their
courts as the laws of the Twelve Tables, or of the Athenian
Senate. And following upon this continued administration
of the law we find the papers of the year 1651 filled with
notices of various lords, gentry, and country people, who
had till then forsaken their houses, returning to their
habitations, living quietly in their homes, and engaging to
do nothing against the existing Government.[3] But the
judges going their first circuits as Commonwealth Judges

---

[1] Burnet, p. 54.

[2] *Ibid.*, p. 40.

[3] See hereon paragraphs in *Proceedings in Parliament* up to
October, 1651.

found great work to be taken in hand. There had
been no judges on circuit from 1642 to 1646. From
1646 to 1648 their appearance had been spasmodic, and
though in the west and the south it had been more
frequent, yet in other parts of the country their absence
had been deplorable.

The duties of a Commissioner or Judge of Assize at this
period were of a far more onerous character than he is
now called upon to discharge. At the present time a
judge on circuit tries the prisoners in the gaol and disposes
of the causes in the lists, and his business is over ; but in
the sixteenth and seventeenth centuries the judge may
almost be said to have administered the county to which
he was sent. He heard appeals from Quarter Sessions and
from orders of Justices of the Peace. He tried questions of
rating and assessments, and when he thought it necessary
or right ordered a rate to be made on the whole county or
on a particular parish for any specific purpose. Numerous
entries, for instance, are to be found in which the Judge of
Assize has ordered rates to be made with a view to
paying the expenses of successful prosecutions to pro-
secutors who could neither themselves afford to pay nor
could recover them from the parish where the offence was
committed. Others in which a parish having been
devastated by fire, or ravaged by disease, funds were
required to rebuild the parish or to tend the sick. He
was, as it were, a grand guardian to the poor, and
as such heard petitions from poor people who complained of the non-administration of parish relief, and at
every assize town he heard and decided disputed settle-
ments of paupers which formed a great part of the duties
of Justices of the Peace. He was constantly inquiring
into questions of county highways and bridges, giving his
orders as to their maintenance and repair, and the proportion in which the cost was to be borne by the various
parishes. He exercised a general control over the Justices

of the Peace, directed the strict enforcement or counselled moderation in the application of penal Acts and Ordinances. He heard reports of crimes and offences that had been committed, and for which no person was in custody, and directed what justices were to undertake the inquiries, what examinations were to be taken, and how and where the offenders were to be tried. He exercised some jurisdiction over the payment of tithes, gave orders as to the repair or rebuilding of parish churches, and as to the rates necessarily to be made for the purpose, and made orders on lay rectors for the repair of their chancels.[1] He heard complaints from the inhabitants of parishes and from the grand juries, of the number of ale-house keepers, maltsters, and others who had to take out licenses, and ordered the local justices to suppress such houses as he found upon evidence to be disorderly or unnecessary. He heard petitions from poor people who by reason of their poverty had been expelled from the towns and villages, and made peremptory orders for their reception upon the inhabitants or the overseers who had driven them out. He entertained complaints of extortion by bailiffs and officers of excise, and appointed certain of the justices to enquire into the complaints and report the facts. He was in effect accessible to all subjects of the realm, and there was no complaint of any wrong, injustice, or misery from one end of England to the other which was not fit matter for the judge to consider if he were to do his duty in that position to which he had been called.

To the Commonwealth Judges on their first circuits, these duties became intensified. The troubles of the time, and the absence of the King's Judges had left the counties without the authority or the guidance of the judge to whom they had habitually looked up for direction and

---

[1] Justices of Assize had power to hear and determine questions as to the repairs of churches and chapels, and the levying of Church rates, under Stat. 1647, c. 105.

advice. They found the counties without coroners, justices, constables, overseers, or churchwardens. Juries were seldom summoned, and the jury lists had remained unrevised since the commencement of the Civil War. The poor rates had not been collected for years, and the poor had thus been without relief except from kindly persons themselves often on the verge of poverty. Gifts, legacies and the profits of lands that had been left by pious people in days gone by for the relief of the poor, or otherwise for the benefit of the parish in which they had lived, had been diverted from these charitable purposes and appropriated by various persons who had refused to account to the parishioners who had been defrauded. The gipsy or counterfeit Egyptian, who swarmed in the land, was almost as great a terror to the countryman as was the witch, and yet the law had declared that for a gipsy to be more than a month within the realm was a felony. Men were plundered and their wives and daughters assaulted by soldiers and sailors wandering about the country without a pass and insisting on money and food, and branded rogues and cheats returning to their roguery infested the country towns and villages, and yet the law that these rogues and vagrants had set at nought declared such conduct to be felony and punishable as such. But the gaols and houses of correction in many counties were in such decay that sturdy rogues and vagabonds could walk out at their pleasure and laugh at the gaolers, who were continually being subjected to charges of escape. The overseers of the highways, unable to collect the rates from the land-owners or the farmers, who beat them if they approached their houses, could not repair the roads or bridges of the country. Men had refused to be constables or church-wardens, so that the few existing constables were old and useless. The parish churches were falling into ruin, and in some cases were closed as dangerous. The various counties had hardly one coroner apiece. The entire

County of Somerset had only one, who was old and sick
and unable to travel, and in some counties the coroners
were men of no means or education, and entirely without
knowledge of the law they had undertaken to administer.
Of the Justices of the Peace, not more than ten per cent.
had been sworn into office, so that those who acted were
few in number, and mostly old, and had borne on their
shoulders for several years the entire burthen of the
county judicature. And above all, the plague in the South
of England and in the Midlands was raging with un-
restricted fury and decimating the population. The
North appears, however, to have been free from the
infection, except in the instance of Liverpool, where,
in 1651-52, the plague was so violent that all intercourse
with Ireland was stopped, and ships from the Port of Liverpool were refused admission to any other ports in the kingdom[1]; and of Chester, where, in May, 1654, the courts were
adjourned to Northwich on account of the plague.[2]
On the Western Circuit I find that there were no less
than six towns[3] subject to isolation, and in respect of
which the several counties were put under contribution by
the Lord Chief Baron; and in the spring of the following
year Baron Gates and Baron Rigby, on the Home Circuit,
were both attacked by the plague while discharging their
judicial duties at Croydon, and died before leaving their
circuit towns. With one and all of these matters the
judges effectually dealt. They took the opinions of the
Justices in grand jury assembled as to the number of
coroners required for the county, and ordered the
under-sheriff to apply for writs *de coronatore eligendo*
to the Lords Commissioners of the Great Seal, and
to proceed at once to an election by the freeholders

---

[1] State Papers, March, 1652.
[2] Ordinance, 16th May, 1654. Scoble, fc. 303.
[3] Langport, Fisherton Anger, Ashbritton, Totnes, Buckland. Wivels-
combe, were the names given in the Judges' orders.

of a sufficient number of duly qualified coroners. On returning again to their circuits they disqualified such of
the elected coroners as had been in arms against the
Parliament, and such as they were satisfied were without
means and not versed in the law of the country, directing at the same time that steps should be taken to supply
the places of those removed. They ordered the attendance of all Justices of the Peace not already sworn,
and directed the Clerk of the Peace to tender them the
oath, and to return the names of those who refused to be
sworn. They issued orders for the election of parish
constables and churchwardens, and directed certain
Justices of the Peace to enquire and report at a subsequent
circuit the best mode of raising money to repair and to
reopen the dilapidated churches.[1] They made similar
orders as to the repair or rebuilding of the county gaols
and houses of correction, with a significant intimation to
the Justices in Quarter Sessions that before their next
circuit they would expect to see these matters taken in
hand. They also, as we may expect, published the
ordinances for the better observance of the Lord's Day,
against profane cursing and swearing, and for the keeping
of the last Monday in every month as a day of fast and
humiliation.

The plague, however, appears to have been almost
entirely confined to the towns, and except in cases where
a poor person left or was driven out of the town and died
on the highway there was little sickness in the country

---

[1] I find the following amongst other orders as to parish churches in
the Order Books of the Western Circuit :—

March, 1649: Order for a rate to repair Broughton Church.

March, 1649: Order to enforce a similar order as to Calne Church.

March, 1649: Similar orders as to Combleton and Idneston Churches.

February, 1651: Order as to the lead taken from Winchester
Cathedral to be valued and restored.

July, 1656: Order for a rate to repair Grewel Church, and that Mr.
Pole, "the impropriate person," repair the chancel.

villages. The course apparently adopted in such cases
was for the inhabitants of the town to be as far as possible
confined within its limits, and for an assessment for the
benefit of the sick and needy to be made upon the lands
of every parish within five miles of the centre of the town.
It happened, however, as would obviously be the case,
that such land was sometimes accommodation land to the
town and belonged to the inhabitants, and in other cases
that it was the property of poor people who were unable to
pay, so that the assessment frequently was of no avail. The
judges, however, taking a broader view of the duty to one's
neighbour, ordered a rate to be levied on every non-infected
parish in the county for the relief of the plague-
stricken spots within it, and at the same time
issued stringent regulations for confining the unhappy
victims within the limits of their infected area. These
rates were collected, as appears from the orders, with great
difficulty, and there was good reason to suspect that much
of the money collected was never paid over to the
authorized recipients. They also made orders suppressing
certain superfluous maltsters, and in other respects endeavoured to keep down the prices of corn and barley in
view of the famine prices that were then anticipated. In
contemplation of which they also by common consent
confirmed previous orders of Quarter Sessions declaring
that in view of the lamentable condition of the poor in this
time of dearth and scarcity, in every market in England
one bushel of every quarter of barley should be sold at a
sum less than the market price for the benefit of the poor.

The amount of work thus thrown on the shoulders of the
judges was almost unlimited in extent; but they took it
boldly in hand, and the numberless orders they made on
an infinite variety of subjects testify alike to their industry,
to their acumen, and to their knowledge of public affairs.
They had to bring order out of chaos; to clear the country
of wandering companies of rogues, vagabonds and highway-

men; to restore order to the various corporations and
other communities who had set up for themselves a law of
their own; to enforce the enactments passed for the
benefit and relief of the poor; and to satisfy the minds of
the public that, under the Commonwealth, law and
order would be restored, private rights respected and
public duties enforced. And to the success with which
they accomplished their task much of the subsequent
quietude of the country was undoubtedly due.

While the judges in the South, in addition to their
ordinary duties, were endeavouring to deal with the plague,
the judges in the North had to deal with the cases of those
who had been sent for trial by Parliament or by the Council
of State for offences arising out of the late troubles. Chief
among these was Colonel Morris, who had held Pomfret
Castle against the Parliamentary troops long after the war
had really terminated. This gentleman was tried at York
by Baron Thorpe and Justice Puleston for being in arms
and holding Pomfret Castle against the Parliament.
When the Castle was surrendered to General Lambert,
Colonel Morris escaped, but he was afterwards captured in the City of Lancaster. His career was not
very creditable. Having been formerly in the service of
the Parliament, he managed by a pretended friendship with
the Governor of Pomfret Castle to obtain command of that
redoubtable fortress, which he thenceforward treacherously
held for the King. While in that position he, in association
with other cavaliers, was concerned in the cruel and
cowardly murder of Colonel Rainsborough, a Parliamentary
officer, in his private lodgings in Doncaster. This last
exploit probably lost Colonel Morris his life, for after a
short trial he was found guilty by the jury and sentenced
to death.[1] At his trial he produced a commission signed
by Prince Charles, and demanded a trial by court-martial,
which was refused. He also protested against the in-

---

[1] State Trials, Vol. IV., p. 1250; Carlyle Letters, &c., Vol. II., p. 79.

dignity of being manacled after his trial, a course which the judges were contented to waive, but the Sheriff declaring he could not hold his prisoner without such security, the irons were riveted on him before he left the court.

But now the judges being home from their circuits and the courts resuming their normal aspect, the Government proceeded to take in hand the reformation of the law. Many flagrant abuses had already been removed. The High Commission Court, the Court of Wards, and the Star Chamber had been abolished, and the judges from the Lords Commissioners to the puisne judges held their offices *dum se bene gesserint.* All the vacant judgeships in England and Wales had been filled up, and the courts were open daily for the transaction of business. The duties which the Commonwealth had in this respect imposed upon themselves were the reconstruction of the courts of law, with the abolition of those that were useless or inconvenient ; the reform of legal procedure so as to remove the scandals of delay, cost, and uncertainty, and the repeal of such of the laws relating thereto as were obsolete or unsuited to the advanced spirit of the times. First, with regard to the reconstruction of the courts : the Court of Chancery had been continued as it had existed during the late years of the Civil War, the Great Seal being in Commission, but being now confided to three instead of two Lords Commissioners. The common law courts were constituted as before, and the benches of the courts at Westminster being filled, the *Twelve Judges* were still continued as an institution of the country, and the regularity of circuits was re-established. But the Prerogative Courts and the Court of Admiralty being originally of ecclesiastical cognizance were dealt with as tribunals tainted with the hierarchy of the spotted dogs.[1] The power of the Lord High Admiral was conferred upon the Council of State, and Acts were passed for regulating the trial of

---

[1] If a Puritan had a spotted dog he called him " Bishop."

Admiralty causes and the granting of probates and letters of administration. Jurisdiction in matters of Admiralty, and during the naval warfare of the Commonwealth such jurisdiction was of a necessary and extended character, was confided to three judges,[1] a common lawyer and two civilians, who were assisted by a very efficient Bar. There was some reason for putting a common lawyer in the post of Chief Admiralty Judge, as in addition to cases of damage, salvage, wages, and other Admiralty suits, he had jurisdiction to try cases of piracy and offences committed at sea, with power of sentencing the offenders to death, of whatsoever nationality they might happen to be. This arrangement being, however, not altogether satisfactory, an Act was passed in July, 1653,[2] to appoint other judges and to declare the jurisdiction of the Court of Admiralty. Under that Act, Dr. Godolphin, Dr. Clarke, and Mr. C. G. Cooke were appointed judges of the Court, not less than two of whom were to constitute a court, and each judge on giving judgment was to deliver in open court his reasons for such judgment.[3] If it could be shown that any such judge had directly or indirectly received a bribe or fee, he was to forfeit his salary, to be removed from his place, and to be henceforward forever incapable of any trust or employment in the Commonwealth of England. The jurisdiction as declared by the Act is that still exercised by the Court. It contains no reference to the trial of felonies by the, Admiralty judges, but the Statutes 1649 c. 61, and 1650 c. 7, show that there was a concurrent jurisdiction to

---

[1] Whitelock, Vol III., p. 88. *Perfect Diurnal of Passages in Parliament*, April, 1651.

[2] Statute, 1653, c. 2

[3] One reason for making all judges give their reasons was the fact that the judges who were believed to have decided in favour of ship money afterwards said they were not in favour of it, but had been overborne by their colleagues. The rule at present is universal except in the Privy Council.

try offences either in the Admiralty or at Common Law.
The Act of 1653 also provides for " the same right of appeal
as hath been formerly used." In the Admiralty cause
"The Sun "[1] taken as a prize and condemned by the judges
of the Admiralty, the Lords Commissioners of the Great
Seal appointed delegates who sat in Serjeant's Inn and
heard an appeal from the owners, and this I suppose was
the usual course of appeal. The salary of the Admiralty
judges was £500 per annum.[2] For the determination of
probates and letters of administration a commission was
appointed, consisting of Sir Anthony Ashley Cooper, Mr.
Steele, Mr. Hale, Hugh Peters, Rushworth, and others,
altogether twenty in number, of whom five were to be a
quorum, with power to sit in divisions of not less than five
each.[3] They were designated by the name, revived
again after a period of two hundred years, of the *Court of
Probate*, and sat at Westminster in the place lately called
the Star Chamber.[4] They held the position of judges and
tried questions of succession and of granting probates or
administrations, and in most other respects exercised the
functions of the old ecclesiastical judges. I am not aware
of any printed record of their decisions, but in one case, of
which there is a MSS. report among the documents of the
Council of State, the case of *Hunck v. Pennoyer and
Others*, in October, 1654,[5] they heard long arguments in a
matter of considerable complication, and ultimately granted
a limited *administration de bonis non administratis*, in
accordance with the recognised practice of the present day. A system of district registries for wills and
administrations was also constituted, and thus the first
step was taken towards that general system of registration

---

[1] State Papers, Vol. XLII. (1653).
[2] State Papers, 6th March, 1653-4.
[3] The Act was passed on he 8th April, 1653.
[4] State Papers, Vol. LXXVI., fo. 58-60.
[5] State Papers, Vol. LXXVI.

of wills and deeds which has gradually but surely been growing up with the general support of public opinion. At the same time also a general registry of marriages, births, and burials was established in every parish throughout England.[1]

The Consistory and other courts, having jurisdiction to deal with matrimonial squabbles, having been abolished, the Council of State was appealed to in some cases to interfere between husband and wife. The only recorded instance of such intervention that I have seen was in February, 1655, and it was not of a character to encourage further ventures. One Mr. John Buck, having petitioned the Council of State, an order was made[2] on the Lords Commissioners of the Great Seal that they should " compose the differences " between Mr. John Buck and Mary his wife. It was further provided that if the Lords Commissioners failed to effect this reconciliation, a committee of the Council should be nominated to do so, and in the event of their failure that Mr. Robert Ashton (presumably a minister) was to try. The Lords Commissioners refused to interfere. The Committee of the Council, on interviewing the lady, were ordered out and informed that " she refused to permit them to meddle in her affairs." Mrs. Buck having a child some few months old, the Council thought to bring her to terms by seizing the child and delivering it over to the husband, and an order was issued to that effect. It appeared, however, that Mrs. Buck, anticipating some such order, had conveyed away the child by means of Mrs. Taylor, her mother, and there the matter appears to have ended. Questions relating to the validity of marriages, apart from questions of separation or alimony, for which there appears to have been no provision unless the Court of Probate had some jurisdiction in the matter, not now easily to be ascertained, were not remitted to the

---

[1] Statute, 1653, c. 6.
[2] State Papers, Vol. CXXVIII.

judges of the Court of Probate, but were dealt with either
by delegates appointed by the Commissioners of the Great
Seal or by Justices of the Peace in Quarter Sessions—a
course which would seem to have been the reasonable
outcome of the statutes which provided that all marriages should take place before a Justice of the Peace
and be regarded solely as civil and consensual contracts.

At Durham, at Lancaster, and at Ely, the Bishops
sitting each as a Pope in his own dominions professed to exercise temporal as well as spiritual power,
but they had in fact permitted gross abuses to corrupt and
obstruct the fountain of justice. These Bishops' Courts
were at once swept away,[1] the process being hurried on by
petitions from these districts, praying that the judges
might be sent down to try the bishops' causes. These
suits, it was alleged by the petitioners, were multiplying to
the number of six hundred, and as they were all sent up to
London to be tried the suitors could not afford the cost,
and thus lost their debts.[2] An order was accordingly made
that the Judges of Assize should take over this business and
ry all such causes at Durham and Lancaster respectively,[3]
and a judge was appointed for the Isle of Ely. At the
same time all the bishops' causes found in the London
lists were sent back to their respective counties to be there
tried. The Chancery Courts of the Counties Palatine of Lancaster and Chester were likewise abolished and their duties
committed to the Common Law Judges, but it was found
that the alteration was not successful, and in 1654 these
courts were re-established. Permanent judges were reappointed, and Justice Hale, as a Chancery man, and
Justice Windham, as a common lawyer, were added to the
staff, with Mr. Fell, the former Vice-Chancellor, as chief

---

[1] Acts, No. 456 and 457, June, 1649.
[2] Whitelock, Vol. III., p. 187.
[3] Acts, No. 456, 19th June, 1649.

judge. North and South Wales still continued each to have a judicial staff of its own, consisting of a chief justice and two puisnes at a salary of £250 a year each. And the Chief Justice of Chester (a post held by Serjeant Bradshaw during the time of the Commonwealth), with his assistant judge, Mr. Fell, still held their courts, and tried on some occasions as many as one hundred causes.

The question of appeals was one not easily to be disposed of. In all countries where the system of judicature is subject to abuse, the power of unlimited appeal is perhaps the greatest evil. It gives greater power to the wealthy suitor than any other engine of the law, and it enables the litigious disputant to wear out his opponent by mere force of delay. The radical spirits of the time attacked these appeals. Let us do away, said they, with these innumerable and unworkable courts of appeal. Let us have competent and independent judges of first instance to decide our cases and abolish all process of appeal whatever. Steady and thoughtful students of law and of statecraft, however, and amongst these Cromwell must be reckoned, while admitting the abuse of appeals, recognised by experience the necessity of some superior tribunal to which the ultimate decision of questions of law should be submitted. And accordingly, in 1654, after some years of experiment, in course of which provisions were made for hearing writs of error, and it was declared there should be no error for matters of form but only for matters of substance established before the judges in open court,[1] a Court of Appeal was established. It was hoped by its constitution and by the conditions of appeal that the advantages could be secured while the evils of frivolous and vexatious litigation would be removed. The Judges of Appeal were the Lords Commissioners of the Great Seal for the time being, and six Common Law Judges, of whom one must be a Chief Justice, or Lord Chief Baron. The court was to consist of

---

[1] Statute, 1649, c. 75.

not less than five of the judges; the appellant was first
to perform the judgment appealed from, and secondly to
pay £50 as security for costs. Means are not forthcoming,
as far as I am aware, for forming any accurate judgment
as to the appeals submitted to this court or the
decisions given by it. It was open to certain obvious
objections. It entertained appeals from Chancery, and the
three Commissioners of the Great Seal formed part of the
court. It heard appeals from Westminster Hall, six of
whose judges sat on the appeals, while the order, which
required the appellant to perform the judgment appealed
from as a condition precedent to his applying for relief,
would in many cases have frustrated the ends of justice.
The rule requiring security for costs to the extent of £50 is
not open to the same objection, though it would have been
more consistent with equity to have permitted the judges
to enlarge or reduce the amount in particular cases.

Appeals from Guernesy and Jersey, which appeared to
be not infrequent, were entertained by the Council of State,
who appointed a committee to hear them and to report their
judgment in due course.[1] Meantime, however, petty courts
of numerous corporations exercised either by custom or by
charter various judicial functions and tried small claims by
the very clumsy and circuitous process which even now to
some extent survives in the trial of questions of ritual and
doctrine before the bishops and in the Court of Arches.
And Courts of Quarter Sessions, to which the administration of justice, criminal and civil, had been almost entirely
relegated during the Civil Wars, still continued to exercise
their functions, acting, however, under the control and
direction of the Judges of Assize.

In November, 1653, the judges in Westminster Hall

---

[1] Several of the judgments are to be found in the records of the
Council of State for 1657. See also *Mercurius Politicus*, No. 385,
which says, the Protector sat with the Council to hear appeals from
Jersey and Guernsey.

had before them one of those cases which are apt to engender difficulties between the executive Government and the Courts of Law. One Captain Streater, who had been committed to Newgate by the House of Commons and also by the Council of State, applied for his *habeas corpus* in the Upper Bench. The judges then sitting were Lord Chief Justice Rolle and Justices Jermyn and Nicholas,[1] who decided unanimously that Parliament having committed the prisoner could alone order his release, and that the Courts of Law could neither bail nor discharge him, nor inquire into the reason of his detention.[2] In February of the following year, 1653-4, after the dissolution of the Long Parliament, on Streater's application being renewed, the Lord Chief Justice and Justice Aske made an order for his discharge, holding that, although they could neither release nor bail a prisoner committed by Parliament, so long as Parliament was sitting, yet that, on the dissolution of Parliament, the order for his committal determined, the Courts of Law had jurisdiction over the matter[3] and were bound to release him. Both these propositions of law have been since upheld as sound, and have been acted upon in various cases.[4]

In the spring of 1655 an occurrence took place which ultimately led to the retirement of the Lord Chief Justice. One of the numerous futile attempts to create a diversion in favour of the exiled Prince and to bring about a rising in the West of England was organized by Sir Joseph Wagstaffe, Colonel Penruddock, and others. The rising was confined to certain gentry of the counties of Wilts and Devon and to a mere handful of adherents whom they induced to follow them. The whole affair was of a very

---

[1] Called in the reports Judge Garmond and Judge Nicholls.
[2] State Trials, Vol. V.
[3] State Trials, Vol. V., p. 402.
[4] This subject is discussed at length in May's Parliamentary Practice.

feeble character, and the insurgents were followed and captured without resistance by Captain Unton Crook with a troop of horse. Amongst other follies, however, Sir Joseph Wagstaffe and his men seized the judges in their beds, ransacked their lodgings, stole their horses, robbed them of their commissions, and were about to hang them, when, better counsels prevailing, they were released with their lives. The Sheriff also and the town crier were threatened with death for refusing to proclaim King Charles II., but stoutly standing to their colours and offering to be hanged rather than make the Royal proclamation, they also managed to escape, not, however, till after the Sheriff had been robbed of £6 in silver and several gold pieces.[1] Charles II. was then proclaimed by others of the party. Looked at from any point of view, these were acts of treason against the existing Government, of which it was bound to take immediate cognizance. Lord Chief Justice St. John, Justice Atkins, and Serjeant Steele (Recorder of London) were at once summoned from their circuits to advise with the Council as to the proceedings to be taken against Penruddock and the rest.[2] The consultations with the Attorney-General and Chief Justice St. John resulted in a determination to respect the views of the Common Law Judges, and to try the various prisoners by a jury of their respective counties, and the Attorney-General, with Mr. Sadler, his assistant, was sent at once to the west to make the necessary preparations. Mr. Ellis (the Solicitor-General), Mr. Roger Hill, and Mr. Richard Graves were afterwards sent down to assist in the preparation of the case. A commission of Oyer and Terminer and Gaol Delivery was then issued, directed to the Lord Chief Justice and Baron Nicholas, being the judges then on that circuit, Lord Commissioner Lisle, Justice Windham, John Glyn (Serjeant to the Lord

---

[1] *Perfect Proceedings*, etc., No. 286.
[2] State Papers, Vol. XCV. Wagstaffe escaped to France.

Protector), and Serjeant Steele (Recorder of London), to hold
assizes for the trial of the persons charged with treasonable
practices in the counties of Wilts, Devon, and Somerset, to
be held at Salisbury, Exeter and Chard,[1] and they were
at the same time to try any other prisoners to be found in
the gaols.   On the 16th April the Commissioners, under
the presidency of Justice Windham, sat at Salisbury, and
tried those engaged in the late rising.   Most of them
pleaded guilty, some pleaded not guilty, and some, including Colonel Penruddock, were sent for trial at Exeter.   Of
those tried at Salisbury three gentlemen were acquitted by
the jury, and thirteen were convicted, after defending
themselves stoutly, and sentenced to be hanged.   Of these
seven were convicted of levying war and treason, five for
felonies (including horse stealing and highway robbery),
and one, Margery Gyngell, for witchcraft.   Of these persons all were pardoned of their lives by the Lord Protector,
except Lucas, who was ordered to be beheaded, and
Thorpe and Kinsey to be hanged.[2]

On the 18th April Serjeant Glyn and Serjeant Steele
opened the Commission at Exeter, and proceeded to
try Penruddock and twenty-five others for treason
and felonies in relation to the late rising.   The account
of this trial (not in the most trustworthy form) comes
from Colonel Penruddock himself.[3]   Such of the evidence
as he has set out makes the case clear enough, and he
defended himself strictly on the lines indicated in the
directions found among his papers.   The Lord Chief Justice
and Baron Nicholas, being possible witnesses in the case,
sat upon the Bench in their robes of office, but neither here
nor at Salisbury took any part in the trial.   The prisoners
were all convicted by the jury, but twelve of them were

---

[1] *Perfect Proceedings in State Affairs*, Nos. 286 and 288.
[2] *Perfect Proceedings in State Affairs*, Nos. 287-288; *Perfect
Diurnal*, Nos. 279.
[3] State Trials, Vol. V., p. 767.

pardoned by the Protector. Penruddock was beheaded and the others hanged, some for treason and some for various felonies committed during the rising.[1] Penruddock, on the scaffold, spoke in somewhat complimentary terms of the Protector, who, as he said, would have given him his life if Colonel Crook had confirmed his articles of surrender, and recognised, in fact, that Cromwell was rather disposed to clemency, when reasonable grounds could be shown, than to act the part of the Roman tyrant and turn down his thumbs upon any victim whose fate was in his hands. This personal violence, however, with a narrow escape from death while in discharge of his judicial office, was a serious shock to the Lord Chief Justice, then verging on his seventieth year, and although his horses were recovered at an expense to the State[2] of £78, paid to the soldiers who rescued them, yet he appears to have determined not again to incur the risk or the fatigue of riding another circuit.[3]

When the judges returned to town, and Trinity Term commenced, an event occurred in the Upper Bench

---

[1] *Perfect Diurnal*, No. 291.

[2] State Papers Warrant, 20th May, 1655.

[3] It is said by Burnet, and quoted by Lord Campbell, that Mathew Hale was ordered to go west to try Penruddock, but that he refused, adding that he had quite enough work to do without it. There is no record in the Council of State papers of his having been communicated with at all, though there are records of communication with other judges. He was at this time riding the Midland circuit, and stopped to finish the business while his brother judge, Justice Windham, went west and tried the prisoners. Similarly, Recorder Steele was called from Essex, where he was on circuit, and his colleague, Justice Aske, was ordered to remain and dispatch the rest of the circuit. (State Papers, Vol. XCV., p. 98.) Nor as these prisoners were to be tried by jury under an Act to which Justice Hale was a party would there seem to have been any reason why he should not have gone.

Justice Windham was reappointed to the Bench after the Restoration in 1670. See Foss's Judges, p. 197.

which has been universally commented on, as showing
Cromwell's disregard of law and of liberty where the
interests of his Government were concerned. Three
of the leading counsel of the day—Serjeant Maynard,
Serjeant Twisden, and Mr. Wadham Windham—were
committed to the Tower for words spoken in court on
behalf of their client, a certain Mr. George Cony. All
writers, including Hallam,[1] speak of the case as
being somewhat obscure as to the facts, it not being
reported in any of the books; but all concur in censuring
the conduct of the Government in regard to the three
counsel. And yet, without a true knowledge of the facts,
no judgment upon the conduct of Cromwell or his Government can be safely arrived at. The immunity of counsel
in defending their clients is doubtless one of the great
strongholds of English liberty, and yet this immunity is
not altogether without restriction. A case would be conceivable where a counsel in his speech might appeal to the
crowd to rescue his client, and thus bring terror and violence
to bear on the judge. Such conduct would not be beyond
the reach of the law. It is a recognised rule of law that
when a counsel, regardless of his instructions or of the fair
limits of argument, goes out of his way to slander any person,
he is subject to an action in respect of words so spoken.
And for misconduct in court the judge may exercise over
counsel the process of contempt either by fine or committal
to prison. I have found among the records of the Council
of State the report upon which their action was taken, and
from that and the newspapers of the day I have gathered
the following facts, which I believe to be accurate, and
from which the reader can draw his own conclusions.

Mr. Cony, a City merchant, dealing in Spanish wine,
whom Clarendon[2] describes as "an eminent fanatik," and
who combined a hatred of the Government with a dislike

---

[1] Constitutional History, Vol. I., p. 670.
[2] Rebellion, Vol. III., p. 649.

to taxation, had refused to pay certain customs' dues, payable under an ordinance of the Protector, continuing an excise duty which had existed since 1647, if not much longer. The power to make such ordinance was conferred on the Protector and his Council by the *Instrument of Government*, which contained the following clauses :—

Art. VI.—The laws shall not be altered, suspended, or abrogated, nor any new law made, nor any tax, charge or imposition laid upon the people but by common consent in Parliament, save only as is expressed in the XXVIIth Article.

Art. XXVII.—That a constant yearly revenue shall be raised . . . . . which revenue shall be raised by the customs and such other ways and means as shall be agreed upon by the Lord Protector and his Council, and shall not be taken away or diminished, nor the way agreed upon for raising the same altered, but by the consent of the Lord Protector and the Parliament.

The Protector was also empowered with the advice of his Council to make other binding ordinances during the intervals of Parliament, and he had in fact by virtue of such instrument and by ordinance appointed all the judges, and had lately conferred on Mr. Twisden and Mr. Maynard the degree of the coif. Mr. Cony, having refused to pay these dues, was committed to the Serjeant-at-Arms by the Council of State, under the powers conferred on them by the Long Parliament. He thereupon moved for his *habeas corpus* in the Upper Bench. The account of the affair, reported to the Council by Mr. Zanchy,[1] the Solicitor to the Commonwealth, was that on Mr. Cony's case being called on for argument of the *habeas corpus*, and the counsel for the Commonwealth being engaged in various other courts, he went out to fetch them, and on his return he found Serjeant Twisden—who afterwards as a judge earned for himself an unenviable notoriety for ferocity of demeanour, and who is specially known for his conduct in that respect at the trial of John Bunyan[2]—arguing Mr. Cony's case.

---

[1] State Papers, 18th May, 1655.
[2] Campbell's Chief Justices, Vol, I., p. 559.

He was contending that the Protector had no power to
make any ordinance in regard to customs and excise, and
accordingly that no duties or customs were then payable
by any law whatever. " He insisted much on the taking
away the Star Chamber, and urged that subjects were not to
be imprisoned nor their goods attached, but in a legal way
and on trial by jury," and he discussed at length the orders
of the Council, and the ordinances under which the commissioners sat at the receipt of custom. The Attorney-
General, in his reply, wondered that the Serjeant should
speak so much against the present authority, being that
under which that court sat, and by which Mr. Cony
expected justice. Serjeant Maynard[1] spoke but little, and
Mr. Wadham Windham said nothing at all. As the result
of Mr. Zanchy's report all these counsel were summoned
before the Council of State, when the Lord Chief Justice
was also requested to attend. Every member of the
council, including the Protector, was present.[2] The
counsel were called in one after the other, when it was
resolved " That all three be committed to the Tower,
and that His Highness sign the warrant for their commitment for using words tending to sedition and subversive
of the present Government."[3] These " three learned
and profound lawyers" accordingly went to the Tower,
whence, on the 25th May following, they humbly petitioned
for their release, and Serjeant Maynard was discharged.
On the 1st June Serjeant Twisden petitioned again for his
release. He pleaded the case of his wife and seven
children, regretted that what he had said in his client's
cause should have excited His Highness's displeasure, and
disavowed any intention to provoke sedition or discontent.

[1] *Proceedings in State Affairs* of 9th February, 1653-4. " Five new
Serjeants were made, who are to be made Judges, viz., Mr. Maynard,
Mr. Steele, Mr. Windham, Mr. Newdigate, and Mr. Twisden."
[2] Attendance of Council of State, calendar 1655.
[3] State Papers, Vol. XCVII.; *Truthful Scout*, 22nd May, 1655.

Mr. Wadham Windham, except for his wife and seven children, petitioned to the same effect, and not long after they also were released. Meanwhile Mr. Cony's case was postponed from time to time. He refused to employ counsel, though several offered their services, and, according to tradition, the matter was settled before the following Term, when Serejant Glyn took his seat as Lord Chief Justice of the Upper Bench. The commitment of these counsel was undoubtedly an arbitrary act on the part of the Council of State, and on general grounds indefensible. But on the other hand it must be borne in mind, not in justification but in palliation of the business, that these two serjeants were among the leading men of the time; that these Ordinances of Cromwell's were authorized by the Instrument of Government which had been accepted by the nation and passed by Parliament: that the proposition of Serjeant Twisden, that no excise or customs whatever were now legally payable (the words that were the gist of the offence) might have given rise to a general repudiation of the payment of customs and excise, and have led to trouble and conflicts from one end of the country to the other.[1] Cony was a firebrand of the Lilburn type, encouraged by the cavaliers for the purpose of injuring the Government, and the combination of Cony, the fanatic, as party, and Twisden, the cavalier, as counsel, supporting his opposition to the payment of any taxes whatever, was one calculated in every way to rouse the susceptibilities of the Protector and the Council of State. It seems improbable that Serjeant Maynard would willingly have lent himself to this course, although his action (if indeed he was correctly reported) in regard to

---

[1] An Act of the Long Parliament (Statute 1653, c. 38) had continued the customs and excise till 26th March, 1654. An ordinance of the Protector and his Council (Ord. 1653, c. 15, 20th March, 1653-4) continued them till 26th March, 1658. The Parliament, 1656, confirmed and again continued the customs and excise.

Lilburn may have given rise to the suggestion, and the three counsel probably had to thank the indiscretion and the Royalism of Serjeant Twisden for their temporary detention in the Tower. At all events it was so regarded at the Restoration, when Serjeant Twisden was at once made a judge as a reward for his loyalty to the Royal family, and Mr. Wadham Windham was shortly afterwards, in November, 1660, also appointed to a seat on the King's Bench.[1] Serjeant Maynard's intervention in the matter seems, however, to have had no very great effect upon Cromwell, who, in May, 1658, appointed him Serjeant to His Highness the Protector, and afterwards, as is suggested, his Solicitor-General, a post which he certainly held under Richard.[2]

A great deal has been made of this case to the prejudice of Cromwell by panegyrists of the Restoration, and by writers on constitutional history, and undoubtedly it can only be justified from the point of view of a ruler, on the ground of necessity and that the injury to the Commonwealth by permitting the course of Mr. Cony and his counsel to pass unnoticed was greater than that of interfering with the privileges and rights of the Bar. I can hardly believe, however, that the public of that day took a very serious view of the position, or that the presence of lawyers in their midst was so lovely in their eyes that they found themselves either pained or outraged by hearing that three of their number had, like so many of their fellow citizens in that generation of troubles, spent a few days in the calm and secluded atmosphere of the Tower. Mr. Cony, who withdrew, or, as is said, was coaxed out of his case, appeared again before the Council in the following autumn under circumstances which seem to favour the suggestion that some sort of a compromise had been made with him. He seems, in disregard of the navigation laws which had, since

[1] Foss's Judges, Vol. VII., p. 198.
[2] State Papers, 21st January, 1658-9.

the time of Richard II., forbidden the importation of foreign
wine in foreign bottoms, to have been in the habit of importing his Malaga wine in any ship, British or foreign,
that happened to suit him ; and, in March, 1655, war with
Spain having in the meantime been declared, he was ex-
pecting the immediate arrival in the Downs of a Dutch ship
with a consignment of Spanish wine. " I and my friends,"
said he, in a petition to the Protector, " cannot safely bring
our goods into the port of London without your leave ;
but you lately promised me your favour on any reasonable
request ; therefore I beg speedy leave to bring in my ship
and goods." Matters of trade and navigation were,
however, matters for the Council of State, and the
petition was accordingly sent on to that body,[1] with
a note of a somewhat similar application to Parliament in January, 1652-3, which had been at that time
favourably received. The Council sent this forthwith
to their Committee, who, on the 16th November, reported
"to signify to George Cony—on his petition to import
Spanish wine in a Dutch vessel—that the Council thinks
not fit to do anything in the matter at present, since the
granting thereof would be contrary to the Act of Navigation."[2] It is said, on what grounds I know not, that the
Chief Justice had scruples in regard to Cony ; if so, he was
not the only judge who showed his independence. Bradshaw,
when required to take oath again as Chief Justice of Chester,
refused to do so, saying he was appointed " *quamdiu se
bene gesserit*," and whether he had demeaned himself
faithfully in his office he was willing to have tried by any
persons the Protector might select.[3] Justice Atkins had
refused, in a paper stating his reasons, to sit on any High

---

[1] State Papers, Council of State, 8th and 16th November, 1655.

[2] He was heard of again in August, 1656, when " the rabble of the
town of Canterbury" were trying to get him chosen as their member.
—Thurloe, Vol. IV., p. 308.

[3] State Trials, Vol. V., p. 366.

Court of Justice when the trial of the prisoners was not by
a jury,[1] and now, on the 3rd May, 1655, two other judges
resigned their posts. "Baron Thorpe and Justice
Newdigate, of the Upper Bench, the two chief of the
Commissioners appointed by commission of Oyer and
Terminer for trial of the risers in the north to sit at
York, etc., attended His Highness and the Council,
and gave in their excuses; after which they had writs
of ease issued out to them and delivered up their patents.
Mr. Newdigate practiseth as a Serjeant at Law." Thus
far the newspaper account of the day.[2] Whitelock[3] says:
"Baron Thorpe and Judge Newdigate were put out of
their places for not observing the Protector's pleasure in
all his commands." The learned ex-Lord Commissioner,
however, was at this particular date very sore about the
Chancery business, and he had not yet become reconciled
to the Protector by his appointment to the Treasury. The
facts appear to have been as follows. Simultaneously with
the rising in the West under Wagstaffe and Penruddock, a
rising had been organised in the North. It had been fore-
seen, and put down with as much ease as that in the West,
and the difficulty arose from the two judges being ordered
to the North for the very uncongenial duty of trying the
prisoners taken during the late rising. For this purpose
the Chief Justice had been requested to go,[4] but had
declined, intending, no doubt, shortly to retire from public
life. Newdigate had just returned from the North, where
he had been Judge of Assize with Serjeant Hatton,[5] and
Baron Thorpe had been on the Oxford Circuit[6] with Glyn.

---

[1] See State Papers, June, 1654.

[2] *Perfect Proceedings*, No. 293.

[3] Vol. IV., p. 101.

[4] State Papers, Council of State, 4th April, 1655.

[5] Serjeant Hatton was cousin to John Evelyn, and lived at Thames
Ditton.—Evelyn's Diary, Vol. I., p. 246.

[6] Baron Thorpe does not again appear as a judge until the Summer
Assizes, 1659, and he then held office till the Restoration. Newdigate

In the meantime the jurors to try the prisoners had been summoned to York for the third week in April, and the trials were expected to begin on the Friday in that week,[1] so that the judges would hardly have been home from their circuits before they were ordered to return again to open the new commissions. The actual grounds of their objections do not appear in their letters, nor am I aware that they have ever been distinctly stated. Lord Campbell says that Justice Newdigate had held, on the trial of Colonel Halsey, that there could be no treason against the Protector,[2] and that he was for that reason removed. But Newdigate did not try Colonel Halsey, and, indeed, such a theory appears entirely inconsistent, both with Newdigate having been made a judge at all, with his having been appointed to try the insurgents at York, and with his re-appointment by Cromwell to a judgeship in the following year. I therefore reject Lord Campbell's story as inaccurate. There is, however, an explanation entirely consistent with Newdigate's position as a Commonwealth judge, and, perhaps, not much more creditable to Cromwell.[3] The evidence against the royalists in the north consisted very much, in the first instance, of their having been seen almost perpetually on horseback and in communication with each other during the time that the rising was being organized in the south. And it seems that Newdigate and his brother judge, Serjeant Hatton, while probably not doubting of the seditious character of these meetings and communications, nor of the object they intended to compass, had expressed considerable doubts whether these ridings and

appears again as a judge at Winchester in the Summer Assizes, 1657, the Winter Assizes, 1657-8, and the Summer Assizes, 1658 and 1659. He was appointed Lord Chief Justice of the Upper Bench in January, 1659-60.

[1] Lawrence to Newdigate and others.—State Papers, 5th April, 1655.

[2] Lives of Chief Justices, Vol. I., p. 444.

[3] See the Judges to the Solicitor-General, and Colonel Robt. Lilburn to Thurloe, 10th April, 1655.—Thurloe, Vol. III., p. 359.

meetings were in themselves such overt acts as are required by law to establish a case of treason. And as the judges at that period and for many years after acted not only as judges to try prisoners, but also as magistrates to take depositions in important cases and to commit the prisoners for trial, their doubts in the first instance on the evidence they had taken would have very fairly indicated the lines upon which they would have directed the juries had they been called upon to try the prisoners. Finding themselves in this difficulty, they made an appointment to meet Baron Thorpe (who was then on the Oxford Circuit with Serjeant Glyn) at Doncaster in order to discuss the matter with him.[1] The two judges and Serjeant Hatton, with Colonel Robert Lilburn, accordingly met, and the three lawyers came to the conclusion that the evidence would not justify a conviction. This being immediately reported to the Council, the two judges, with their respective serjeants, were summoned to town, with the result that has been already stated. If, for this reason, Justice Newdigate and Baron Thorpe felt themselves called upon to resign rather than risk a collision with the Protector, their conduct was honourable both to themselves and their profession. But the story is not so absolutely clear as one might desire to find it, and there may possibly have been some other motive on the part of these two judges to which we have no clue. If, however, these were the judges' objections their scruples were given effect to, for the Commission was abandoned and the Cavaliers were discharged.

In November, 1657, Serjeant Thorpe, then practising at the Bar, appealed to the Council of State for payment of £1,550 due to him for arrears of salary as a Baron of the Exchequer, for which payment he had a warrant, but having only received £250 on account he begged that the rest might be made good. He " knows he has incurred

---

[1] Strickland to Thurloe.—Thurloe, Vol. III., p. 385. "Doncaster, 17th April, 1655, 12 at night."

his Highness's displeasure though he desired to serve him, and now that he has returned to the practice of his profession, from which he was called to the public service, desires that such displeasure may be removed."[1] The Council, however, had no money to pay anyone, and accordingly no immediate order was made on his application.

In the summer of 1655 Chief Justice Rolle resigned, retired into private life, and died at his country seat within a few months of his quitting office. Serjeant Glyn was appointed Lord Chief Justice, well-known serjeants were appointed to the vacant judgeships, and no matters of interest in connection with the law and its administrators arose till after the death of the Protector. All things seemed to go well with him, says Clarendon,[2] both at home and abroad. The decimation of the Royalists' incomes had ceased, the iron hand of the major-generals had been uplifted, sequestrations for payments of fifths and twentieths had been discontinued, all actions and orders in reference thereto had been stayed, and even, according to Clarendon, an era of peace and contentment had arrived which the sudden death of the Protector seemed only to intensify.[3] How far the Commonwealth Judges, by their learning, their industry and their independence, contributed to this result the present generation may judge for themselves by the perusal of the foregoing pages.

---

[1] A similar application for £1,050 was made by Serjeant Keble for arrears as Lord Commissioner, with the same result.—State Papers, Vol. CLVII.

[2] Vol. III., p. 646.

[3] Rebellion, Vol. III., p. 655

II.

I HAVE referred elsewhere to the endeavours made by Parliament to reform the social position of the people by means of Acts turning vices into crimes, and to the scanty success which they seem to have achieved. The attempts of the Commonwealth, under the Parliament and under Cromwell, to reform abuses of the law, though not attended with much good effect for the half century immediately succeeding the Restoration, were in fact the foundation to a great extent of our present system. No endeavour was made or even suggested to reduce the Common or Statute Law to a code, but each offending branch of the law was attacked in its turn and separate Acts were passed dealing with each particular subject. The recommendations and the Acts of these reformers have been one by one adopted by succeeding generations, and few now remain unaccomplished.

To inaugurate this important task it was necessary to appoint a committee, and the discussion of that proposal gave rise to a debate in which many opinions were expressed adverse to the presence of lawyers in Parliament. Whether this arose from the inherent opposition to practitioners of the law by soldiers who preferred cutting the knot of difficulty to untying it, by fanatics who hated the idea of their various monomanias being discussed and exploded, or whether it arose from the feeling that the lawyers spent too much time over their cases and too little over the Parliamentary debates, cannot now be known. But the feeling was strong, and a motion was made that no lawyer be permitted to sit in Parliament and at the same time to carry on the practice of his profession. The account of the debate comes to us from Whitelock,[1] who sets out *in extenso* the long and learned speech he made on the occasion. The most practical argument, however, is to be found in the concluding sentences in which he declares that Parliament has no more right to debar a lawyer from exercising his profession than it has to declare that a physician shall not attend his patients, a country gentleman sell his corn or his wool, a soldier drill his troops, or a merchant barter his goods. No such law was passed, but a draft of an Act was presented to Parliament declaring that it should not be lawful for any Member of Parliament, being a lawyer (other than the Counsel for the Commonwealth), to practise in any court of law during the time that he continued a Member of that House. Nothing, however, came of the proposal. I do not find that the draft was ever taken into consideration, and the lawyers continued to take the same leading and fearless part in the politics of the day that they had occupied ever since the first outbreak against Divine right. The debate also brought up the question of allowing all prisoners to be defended by counsel, and the general agreement appears to have been with the sentiment expressed by Whitelock,[2] that he never could answer the objection "that for a trespass of sixpence value a man might have a counsellor-at-law to plead for him, but where his life and posterity are concerned (as in cases of high treason) he is not admitted this privilege and help of lawyers. A law to reform this would be just and give right to the people." I find nowhere, however, among these proposals any suggestion that a prisoner should be allowed to give evidence on his own behalf, although the same reason applies to the one proposal as to the other, and it is only within the last few years that Parliament appears to have come to the conclusion that if a man is to be admitted to deny on

---

[1] Vol. III., p. 118.
[2] *Ibid.*, p. 124.

oath a claim for a few pounds, or an assault for which damages are claimed, it is only equitable and just that he should be permitted to deny upon oath facts tending to deprive him of life or to bastardize his issue. But now, as under the Long Parliament, reforms of the law, not appealing to popular passions, are easily laid aside, and it may even yet be many years before this desirable reform is introduced into our procedure. A Law Committee having been appointed by the House, schemes were laid before them by the attorneys and officers of the several courts,[1] by the committee of officers of the army, and by various volunteers, most of which contained some grains of gold amongst many tons of sand. The Committee was ordered to sit every Wednesday afternoon,[2] and they appear, in the beginning, to have worked well at their business. The first great subject of discussion was the language and text in which the laws and proceedings of the court should be written. The conduct of law proceedings in the so-called Norman-French was compared to the Latin Services in the Church, and it was said that in the one case as in the other, the people had a right to know what was going on and to be able to take an intelligent interest therein. Whitelock made again a long and learned speech,[3] giving an interesting history of the English law and its growth, showing how each succeeding governor, whether Roman, Saxon, or Norman, took over our laws as they were, and rather assimilated their foreign manners and customs to our ancient laws than modelled those laws to suit their foreign fancies. More successful than in his defence of the lawyers, the House, struck perhaps by his reference to Moses, who brought down the tables of the law written in the Hebrew character, which all Jews

---

[1] Whitelock, Vol. III., p. 194.
[2] *Public Intelligencer*, No. 50.
[3] Vol. III., pp. 260-273.

'could read, passed *unanimously* the resolution he proposed, which was in the following terms :—

It is ordered by the Parliament of England[1] that all books of the law be put into English, and that all writs, process, and returns thereof, and all patents, commissions, indictments, inquisitions, certificates, judgments, and records whatsoever, and all other rules and proceedings in courts of justice within the Commonwealth of England, shall be in the English tongue only, and not in Latin and French or any other language than English, and that the same be writ in an ordinary legible hand, and not in any court-hand; and that it be referred to a committee to bring in an Act upon this vote.

An Act[2] was accordingly brought in and passed on 22nd November, 1650, to come into operation on the 1st January following. In the next year, however, an amending Act[3] exempted, from the operation of the English rule, proceedings in the High Court of Admiralty. In that Court, which was of an international character, dealing with foreign vessels and sending its judgments and certificates into foreign countries where English was but little understood, Latin, which was still the language of diplomacy, and that in which all Admiralty proceedings and sentences had hitherto been expressed, was, for the general convenience, restored.

On the same day that the House passed the last-mentioned order they passed also the following :—

For the easing of the people of charge in law suits and prevention of long and tedious delays, it is ordered that after 20th November

[1] *Intelligencer of Parliament*, 5th November, 1650.

[2] Statute, 22nd November, 1650: As an instance of the polyglot language employed before and after the Commonwealth, and turned into good English during that period, take the following from Rolle's Abridgment, p. 3: The friend of an innkeeper is invited to supper, gets too drunk to go home, is given a bed by his host, and during the night has his pocket picked of a jacobus. He tries to make the innkeeper liable for his loss, and the judgment is recorded as follows : " Si un Hoste invite un al supper et le nuit esteant farr spent il lui invite a stayer la tout le nuit, sil soit apres robbe encore le Hoste ne serra charge pur ceo, car cest guest ne fuit ascun Traveller."

[3] Statute 19, April, 1651.

next it shall be lawful for any defendant or tenant in any action, real, personal, or mixt, to plead the general issue of not guilty or any like issue, and to give any such matter in evidence to the jury that shall try the same, and the said matter shall be available to such persons to all intents and purposes, as if the said matter had been specially pleaded, set forth, or alleged in Bar of such action.[1]

The right to plead the general issue and give special matter in evidence conveys very little to the mind of the public of to-day. · In 1650 it was, I take it, very generally appreciated. It meant in substance that the parties could get to trial at once, and that vexatious delays over matters of pleading were no longer possible. It was regarded, and rightly, as the first great step towards trying the substance of a cause and dispensing with useless and obfuscating technicality.

The Committee also took in hand the task of reforming the jury laws, and for this purpose caused a general inspection to be made, by their nominees, of the freeholders' books in each county, in order that a full and impartial return of juries to try cases between party and party might be made, and that so large a panel should be returned that litigants might be sure of " indifferent justice " in their causes.[2] This order was strictly enforced, as will be seen from the various order books of the Judges of Assize, who dealt summarily with sheriffs and their officers who did not comply with their direction as to the summoning of juries.

By the end of the year 1651, however, owing to other matters that had occupied the attention of Parliament, very small progress had been made, and when Cromwell returned in triumph from the Battle of Worcester and it was found that the reform of the law stood where it did in the spring, great discontent was shown. To urge the matter more vigorously on, a second committee was appointed by the Council of State, independent of the House,[3] to whom the

---

[1] *Intelligencer of Parliament*, 5th Nov., 1650.
[2] Whitelock, Vol. III., p. 254.
[3] Whitelock, Vol. III., p. 381.

subject was committed with directions to consider and
report drafts of such Acts as they might find necessary to
remove the inconveniences of the existing law. It sat first
in January, 1651-2, and consisted of the following members :
Mathew Hale, Esq., who was chairman and settled most of
the drafts; W. Steel, Esq., Recorder of London; Charles
George Cock, Esq.; Thomas Manby, Esq. ; John Sadler,
Esq.; Colonel Thomas Blunt; Josiah Berners, Esq.; Major-
General Desborough; Samuel Moyer, Esq. ; Colonel
Matthew Tomlinson; John Fountain, Esq. (afterwards
Serjeant-at-Law and Justice of the Upper Bench under
Richard Cromwell); Alderman J. Fowlk; Mr. Hugh
Peters; Major W. Parker; Sir W. Roberts,[1] Mr. W.
Methwold, Mr. John Maunsell, Mr. John Rushworth, Mr.
James Sparrow, junior, Sir Anthony Astley Cooper (after-
wards Lord Shaftesbury). Seven to be a quorum, and the
Committee to meet in the House, " heretofore called the
Lord's House."[2] The names of Dr. Walker and
Dr. Turner, two learned civilians, were afterwards added
to the Committee. They sat *de die in diem* and
advised much with Whitelock[3] and with Selden,[4] who was
also much consulted by the Council of State. Concurrently
with the deliberations of Mathew Hale's committee, the
House also considered the law, and on the 27th January,
1651-2, passed a vote,[5] which lies at the root of all our
judicial system :—

It is ordered that no fee, perquisite, or reward shall be taken by any
of the judges of Westminster Hall or their servants but such salary
as shall be allowed them by the State.[6]

---

[1] A lawyer and member of the Inner Temple.
[2] *Proceedings in Parliament*, 22nd January, 1651-2.
[3] Whitelock, Vol. III., p. 387-408.
[4] Selden died 30th November, 1654, and was magnificently buried in
the Temple Church.
[5] Whitelock, Vol. III., p. 387.
[6] Under the old system of James and Charles, judges had often
bought their places at considerable prices, and looked to fees and
extortions for recouping their outlay and providing for their families.

This salary was fixed at the sum of £1,000 per annum, and they were allowed circuit-money for defraying the necessary expenses of their several circuits ; so that relatively the judges of Westminster Hall, during the Interregnum, received nearly the same salary as those that occupy the same position under Queen Victoria. Although, however, the judges' salaries were thus fixed, they were not regularly paid. In February 1651-2, the Council of State, in view of the arrears due to the Lords Commissioners of the Great Seal and to the judges in Westminster Hall, ordered the Revenue Committee to pay £500 to each of the judges, and to see that their arrears of circuit-money were paid, and appointed Colonel Purefoy and others a committee to consider where the money was to be had for making the payments.[1] In October of 1652, reference was made by the Council of State to the Irish and Scotch Committees to see where the money could be had to pay the judges.[2] In June, 1653, the judges of Westminster Hall obtained an order for £200 each on account of their salaries.[3] In April, 1654, the salaries of the judges in Wales (£250 per annum) were one year and a half in arrear, and they clamoured for some payment on account.[4] In August, 1654, after Cromwell's assumption of the Protectorate, an order was made by the Council of State on the Customs Committee to pay the arrears of the judges out of the receipts of the Customs,[5] and from this time forward they appear to have received their salaries with reasonable regularity.

Meantime Mr. Hale's Committee proceeded with much labour, but with at first no great despatch of business. " I was often advised with by some of this Committee,"

---

[1] State Papers, February, 1651.
[2] *Ibid*, October, 1652.
[3] *Ibid*, June, 1653.
[4] State Papers, 15th April, 1654.
[5] *Ibid*, 27th August, 1654.

says Whitelock,[1] who appears to have been much bothered with the Reverend Hugh Peters and his views of the laws of Holland, " wherein he was altogether mistaken." But they discussed the inconveniences of estates tail and copyholds, and provided that they should in future be made liable to the payment of debts. They obtained a return from the Courts of Justice of the various officers, what fees they received and what duties they discharged, with a view to abolishing their fees and putting them upon salaries.[2] They reported a resolution that for the future all personal actions should be commenced by a writ of summons, with the cause of suit endorsed upon it, and further that a defendant should in all cases be at liberty to make a tender of amends with costs of suit, and that if the jury found his tender sufficient he should have judgment in his favour with costs.[3] These propositions seem so elementary and their propriety is so obvious that one can hardly reconcile oneself to the idea that they amounted almost to a revolution of the legal procedure as it then stood.

The Committee proceeded, says Whitelock, "with great debate but little done ";[4] but the Lord Commissioner hardly did them justice, for, on the 23rd March, 1651-2, they forwarded to the Committee of Parliament, for presentation to the House, the drafts of several Bills dealing with the reformation of the law.[5] The drafts so presented were as follows :—

A draft of an Act to take away Fines upon Bills, declarations and original writs ;

---

[1] Vol. III., p. 388. Mr. Peters was not typical of the Commonwealth. Whenever a matter of law reform is moved in the House of Commons there are plenty of well-meaning Peterses to chatter and obstruct its passing.

[2] A course almost universally followed at the present day.

[3] Whitelock, Vol. III., p. 293.

[4] *Ibid*, Vol. III., p. 396.

[5] *Perfect Diurnal*, 29th March, 1651-2; Whitelock, Vol. III., p. 408.

A draft of an Act against customary oaths of Fealty and Homage to Lords of Manors.

A draft of an Act for taking away common recoveries and the unnecessary charge of Fines, and to pass and charge lands entayled as lands in fee simple, etc.[1]

A draft of an Act for ascertaining arbitrary fines upon descent and alienation of copyholds of inheritance.[2]

A draft of an Act for the more speedy recovery of rents.

A draft of an Act for the more speedy regulating and easier recovery of Debts and Damages, not exceeding £4 and under.[3]

A draft of an Act against the sale of offices, providing that no office for life or during good behaviour should be granted to an infant or to any one unable to execute it, or granted in reversion, or bought or sold. Any offender to forfeit double the sum promised or paid, and to be incapable for the future of holding any office of profit.[4]

A draft of an Act regarding pleaders and their fees. That no member of Parliament should plead in any Court of Justice except the counsel for the Commonweath. No one shall receive in any one cause wherein he is retained counsel more than £5 nor any other thing valuable. Yet he shall give his advice and assistance till the case be ended.[5]

The Parliamentary Committee having received these drafts ordered that they be considered and debated every Thursday.[6] The only outward sign of their existence, how-

---

[1] The Act to abolish Fines and Recoveries, and to provide a simpler mode of conveyance based on this scheme, was not made law till 1833.

[2] An Act to this effect was passed in 1885.

[3] This was carried into effect by the County Court Act of 1846, which, in the first instance, confined the jurisdiction of the Courts, except by consent, to £20 and under: nearly equivalent to £4 under the Commonwealth.

[4] State Papers, XLII., fo. 145 (1653).

[5] Draft of an Act for better regulation of pleaders and their fees.—State Papers, Vol. XLII., fo. 145 (1653). Nothing more was ever heard of this draft.

[6] *Perfect Diurnal*, 29th March, 1652.

P

ever, which the Parliamentary Committee made, appears to
have been that for some reason not now to be arrived at
they removed the Courts of Chancery and of the Upper
Bench from the end of Westminster Hall, where they had
always been located like a twin cherry, to the northern side
of the Hall,[1] thus placing the four Courts in a
row, leaving the southern side for the shops and
the western end unoccupied.[2]

This state of things, however, was by no means satisfactory, either to the army or to the Independent party.
It was a fact as remarkable as it was creditable to the
great army of the Commonwealth that they were all,
whether commanders, officers, or troopers, enthusiastic
in the cause of law reform. They regarded it as one of
the main objects for which they had imbrued their hands
in the blood of their fellow-countrymen. They had obtained
through their prowess the removal for ever of the Courts
of Star Chamber and High Commission, of the Marches
in Wales, and of the Council of the North. They
nad secured the appointment of all judges to be during
good behaviour and not during the good pleasure of the
Crown. Their petitions and remonstrance had led to the
English language being substituted for the barbarous
Norman-French or dog Latin, and now, peace being assured,
they looked forward with longing eyes to the crowning of
the judicial edifice of which they had thus set the corner-

---

[1] Whitelock, Vol. III. p. 383.,

[2] Among various visitors to the courts as thus established was
one whom prudence and good taste should have combined to keep
away. According to Whitelock, quoting from letters from Paris,
Charles II. stated to his mother and others that after his escape
from Worcester, he lay some days in London disguised as a woman,
during which period he visited the courts in Westminster Hall, where
he saw the Arms of the Commonwealth, and the colours taken from
the Scots. (Vol. III., p. 361.) It is not consistent, however, with the
story of his escape dictated by the King to Samuel Pepys, and published in the Boscobel Tracts.

stone. In answer to their further demands Parliament had appointed committees and had set apart certain days to take in hand the reformation of the laws of England. But in itself it had done little, and Mr. Hale's Committee, which had shown its good will in the cause and had sent up to the House drafts of good and useful reforms, was likely to prove abortive through want of the necessary vigour in Parliament to pass its measures into law. In this state of things, therefore, the army came forward in support of Mr. Hale and his proposals, and thus it happened that the first public appearance of the future Chief Justice of King Charles, in relation to his schemes for law reform was, with the army of Independents at his back, clamouring for the passing of the Bills that he had drawn. On the 12th August, 1652, a petition was presented to Parliament by a committee of officers of the army praying, amongst other things, that a speedy and effectual course might be taken for the regulation of the law both in the matter of the form and of the administration of it in all those particulars in which it was unjust, unreasonable, needlessly vexatious, grievous or burdensome to the people. To this purpose they prayed that the several results agreed on by the committee, over which Mathew Hale presided, might be speedily taken into debate and consideration in Parliament; that what should be found to make for such regulation be speedily enacted, and that thus the committee be encouraged to proceed in the said work until the same be perfected. This petition was presented by Commissary-General Whalley, a stout Parliamentary officer, who afterwards showed his courage and resolution in the matter of the Spanish Ambassador's brother, who said that he and the other gentlemen with him (meaning a goodly company of redcoats, and steelbacks and breasts, who had accompanied him to the Bar of the House) were commanded by the Council of the officers of the Army to attend

upon the Parliament with this their humble address. In
answer to which the Speaker was ordered by the House to
present to the officers the thanks of the House "for their
care and love to the publique."[1] But civil words were not
enough for these stalwart reformers, who continued, as
Whitelock says, "to grumble" at the delay of Parliament,
and before very long made their voices heard in very
resolute fashion.

In January, 1652-3, Parliament spent the day in reading
drafts of Acts sent up from Mr. Hale's committee, and as
we now know settled by himself.   These were for the construction of district registries for wills, deeds, and letters
of administration in every county in England ; for the
reform of the Court of Chancery and of the Common Pleas ;
for the better procedure in causes civil and criminal, and
in other particulars[2] for a general amendment of the law.
But having begun to discuss Mr. Hale's Bill for county
registries, which law reformers even now desire
to see carried into effect, they were still found
discussing it on the following 23rd April, when Cromwell
in his worsted stockings, and his Ironsides, in their leather
and steel, turned the Parliament out of doors and took the
further reform of the law into their own hands.

Very little in the way of law amendment was done by
the Convention or Barebones Parliament, and upon their
resigning their powers to Cromwell he appears to have
taken the important step of consulting the judges as to the
course to be pursued.   These had hitherto acted on the
mandate of the Long Parliament, and its successor, the
Convention of 1653, but the latter having abdicated its
functions it became necessary in the view of the judges
that there should be some supreme authority not liable to
the changes and fluctuations of a Parliament, from whom
they could receive their commissions as judges, in whose

---

[1] *Perfect Diurnal*, 16th August, 1652.
[2] *Proceedings in Parliament*, 24th January, 1652-3.

name writs and processes might run, and who might
be the final appeal in all cases where pardon or
clemency might properly be exercised. In his speech
of 4th of September, 1654, Cromwell referred with
pride to his having taken care to put the administration of the laws into the hands of "just men; men
of the most known integrity and ability."[1] And in
his speech of the 12th September, 1654,[2] in alluding to the
circumstances under which he had assumed the Protectorate
in December of the previous year, he says: "The judges
thinking that there had now come a dissolution to all
Government, met and consulted; and did declare one to
another that they could not administer justice to the satisfaction of their consciences until they had received Commissions from me. And they did receive Commissions from
me, and by virtues of those Commissions they have acted;
which was a little more than an implied approbation."
Acting upon this advice, which ran probably in accordance
with his own inclination, Cromwell assumed the reins of
Government as Lord Protector, and proceeded to govern on
the lines of the Instrument of Government published by
him and his Council of State on the 16th December, 1653.
Foremost amongst those who favoured this course was Mr.
Mathew Hale. Burnet has written a life of Hale, distinguished by numerous inaccuracies and instigated by a
desire to show that the then Lord Chief Justice was
a man attached by nature and instinct to the cause
of the Cavaliers, resenting the usurpation of Cromwell, and accepting office under the usurper only that
he might secure as far as in him lay justice and mercy
to the persecuted Royalists. Lord Campbell, while
guarding himself against the exaggerations and errors of
Burnet, proceeds somewhat on the same lines. He is, I
think, too much bitten with his hero's various meditations,

---

[1] Carlyle, Speech II.
[2] Carlyle, Speech III.

and pays too little heed to the fact that in that age, and among the Puritan party (to which Hale was to the last attached), these solemn meditations and exercises were the duties and the pastime of men's leisure hours. And while he eulogises and expounds Lord Hale's celebrated programme of duties and of demeanour to guide his conduct in the office of a judge, he overlooks the fact that these laudable sentiments had somewhat the appearance of being prepared for the press, and were in any event written after he had performed the duties of a judge of the Court of Probate, of the Court of Common Pleas, and of the County Palatine of Lancaster for a period of nearly five years. Recent disclosures of the order books of the Council of State show Mr. Mathew Hale in a position altogether opposite to that assumed by Burnet and not altogether in accordance with that of Lord Campbell. Hale had in his youth been educated in the strictest sect of the Puritans.[1] He had in 1643 taken the Solemn League and Covenant, and though one of the counsel for the defence of Laud, he never agreed with that prelate in his views on public affairs. In May, 1644, he was assessed by the Parliamentary Committee at £400, being one-twentieth of the value of his real estate, but his assessment was respited on the ground that *his lands were occupied by the enemy*, and on his being again assessed at £800 in November of the same year, he appears through the good will of the Committee to have had his assessment vacated, "having been before assessed and respited,"[2] and he does not appear to have been again put under any contribution. He

---

[1] He was, however, always fond of good society, and he is put by Sir John Suckling, the amatory poet of King Charles's body-guard, in a session of the poets and wits, cheek by jowl with Selden, Jack Vaughan, Thomas May, and other Puritans of the Temple, and Davenant, Selwyn, Sandys, Endymion Porter and others of the King's party.—"A Session of the Poets," published about 1640.

[2] Committee for Advance of Money, p. 384.

was at this time also frequently consulted both by the Parliament and by the cavaliers, and although he advised King Charles as to his conduct before the High Court of Justice in January, 1648-9, he did not hesitate in the following month of March to accept a retainer from Cromwell to draw the marriage settlement of his eldest son Richard with Dorothy, daughter of Mr. Mayor of Dursley. He was among the first to take the engagement to be " true and faithful to the Commonwealth of England as it is now established without a King or a House of Lords." " I have done it," he said, at the trial of Love in 1651, when not one of his colleagues had put his hand to the document. He accepted the position of chairman of the committee for the amendment of the law in December, 1651. He appeared with Serjeant Maynard as counsel for the Commonwealth at the trial of Falconer before the Upper Bench in May, 1653. He advised the Council of State, as we have seen, on various questions as to the postmasters and others. He took office under the Long Parliament in April, 1653, and was appointed, together with Sir Anthony Ashley Cooper, Mr. Steel, Peters, Desborough, and other regicides, one of the judges of the new Court of Probate, with power to grant probates and administrations, and to exercise all the functions of the late Sir Nathaniel Brent, judge of the Prerogative Courts of Canterbury and York.[2] In the course of the same year, 1653, he, together with Serjeant Maynard, advised the Council that Philip King of Spain having become indebted for monies lent to his Ambassador in London for the use of his master and so employed, goods of the King of Spain found in London could, according to the custom, be lawfully attached.[3] He was among those who, in December,

---

[1] Carlyle, Letter XCVI.
[2] Statute 1653, c. 2. Sir Nathaniel Brent had been appointed by the Parliament in November, 1644.
[3] Thurloe, Vol. I., p. 604.

1653, favoured Cromwell's assumption of the office of Protector, and at once accepted from him the offer of a judgeship being the very first person nominated by the Protector to that post. On the 19th January, 1653-4, he was made a serjeant-at-law by special order of the Council of State,[1] and thereupon took his seat on the Bench. He was, however, still employed in preparing ordinances for the amendment of the law, and was accordingly excused by the Council of State from riding the spring circuits "in respect of some special occasions for the public wherein he is employed."[2] He swore allegiance to Cromwell on taking his seat as judge, and received the oath from Lord Commissioner Lisle, whose name was on the warrant for the execution of the King, and who sat as one of the assistants to Bradshaw at the trial. In September, 1654, he swore, as member for Gloster, to be true and faithful to the Lord Protector and the Commonwealth of England, Scotland and Ireland, and not to propose or give any assent to alter the Government, as it is now settled in a single person and a Parliament. He again swore allegiance to the Protector, sitting with the other judges, at the Lord Protector's installation, in July, 1657, and he remained his loyal and faithful servant till his death. He went alone to Warwick and other midland towns on the first circuit after the appointment of the Major-Generals in 1655, trying civil and criminal causes, and he so demeaned himself in reference to the Protector's interest that Commissary-General Whaley, who was Major-General in command of that district, specially commended him to Cromwell, whom he desired to give the judge more than ordinary thanks, declaring at the same time that he never

---

[1] State Papers.

[2] State Papers, 17th February, 1653-4. I do not know the actual date of his appointment, but the "*Proceedings of State Affairs*" for 7th February, 1653-4, refers to Justice Hale as then sitting in the Common Pleas with Lord Chief Justice St. John and Justice Atkins.

knew anyone, at his own cost, more willing to serve the present Government than Justice Hale.[1] During the whole time that he held judicial office he sat on the Bench with Justice Aske, one of the counsel for the Commonwealth at the trial of the King, and for a considerable period with Lord Chief Baron Steele, the Attorney-General on that memorable occasion. To describe him, therefore, as a Royalist in disguise, to assume that while serving under Cromwell he regarded him as a sanguinary usurper, and many of his colleagues on the Bench as rebels and murderers, and to suggest that his conduct under the Commonwealth was guided by or at the least consistent with a fervid loyalty and longing for the restoration of the Royal Stuarts, is to proceed in direct contradiction to every action of his life for the twelve years of the Interregnum. Whatever views he may have entertained as to the execution of the King, his early training and his religious sentiments attached him to the Puritan cause, and there is in my judgment less surprise and less fault to be found with his ready acceptance of the Government of the Protector than with his somewhat effusive adoption of the politics of the Restoration. He was not perhaps altogether of the type of the late Lord Wensleydale, who, being asked what were his politics, replied that he was a special pleader, but he took little part in political warfare, and the two occasions on which he is remarked as having intervened, first to move the imposition of conditions on the return of Charles II., and, secondly, to propose a form of church establishment— somewhat after Cromwell's idea—which would embrace all shades of Protestant thought, were both inopportune and unsuccessful. Looking upon Mathew Hale as a great judge and as a great and good man, I confess to a feeling of pain and humiliation at finding him in October, 1660, sitting as a judge at the Old Bailey,

[1] Thurlow, Vol. III., pp. 663, 686.

trying and condemning to death batches of the regicides,
men under whose orders he had himself acted, who
had been his colleagues in Parliament, with whom he
had sat on committees to alter the law, and had been for
years on terms of personal friendship. It was doubtless the
price that he and his brother judge, Mr. Justice Atkins, had
to pay for their re-appointment to office, but it was, none the
less, a degrading and a saddening spectacle. He lived in
times of trouble, was devoted to his profession both as
counsellor and judge, and by reason of that devotion he
accepted from time to time the existing order of things,
swearing in his time so many oaths that if they had all
been written on one sheet of paper he would probably have
been ashamed to look them in the face.[1] And it is fair to
say that he was not alone in his conversion, for among his
colleagues of the Commonwealth he found beside him at
the Restoration Justices Atkins, Glyn, and St. John, Sir
Anthony Ashley Cooper, Ingoldsby, and Monk.[2]

[1] "Oaths," said Selden, in the little book dedicated to his friend and
executor, Mr. Justice Hales, "are so frequent they should be
taken like pills, swallowed whole ; if you chew them you will find them
bitter; if you think what you swear 'twill hardly go down."

[2] The difficulty of arriving at the truth in regard to the affairs of the
Commonwealth may be exemplified by the case of Sir Edward Atkins.
It is beyond a doubt that this judge was a Baron of the Exchequer
under the Long Parliament, that he was afterwards Justice of the
Upper Bench from 1649 to Cromwell's death in 1658, that he was
appointed to the Exchequer by Charles II., and died in 1669. And yet
in the face of these facts his great-grandson, Edward Atkins, Esq., of
Ketteringham Hall, has carved the following epitaph, to be found in
Poets' Corner, Westminster Abbey.

TO THE MEMORY

of Sir Edward Atkins, one of the Barons of the Exchequer in the
reigns of King Charles I. and King Charles II. He was a person
of such integrity that he resisted the many advantages and honours
offered him by the Chiefs of the Grand Rebellion. He departed this
life A.D. 1669, aged 82.

The *suppressio veri* could hardly be carried farther.

The Common Law was administered in a mode entirely unfamiliar to us at the present day. It was technical almost beyond our conception. Its source, as was said by Hale, was as undiscoverable as that of the Nile. Except for digests or abridgments, one by Glanvil, another in the reign of Henry VIII., and Lord Bacon's in the reign of James I., there was nowhere a definite statement of the law of England, which had to be found after great search and many years of labour in the chambers of old pleaders and conveyancers. Judges who had habitually attended upon Parliament and were consulted as to Bills before they passed the House of Lords, obtained by this means a sufficient knowledge of statutes actually passed during their tenure of office, and of others necessarily bearing upon them. But for students and for ordinary practitioners of the law, it consisted in a great measure of legal tradition handed down from father to son through succeeding generations of lawyers, together with one or two collections of statutes and of cases of very doubtful authority. The doctrine that the best way to get at the substance of a dispute is to hear what the parties themselves have to say about it, had found no place in the legal ethics of the day, and so great was the fear lest any possible personal interest might influence the evidence of a witness that, in the desire to obtain the truth pure and undefiled, a system was constructed which frequently banished it altogether. The one great object of the plaintiff's lawyer was to make out a *primâ facie* case, such a case, in other words, as was just sufficient to call upon his opponent for an answer. In this difficulty the defendant, unable to give his own evidence and hampered by innumerable restrictions and estoppels, was usually unable to make effective reply ; and his lawyer's energy was then directed to breaking down by technical objection the *primâ facie* case of his opponent. This legal warfare, as may well be conceived, brought into play the finest features of legal subtlety and wit, and the victory was commonly enough that of the strongest and acutest lawyer rather than that of the most righteous cause. To aid the law in these forensic struggles came the doctrine of presumptions, and these again led to endless discussions as to their proper and seasonable application. Presumptions in favour of innocence, of death after a prolonged and unexplained absence, of the legitimacy of all persons born in wedlock, that things will continue as in their last ascertained condition, these and some others, presumptions not only of law but of natural justice, have been from time immemorial part and parcel of our jurisprudence, and like the axioms of Euclid serve to work out the problems of the law. They formed a great part of every plaintiff's case, and led to prolonged and learned discussions as to whether, or how far, these various presumptions had been weakened or rebutted by the consideration of surrounding circumstances. Substantial reforms in the common law were therefore necessary, not only for the good government of Great Britain, but for the benefit of the colonies that were then becoming an integral and important part of our Empire. Where the Roman soldier planted the eagle, the law of old Rome was planted with it, and when in a new country our colonists raise our flag, there the law of England attaches itself to the soil. How, then, was this jargon of languages, these intricacies and technicalities, unintelligible and detestable even in our own country, to be applied by our British settlers to the soil of Virginia, to the islands of the Pacific, or to the tracts of country soon to come under our hands in the vast continent of Asia? These considerations bore hard upon the minds of the Protector and his Council, and demanded and received their most serious attention.

Under the Instrument of Government the Protector and his Council had power when Parliament was not sitting to make all necessary laws by way of Ordinances, which had the effect and operation of laws until otherwise decreed by

Parliament. Under this power, therefore, the Protector and his Council at once dealt with a matter which was raising questions in all parts of the country. The condition of the law of treason was considered open to doubt, it not being very clearly understood whether acts that would be treasonable against a king would be treasonable against the Protector. An Ordinance,[1] having the virtue of an Act of Parliament, was accordingly issued in January, 1653-4, enacting that the Statute of Treason was only declaratory of the Common Law : that it did not of itself constitute the offence of treason, and that it was high treason for any person to compass or imagine the death of the Lord Protector for the time being. This was afterwards adopted by Parliament and became the Act under which trials for high treason subsequently took place. It was one of the first of these Ordinances, its necessity and propriety were obvious, and it received the assent of the judges of the various courts.

Complaints being made of the judge's marshals that they took fees to call on causes out of their turn, inquiry was ordered and some attempt made to put an end to the abuse. And the same committee which inquired into this, called together the judges and counsel to propose some plan by which it would be possible to avoid the anomaly of plaintiffs who recover very small damages being allowed enormous costs, and of small fines being followed by excessive costs.[2] An attempt was also made to deal with what was then a crying injustice, and is even now a subject of just complaint, viz., the great expense cast upon High Sheriffs in respect of the reception and entertainment of the judges. In

---

[1] Ordinances, 1653, c. 8, printed in Hughes' Collection.

[2] State Papers, 20th February, 1655-6. The former of these anomalies as to costs has been somewhat remedied by recent legislation, but the system by which a defendant is fined *a shilling* and the costs amount to a pound is still in full vigour in every county in England.

February, 1655-6, an order was made and published that for the future relief of High Sheriffs, the judges should be entertained at the expense of the county and not of the Sheriff, and that a guard of soldiers should be supplied to attend the judges and the Sheriff in place of the old javelin or pikemen, and that no fee or payment should be made in respect thereof.[1]

But the great object of all law reform was, as it has ever been, the Court of Chancery. The rooks that cawed morning and evening as the Protector left and returned to his lodgings in Hampton Court were not more persistent in their cry than was the great flock of soldiers and civilians, laymen and divines, who incessantly clamoured for the abolition of the Court of Chancery. "Away with it," said they; "no greasing of the wheels, no patching and mending of the machine; destroy it, bolt, crank, and lever, and end this engine of oppression and corruption." Chancery in their opinion had a bad origin and a worse record. It was associated in the public mind with the prelates who had been the early chancellors and the monks, whose tonsures still mark their origin on the serjeant's coif. Its officers and its practitioners were locusts, flies, caterpillars—all the plagues of Egypt rolled into one. And there was, or, at least, there had been, some solid ground for this general denunciation of the court, for there was then no definite system of equity. Each Chancellor, Keeper or Commissioner of the Great Seal was credited with doing what was pleasing in his own sight, with extending his jurisdiction without authority, with interfering arbitrarily with the proceedings of the judges in Westminster Hall, and with granting injunctions and prohibitions collusively, fraudulently and corruptly. Equity was in effect, as Selden puts

---

[1] *Mercurius Politicus*, No. 296.

it, the length of the Chancellor's foot.[1] Whitelock and his two colleagues had worked assiduously. They had introduced great reforms in the pleadings and procedure of the Court, and had, by sitting early and late, brought the cause list into reasonable limits. But this valuable instalment of reform was too slow and restricted in its operation for the energies of the Chancery reformers, and even the Little Parliament had voted its abolition. On the 5th August, 1653, that House, after a long debate lasting over two days, voted without a division[2] that the Court of Chancery be taken away, that the Committee on Law bring in an Act accordingly, together with another for causes now depending there, and another for future relief in Equity.[3] On the 5th November following a Bill was read a second time and committed[4] for taking away the High Court of Chancery, and constituting Judges and Commissioners for hearing causes now depending in Chancery and future matters of Equity, and for reforming abuses in the Courts of Common Law. The Bill passed through Committee, but on its report to the House it was found that the amendments inserted with a view to make the scheme practicable, had rendered it distasteful to these ardent reformers. It was declared

---

[1] "Equity in law is the same as the spirit in religion : what everyone pleases to make it. Sometimes they go according to conscience, sometimes according to law, sometimes according to a rule of court. Equity is a roguish thing ; for law we have a measure ; know what to trust to. Equity is according to the conscience of him that is chancellor, and as that is larger or narrower ; so is Equity. 'Tis all one as if they should make the standard for the measure we call a foot a Chancellor's foot. What an uncertain measure this would be ! One chancellor has a long foot, another a short foot, a third an indifferent foot. 'Tis the same thing in the chancellor's conscience."—Table Talk ; Equity.

[2] Hansard Parliamentary History, Vol. III., p. 1412.

[3] Whitelock, Vol. IV., p. 29.

[4] *Ibid.*, p. 47.

to be of no use, to be only "washing the blackamore," to be cutting off one hydra's head where five more would immediately grow, and it was thrown out by a small majority on the third reading.[1] It formed, however, in its unamended condition the basis of the Ordinance that Cromwell, under the power conferred by the Instrument of Government, subsequently issued.

Like many other legislative attempts during the Commonwealth, this ordinance was framed with more zeal than discretion. It substituted hard and fast rules for the flexibility necessary to a due administration of equity, and it was defeated by that absence of moderation which had defeated so many proposals otherwise excellent in themselves. The subject of the Ordinance is discussed at great length by Whitelock,[2] and the defects of the scheme are lucidly and temperately pointed out. When, indeed, the matter had been taken in hand with a view to practical legislation, it was found an easier task to cry for, than to accomplish the abolition of the Court of Chancery. And, accordingly, Cromwell and his Council were speedily made aware that without a system of equity to soften the rigours of the common law, to enforce and protect the operations of trustees and of mortgagees, and to interpose for the prevention of frauds, the judicial business of the country could not be carried on. His celebrated Ordinance was, therefore, framed on the footing of accepting and continuing the Court of Chancery, and of recognising the succession of Lord Chancellors and Lord Keepers, and was restricted to the comparatively innocuous process of applying a remedy where all agreed that a remedy was required. "For the better regulating and limiting the jurisdiction of the High Court of Chancery and to the end that all proceedings touching relief in equity to be given in that court may be with less trouble, expense, and

---

[1] An Exact Relation, etc., published 1654.
[2] Vol IV., pp. 191-207.

delay than heretofore," was the preamble of the celebrated Ordinance which was passed on the 21st August, 1654. In the following November its operation was suspended for a time,[1] and on the 23rd April, 1655, an order was served on the Commissioners of the Great Seal to proceed forthwith to the enforcement of the new procedure.[2] Among very many provisions, some of which appear to have been accepted as necessary and useful reforms, it endeavoured to deal with vexatious actions by requiring the plaintiff in every case to give security for costs, with one surety at least to the satisfaction of a Master in Chancery before a defendant could be required to answer. To relieve a defendant from the necessity of hunting for a Master in Chancery, before whom to swear his answer it enabled him to make his affidavit before a Justice of the Peace in any county where he happened to be. To obviate delays in pleadings it required a defendant peremptorily to answer within eight days, and provided that unless the plaintiff replied or set the cause down for hearing within eight days of the answer, the cause should be dismissed without motion for want of prosecution, with costs to be paid by the plaintiff. One of the scandals of the Court was the number of Commissions to take evidence issued from time to time in the course of a cause, thus causing great expense and delay. To remedy this it was provided that there should not be more than two Commissions at the most for the examination of witnesses in any one cause to be executed in England and Wales, and a second Commission was only to be issued by order of the Court upon sufficient evidence of the discovery of new witnesses, etc.

To deal with the evil of inofficious injunctions, it ordered that no interlocutory injunction was to be granted and no injunction to stop an action of law was to issue after plea. No relief was to be given in equity against any bond for

---

[1] Whitelock, Vol. IV., p. 158.
[2] Whitelock, Vol. IV., p. 191.

payment of money entered into after 25th March, 1655; and no trust created after that date was to be recognised unless in writing produced in Court. Legacies were to be sued for at Common Law and not in Chancery.

All causes were to be set down for hearing in order as they were published, without preferring one cause before another, and they were all to be heard in the same order. Every cause was to be heard the same day on which it was set down : and "for that purpose the Lords Commissioners, if there be cause, shall sit for hearing such causes in the afternoon as well as in the forenoon, except upon Saturdays." It regulated the number of attorneys to be employed in Court, and further provided that, if any counsel should misinform the Court of any matter contained in the pleadings, proofs, or evidence whereof he might have the perusal, or of any other matter whereof his client did not inform him, and thereon obtained an order which the Court should afterwards see cause to discharge, the counsel so misinforming should be reprehended openly in Court, and before being heard any more in Court pay 40s. to the party wronged by such information and 20s. to the use of the Lord Protector. But if such information were of matter of fact, whereof the counsel could not be otherwise certified than by information from his client, then the client, attorney, or solicitor who gave such information should pay 40s. unto the party wronged, and stand committed by order of the Court till he paid the same.

The provision for appeals was on the lines already indicated. An appeal might be made against any decree within three months, the decree being first performed and £50 deposited as security for costs. If the decree were to pay money, the money was to be paid into court. When notice of appeal was given, the Lord Chancellor, the Lord Keeper, or the Lords Commissioners of the Great Seal were to send to the Upper Bench, the Common Pleas, and the Exchequer, who should send six judges, two of each court, so that one of the six judges was a chief, to sit with the Chancellor, the Lord Keeper, or Lords Commissioners to hear such appeal.

There was also appended to the ordinance, what was no small matter of reform, a comprehensive table of fees regulating the maximum amounts to be taken by every officer and practitioner in the court.[1]

Of the three Commissioners of the Great Seal, Lisle was all for trying the experiment and working out the ordinance. Whitelock and Widdrington held it impossible of execution, and likely to lead to much injustice. They pointed out the evil that might accrue from depriving the judges, by statute, of any discretion as to enlarging the time for pleadings, or for the reception of evidence. They insisted on the absolute necessity that sometimes arose for granting an *ex parte* and interlocutory injunction to prevent immediate injury to property or to persons. They showed how the scheme for security for costs in every case would operate in favour of wealthy defendants, and might deprive a needy plaintiff of obtaining justice in a perfectly honest and meritorious cause. They laughed at the idea of trying every cause on the day it is set down, pointing out that such causes by reason of complicated questions of frauds and of trusts often required three or four days for their orderly hearing, and to impose such a duty on the judges was to impose on them an impossibility, while Lenthall, Master of the Rolls, signed the objections of the Lords Commissioners, and vowed that he would be hanged at the Rolls Gate before he would execute the Ordinance.[2] These detailed and reasoned objections of the two senior Lords of the Great Seal disconcerted the Protector and his Council, who had the

---

[1] Counsel's fees were regulated as follows : To every Counsel under rank of Serjeant, for a motion, 10s. ; for a hearing, £1. To Counse for the Lord Protector and Serjeants, for a motion, £1 ; for every hearing, £2.

[2] Whitelock, Vol. IV., p. 206.

matter again under their consideration from April till 6th June, 1655, and in the meantime matters proceeded in Chancery as before. It was impossible, however, to withdraw the Ordinance of which so much had been made before the country, and of which Cromwell himself was proud, and accordingly on the 6th June the Commissioners Whitelock and Widdrington were summoned by the Protector, to whom, having again explained their objections, they resigned the Great Seal, and Lisle and Fiennes were appointed in their place. But these gentlemen, like their predecessors, found the Ordinance impracticable, and though accepting the new system refrained from carrying it out. And according to Whitelock the reasons which he and Widdrington gave to the Protector and the Council were the means that it was not exacted from their successors, who were thus connived at in their default.[1] Notwithstanding, however, the attacks upon the new procedure it contained many valuable reforms. The attempted discouragement of appeals was worthy of all praise. The institution of suits by a summons, stating the nature of the relief sought (in place of the old subpœna), to be served in the first instance upon the party sued, is the actual procedure of to-day; while the provision that no trust was to be enforced which was not in writing was probably the foundation for the Statute of Frauds passed in the succeeding reign,[2] which declared that no contract for the sale of lands or of goods of the value of £10 and upwards shall be enforced by the courts unless in

[1] On 30th June, 1655, Mr. Attorney-General Prideaux wrote to Thurloe complaining of the non-attendance of the Master of the Rolls and the consequent inconvenience to the suitors in his court. Adding, however, that the whole course of justice seemed to be obstructed by reason of the new status given to the Masters in Chancery and the uncertainty as to the matters over which they were to have jurisdiction.—Thurloe, Vol. III., p. 598.

[2] 29 Charles II., c. 3.

writing signed by the party to be charged therewith—a statute of which the benefit to commerce has been great and lasting, and of which the principle is even now sus- ceptible of greater extension.

The conduct of the Protector towards the retiring Com- missioners was of a part with his conduct to others of his judges and officers; for feeling that they had lost their places for keeping to that liberty of conscience, which he himself held to be everyone's right, he appointed them to be Commissioners of the Treasury with a salary of £1,000 a year,[1] and a residence at Whitehall, so that from a material point of view they lost nothing by their honesty, and were personally much raised in the public estimation. As for Lenthall, after his valiant declaration that he would be hanged at the gate of his own court rather than accept the Ordinance, so soon as he found it was a question of losing his place he went back upon his former declarations, held on to his office as Master of the Rolls, administered the Ordinance which he had so vigorously condemned, and received in addition for his pliancy the lucrative office of one of the six Masters in Chancery.[2] The conduct of Whitelock and Widdrington in reference to this subject was probably dictated by public spirit, but considering the serious abuses to which the administration of the Court of Chancery had given rise, and the difficulties of so dealing with its reform as to give satisfaction to the public as well as justice to the suitors, their public spirit would equally well have shown itself in some attempt to carry out the Act and to have its provisions modified from time to time to meet the public needs. It seems, however, from some expressions of Whitelock's that his stiffness in the matter was very much accentuated by the fact that the ordinance

[1] Whitelock, Vol. IV., p. 207.
[2] Whitelock, Vol. IV., p. 203. Masters in Chancery sat on the Woolsack beside the Lord Chancellor in the House of Lords, but were not permitted to take part in the debates.—Hargrave's Tracts, p. 39.

was settled during his absence in Sweden and without his opinion having been taken on any of its details.

The Court of Common Pleas was also a favourite subject for projected reforms. " The Common Shop for Justice," as Sir Orlando Bridgman called it in the following reign, was a happy hunting-ground, having the exclusive jurisdiction over real actions, in which serjeants-at-law were alone entitled to practise. It was proposed and a Bill was drafted in 1655 to throw this Court open to all barristers and attorneys, giving to every qualified practitioner the same right to conduct cases there as he had in the Exchequer and the Upper Bench. The change was not popular, however, in Westminster Hall, and an unhappy attorney endeavouring to assert this inchoate right was laid hold of by the serjeants and thrown over the spiked iron bar which divided their Court from the floor of Westminster Hall. " Whereof we shall probably hear more," said the daily paper. But nothing more was heard of the attorney or indeed of the proposal for just one hundred years, when in 1755 Chief Justice Willes endeavoured again to have the Court thrown open to all members of the Bar. But the proposal was not even then popular with either the public or the Bar, and the monopoly of the serjeants continued for nearly another hundred years, when the scheme of the reformers of the Commonwealth was carried into effect by an Act of 9 and 10 Vic. c. 54 (1846), a reform which has had the natural result of bringing to an end the dignity of Serjeant-at-Law, a degree as ancient as the Law of England and intimately associated with all its changes and traditions.

Other reforms also were proposed and were well received, although they were never actually carried into effect. The cruelty and inequality of sentences which even to a recent date disgraced our Statute book and degraded our administration of the Criminal Law were the subject of much debate and animadversion under the Commonwealth.

Every felony was a capital offence, and men, women and children were put to death for stealing, for clipping coin, for returning home from transportation, and for other more or less venial offences, while such a crime as perjury was not a felony, and punishable only as a misdemeanour. "The truth of it is," said Cromwell in his address to the Parliament of 1656, "there are wicked and abominable laws which it will be in your power to alter. To hang a man for six and eightpence and I know not what: to hang for a trifle and acquit murder, is in the ministration of the law through the ill framing of it. I have known in my experience abominable murderers acquitted and to see men lose their lives for petty matters: this is a thing God will reckon for."[1] Following these advanced and statesmanlike utterances of Cromwell, a proposal, which met with general favour, was brought forward by Whitelock, who suggested that no offences should be capital except murder, treason, and rebellion; that in cases of justifiable and excusable homicide the prisoner should be acquitted without the trouble, expense and delay of suing out a pardon of course under the Great Seal,[2] and that under these circumstances "benefit of clergy" should be abolished. This process of "praying his clergy," though smacking of ecclesiastical savour, had at that date very little of the Church about it. It was a procedure in the interest of mercy, being a cumbrous mode of enabling a first offender

---

[1] Carlyle, Speech V. To what instances the Protector referred I know not; but there had been some cases of murder in the Cinque Ports which the law, by reason of a conflict of jurisdiction, had not been able to reach. Justice Hale is said to have given great satisfaction to the country by reprieving various thieves and felons, with a view to their being transported instead of being hanged. —Thurloe, Vol. III., p. 686.

[2] If a prisoner was found guilty of justifiable homicide he was bailed to the next assizes that he might in the meantime obtain and produce to the Court his pardon under the Great Seal.

in every capital case, except murder, treason, witchcraft and some other offences expressly declared to be without benefit of clergy, to be discharged without punishment if he could read a passage from the Psalms ; precautions, however, being taken for his identification in the future by burning him with a letter T on the left thumb.. It is remarkable that this provision for the relief of first offenders in cases of previous good character, which was of old the practice of this country, and has for many years formed part of the Criminal Code of New York, has only within the last Parliament (1887) become once more the law of England.   It was also proposed to abolish the *peine forte et dure*, otherwise the penalty of pressing to death in default of pleading, and in its place to authorise the Court who was to try the indictment to order a verdict of guilty to be entered in all cases where the prisoner refused to plead.   To some extent this recommendation was carried out, as it will be found that in all the Ordinances or Acts for trials by the High Court of Justice, a provision was inserted that in the event of a prisoner refusing to plead, judgment and sentence might be pronounced, as was actually done in the case of Dr. Hewett.   It was also proposed to alleviate the position of accessories before and after a felony, and to repeal the law by which wives who had murdered their husbands were sentenced to death by burning, substituting for that punishment the ordinary penalty of hanging.[1]   It was also proposed to allow prisoners to be defended by counsel, to give them in all cases copies of their indictments, and to allow their witnesses to be heard on oath.   The last of these provisions, as may be seen, was introduced into more than one of the Acts and Ordinances constituting new criminal offences.   But with all Cromwell's anxiety for these reforms, and although they were generally accepted in principle as reasonable and desirable amendments

---

[1] Selden was not favourable to any mercy on " these baggages."

of the law, yet the Parliament to which they were expressly
remitted was so much engrossed in the discussion of its own
personality that it either could not or would not find time
for the discussion of these, amongst other matters, specially
affecting the great masses of the people. Whether the
Parliament, in course of being summoned at the period of
the Protector's death, would have paid more attention to
his wishes, and have legislated in this direction, it is useless to speculate. It is sufficient to say that nearly all
these scandals with which Cromwell wished to deal remained unredressed until the commencement of the present
century ; that general pardons of offences visited with the
penalty of death, but from the infliction of which even the
most cold-blooded of rulers would shrink, continued to be
issued after every Assize, and that the Recorder's report at
the Old Bailey, giving the names of those prisoners who.
alone out of some hundreds sentenced to death he thought
it would be right to execute, was issued after every monthly
session within the memory of thousands of persons now
living.

Much of the success of the administration of justice in
every civilised community depends on the temper and the
character of the advocates who practise in the Courts, and
give by their learning and their demeanour a tone to the
conduct of judicial business. And it is to be remarked
with regard to the counsel of the Commonwealth period
that they conducted their cases with independence and
decorum, that they showed great industry and learning on
the various questions that were raised, and that they are
one and all honourably distinguished by an absence of
those insults and brutalities which gained so unenviable a
notoriety for some of the counsel of succeeding reigns.
And never was a government better served by its law
officers and its other legal advisers than the Long Parliament and the Commonwealth were by the eminent men
who then led the legal profession. In addition to the

judges who from time to time, as requested, gave their
advice to the counsel of State, they had the assistance of
Selden, in himself a tower of strength, of Prideaux, of
Maynard, of Hale, and of Whitelock, and it will be found as
the result that the conduct of business under the Commonwealth was satisfactory in the extreme, and that in great
constitutional questions such as the various applications for
writs of habeas, the privileges of ambassadors and their
retinue, or the effect and abatement of orders of the House
of Commons, the course pursued by the Government
was in accordance with the spirit of enlightened jurisprudence.

The Attorney-General of the Commonwealth, Mr.
Edmund Prideaux, the younger son of a Devonshire
baronet, whose family traced back to the Norman Conquest,
was a learned man of extraordinary vigour and resource,
and he occupied a position inferior to none during that
troubled time. He came from Oxford to the Chancery
Bar, and as a good Chancery man is spoken of in terms of
eulogy by Whitelock.[1] He was during the whole of his
term of office M.P. for Lyme Regis; he was for many years
a member of the Council of State, and he was consulted
on every matter of importance from his appointment to his
death. He was Recorder first of Exeter and afterwards of
Bristol,[2] was a Governor of Westminster School,[3] was
elected a Bencher of the Inner Temple, and was treasurer
of that Inn for eleven consecutive years.[4] When the
Long Parliament, in 1643, appointed Commissioners of the
Great Seal to execute the office of Lord High Chancellor,
Mr. Prideaux, who even then as a young man had a great
reputation as a Chancery lawyer, was amongst the

[1] Vol. IV., p. 358.
[2] State Papers, 29th October, 1649.
[3] Whitelock, Vol. III., p. 189.
[4] He was elected Treasurer in November, 1648, and was still
Treasurer at his death in August, 1659.

number. He occupied this post till 1646, when Parliament put the Great Seal into the hands of the Speakers of the two houses, the Earl of Manchester as representing the Lords and William Lenthall the Commons. On his retirement from the post of Lord Commissioner he resumed his practice at the Bar, having precedence over all counsel except the King's Serjeant and the Attorney and Solictor-General,[1] and was, subsequently, one of the Parliamentary Commissioners to treat with the King at Uxbridge.[2] In October, 1648, he was appointed Solicitor-General on the removal of Oliver St. John, the then Solicitor-General, to the Chief Justiceship of the Common Pleas. He appears, however, to have joined many of his brethren at the Bar in objecting to the King's trial, and for a short time he was superseded in his office by Mr. Cook. But Parliament recognised his abilities and his independence, and appointed him Attorney-General in April, 1649, with Mr. Reynolds, and afterwards Mr. Ellis, as his Solicitor-General. He was thus, from his earliest days to his latest, in the service of the Parliament, and no more careful, painstaking, or trustworthy official could anywhere have been selected. A certain amount of hospitality has always been and is expected of an Attorney-General. When the number of his colleagues was less than at present it was the habit of the Attorney-General of the day to entertain them on stated occasions in the same fashion that judges on circuit are required by a prescriptive custom to entertain the Bar at certain circuit towns. Mr. Prideaux, according to the reports, was a man like the typical bishop, " given to hospitality," and we find the Lords Commissioners of the Great Seal and others speaking of the "great entertainment " given by the Attorney-General on the occasions of various public functions.[3] What his salary or emoluments

---

[1] Foss's Judges, Vol. VI., p. 356.

[2] Thurloe, Vol. I., p. 59.

[3] Whitelock, Vol. III., p. 89.

amounted to there is no means of ascertaining.[1] But he had great opportunities of increasing his store, for the Commonwealth, in one form or other, was engaged in litigation from its cradle to its grave. " According to the duty of my place," as he said, he personally took the examinations of all persons charged with treasonable practices or other serious offences. He arranged the details and the procedure of all the trials in which the Commonwealth was represented, selected the counsel, and was responsible for the result, which, except in the case of John Lilburn, was always satisfactory. His position at these trials was not that of a law officer of the present day. After his first year of office, he individually took small part in court, but left the cases to be conducted by other counsel for the Commonwealth, only intervening personally when some incident occurred to make it necessary that he should throw himself into the fray. With Mr. Reynolds or Mr. Ellis as Solicitor-General, with Mr. Hall the Chancellor of the Duchy, with Serjeant Maynard, and with the occasional assistance of Mr. Matthew Hale and others, he had able and trustworthy lieutenants, and it was his practice, as we find from the reports, to sit beside the judges on the bench, and to represent the dignity of his office by wearing his hat while the case was being tried.[2] Contrary to the practice of the present day he was in constant communication with the Council of State and with the judges in reference to all pending cases, and he settled, after consultation with the latter, what special form of indictment would be applicable to the case, and how far the facts that could be established would amount to any and what offence. This

---

[1] Foss (Vol. VI., p. 357) says his practice was worth £5,000 a year, and as postmaster for all inland letters, at 6d. a letter, he calculates that Prideaux netted £15,000 a year. But he did not hold that post, and inland letters were not 6d. a letter.

[2] See his description in Lilburn's case.—State Trials, Vol. V.

"hugger-muggering" was denounced by Lilburn, but no judge raised any objection. The summons to the judges to advise with the Attorney-General seemed to be almost a common form, and the practice was one doubtless sanctioned by long usage. The Attorney-General of the day was, in fact, a minister of justice and a public prosecutor after the style to be met with in every capital of Europe. References were constantly made to his great position in Parliament. Great deference was shown to him by all courts and officials. Prisoners appealed to him for his opinion. He was supposed to lay down the law for the courts, and judges on circuit awaited his convenience. He appears, withal, to have given very general satisfaction in the discharge of his office, and to have created little, if any, personal animosity, for when the vials of wrath were emptied upon the heads of nearly all the leaders and officials of the Commonwealth the name of Mr. Attorney-General Prideaux was treated with respect.

But the legal business which he was called upon to transact was perhaps the least onerous part of his employment. He was in almost daily attendance upon the Council of State, and when he ceased to be a member of that body he was nearly as often at the Board on their summons to attend. He had also placed in his hands the reorganisation of the Mint, with the appointment of the officials and the composing of the disputes between Thomas Simon, chief engraver, and Pierre Blondeau, who had a new system of coinage which he desired to introduce. He had the entire organisation and arrangement of the new postal scheme over the whole of the United Kingdom, and although Manley at one time and Thurloe at another farmed the business at a fixed rental, yet Prideaux was the responsible head of the new department. He was applied to on every difficulty, was consulted on every emergency, and the mass of documents pouring in upon him from all parts in reference to the affairs of the

posts forms a not inconsiderable portion of the State Papers
of the period. He was called upon, amongst other duties,
to advise the Council as to the best mode of suppressing
thieves and robbers;[1] to arrange for the issue of letters of
mark, by the Admiralty judges, to merchants plundered by
the French;[2] to frame regulations for printers and
stationers so as to protect them in the free exercise
of their trade, while obtaining for the Government security
against the publication of scandalous and seditious pamphlets;[3] to stop the carrying of daggers and pocket-
pistols,[4] and to provide for the due administration of
justice in the Cinque Ports.[5] He prepared and settled
charters for the incorporation of Durham College,[6]
and for the College of Physicians in Edinburgh.[7] He
inquired into and issued ordinances and advice for the
reparation of York Minster and the school.[8] He enforced
the due impressment of seamen[9] and read and advised
upon the articles in *Mercurius Pragmaticus.*[10] And in
addition to various other duties he issued licenses for the
exportation and importation of various articles of consumption, until he declared that he had so much other business
that the licenses must be got elsewhere.[11]

In August, 1658, Cromwell, in appreciation of his great
services to the Commonwealth, made him a baronet;[12]
having some three years before appointed him on a special

---

[1] State Papers, 30th October, 1649.

[2] *Ibid*, 22nd October, 1649.

[3] *Ibid*, 18th September, 1650.

[4] *Ibid*, 25 March, 1656.

[5] *Ibid*, 17th March, 1653-4.

[6] *Ibid*, 5th September, 1656.

[7] *Ibid*, 17th February, 1656-7.

[8] *Ibid*, 16th May, 1654.

[9] *Ibid* 19th March, 1654.

[10] *Ibid*, 3rd June, 1650.

[11] *Ibid*, 22nd April, 1655.

[12] Whitelock, Vol. IV., p. 334.

mission to Russia, as the bearer of confidential communication to the Emperor of that country.[1] On the sudden death of the Protector in September, 1658, he was at once consulted as to the course to be pursued, when he advised the immediate proclamation of Richard, and with his own hand signed the proclamation that was affixed to the Royal Exchange.[2] Richard's position being peacefully secured, Prideaux remained in office as his Attorney - General, having Serjeant Maynard as his solicitor. He died in harness on the 19th August, 1659, at the age of nearly seventy years, leaving a wife and several children, with a very ample fortune to maintain them.[3] He was a man of unexceptionable character, a stout Presbyterian, and devoted to Cromwell, and I am not aware of any action during the course of a long and active career which would disparage him as a man of honour and of integrity, or in any way derogate from the position he held for over ten years as head of the Bar and Minister of Public Justice.

Among other counsel of this period, however, there was no one more popular or more powerful than Serjeant Maynard. He was the only public man who saw the entry of the first Stuart and the exit of the last, and who took part in every great movement during the three-quarters of a century that they occupied the throne. He was born under Queen Elizabeth in 1602. He took his Oxford degree under King James in 1620. He was called to the Bar under King Charles I. in 1625. He was made a Serjeant-at-Law by Cromwell in 1654,[4] and Protector's Serjeant in May, 1658, Solicitor-General by Richard in September, 1658, was knighted by King Charles II. in 1660, was appointed Kings' Ancient Serjeant by King James II.

---

[1] State Papers, 22nd June, 1654.
[2] Whitelock, Vol. IV., p. 336.
[3] His widow lived till 1683 at White Lackington, Somerset, and was always known as the Lady Mary Prideaux.
[4] *Mercurius Politicus*, No. 413.

in 1685, and Lord Commissioner of the Great Seal by King
William III. in 1689. He was in nearly every Parliament
that sat from 1625, when he was M.P. for Chippenham,
to 1690, when he was M.P. for Plymouth, and he was
retained on one side or the other in every important
cause. He was a staunch Presbyterian by conviction and
by party ties, and, never having swerved from his religion
or his party, he earned a well-deserved respect. He lived
till 9th October, 1690, and left behind him a large fortune
and a great reputation, which has survived even to the
present day.[1] Some specimens of Serjeant Maynard's
style are left to us in the Parliamentary History, where his
speeches are recorded, and in the State Trials, which report
his arguments. He appears, so far as one can judge, to
have been prolix and rather dull, but to have exhibited
great industry, courage, and perseverance. Perhaps the
best thing he ever said was his last, which showed him at
once as a patriot and a courtier. In a conversation with
King William III., who suggested that at his great age he
must have outlived all his contemporary lawyers, he replied
that indeed he was like also to have outlived the law itself
if His Majesty had not come to the rescue.

But, indeed, counsel in those days had great opportunities
for making both fortune and reputation. There were, in
addition to long lists of causes in Chancery and at Common
Law, numerous State trials and capital felonies which
attracted much public attention, and in which several
counsel were usually engaged. The Courts of Chancery
(the High Court and that of the Master of the
Rolls), together with the three Courts in Westminster Hall sat regularly for the dispatch of business.

---

[1] See Lord Campbell's Lives of Chancellors, Vol. IV., p. 1; Foss's
Judges, Vol. VII., p. 325. Maynard was for many years leader of the
Western Circuit, and to him and Serjeant Glanvil causes were fre-
quently referred. Mr. Foss says on some occasions he made £700 a
Circuit (£2,800).

Causes on circuit were frequently referred to arbitration, and in addition to the circuits held according to Magna Charta by judges or serjeants, the north and south Wales circuits with a special staff of judges, an institution which survived into the present century,[1] were periodically held. Other and inferior tribunals also demanded the assistance of counsel, and of these there were two that did great business during the Commonwealth, but did not survive its fall. These were the *Commissioners for ejecting Scandalous Ministers* and the *Committee for the advance of money.* Before both these bodies counsel were heard. We have in the State Trials[2] some specimens of the cases tried before the first-named of these tribunals, and if, as is there suggested, they are a fair sample of the investigations that took place, there never was a time when a clergy discipline Act of stringent and comprehensive character was more truly needed.

The Court of the Committee for the advance of Money was of a different character. In the great outburst of enthusiasm which sent the Parliamentary Army to the field, liberals of all shades of thought came forward voluntarily with money, horses, arms, and ammunition for the equipment, the pay, and the maintenance of the troops. To all those who had so helped the party with their gold and silver, either in money or in plate, the public faith was pledged for repayment with interest at eight per cent. But when the first clash of arms was over and the nation settled down to what promised to be a long and doubtful struggle, the want of means was sorely felt by both the combatants. The King and his party, though more favourably situated in this respect than their opponents by reason of the great wealth of many of their adherents, had before very long melted down all available metal, issued their coins from siege to siege, plundered their enemies, and even then could

---

[1] They were abolished in 1830.
[2] Vol. V., pp. 539-768.

R

with difficulty find the sinews of war. The Parliament, on
the other hand, though no less straitened at times, had the
City of London at its back, and proceeded to replenish its
exchequer in a resolute and business-like fashion. Until
Cromwell had effectually re-established the customs and
excise, and the country had settled down to peace and
quietness, Parliament mainly obtained funds for carrying
on the war by means of the *Committee for the Advance
of Money*, appointed by the Long Parliament on 26th
November, 1642. To raise the necessary supplies, an assessment was ordered upon all persons indifferently of whatever party, of the value of one-twentieth of their real
or one-fifth of their personal estate. For the money
so advanced a Public Faith or Exchequer Bill was given,
recognising the advance and pledging the nation to a
repayment in times of peace.[1] This assessment, which
began in London and the suburbs, was gradually extended
to all parts of the kingdom as the Parliament became
victorious in successive campaigns. A committee sat at
Haberdashers' Hall every Tuesday and Friday as a Court
of Appeal from the orders of assessment made from time
to time by the district or local assessors. Persons thus

---

[1] The following was the form which was first given of Publique
Faith Bills, of which many hundreds of thousands were issued:—
   "These are to certifie that   hath paid
unto the Committee of Lords and Commons for Advance of Money
sitting at Haberdashers' Hall, London, the summe of   .
   upon the Twentieth part of his whole estate and revenue
assessed by vertue of an Ordinance of Parliament in that behalfe, for
repayment of which summe the said
hereby hath the publicke faith of this Kingdom by vertue and according to an ordinance of both howses of Parliament of the Twelfth of
August, 1645, authorising us whose names are subscribed to signifie and
attest the same."
   In 1653 numerous copies of the above, duly filled in, were given to
applicants on affidavit that the original certificates had been lost, and
on reference to the dates and particulars of the sums paid.—State
Papers, Interregnum, A 59, on the last page of the book.

assessed could appeal upon notice, and were then heard on affidavit, and upon their application were allowed to appear by counsel. And according to the records of this committee there was hardly a case of any importance where the parties were not represented and their interests protected by the leading counsel of the day. Very many reductions were thus obtained, and, as a rule, the affidavit of the party as to the amount of his property was accepted as sufficient evidence of his means. Before, however, the party could lodge an appeal, he was compelled, by the practice settled by the committee, to pay into court half the sum in which he was assessed, and he afterwards either paid or received back according to the judgment of the committee. He also obtained a mitigation of his assessment if he could show that he had rendered substantial services to Parliament or that he had incurred losses in the war, and when his property did not in the whole exceed £100 in value he was exempted altogether. If he were assessed a second time, he could plead his former assessment and thus obtain a total or a partial relief, unless a subsequent case of delinquency (or appearing in arms against the Parliament) could be established against him.

Cases of delinquency, viz., the fining of Royalists and sequestering their estates, were entrusted to the *Committee for Compounding with Delinquents*, which gradually became merged in the *Committee for the Advance of Money*. Delinquents under various orders of Parliament were required to compound for their estates, and the same form of procedure was adopted with them as under the original assessments. The combined Committees after a time sat as a Court sometimes at Haberdashers' Hall, sometimes in a house at Whitehall, for which they paid a rent of £46 a year,[1] with treasurer, registrar clerks, and legal advisers and other salaried officials, and heard the parties either in person or by their counsel. Cases of delinquents were

[1] Warrants.

brought before them upon sworn information, and an order
was then made upon the district or county authorities to
inquire and report upon the value and particulars of the
delinquents' estate. On this report a summons issued to
the delinquent, evidence was taken by the examination of
witnesses *viva voce* if desired, otherwise by affidavit,
arguments of counsel were heard and orders were made,
subject to confirmation at a subsequent meeting. At each
of these steps counsel were heard and fresh evidence was
frequently imported. Some of these cases, owing to their
intricacy, to the amount of business before the court, and to
the pertinacity of the defendants, lasted for months or years,
and an enormous number were actually pending when the
Act of December, 1651, wound them all up and released all
further claims for contribution.

A discovery of undisclosed delinquents' goods was a
favourite source of triumph and of revenue to fanatics and
informers. But the process was found to be of so inquisitorial and so hateful a character that to check as far as
possible the license, and the extortions practised by unauthorised intruders into the homes of quiet and unoffending
Royalists, a resolution was passed in April, 1645, that no
order should issue to enable any person to search for or
discover goods or estates of a delinquent concealed or not
compounded for, except upon certificate of a Member of
Parliament countersigned by the Speaker, recommending
the claim and vouching the applicant. Upon any such
discovery it was the practice of the committee to give from
one-eighth to one-half of the property so discovered to the
party having the carriage of the order, reserving, however,
in all cases, at least one-fifth for the delinquent or his
family, and the remainder going to the Government. The
person applying for such an order was usually one who,
having advanced money to the Government on a Public
Faith Bill or having an overdue claim for pay or salary,
resorted to this as the only means of obtaining payment.

In all these cases, both of ordinary assessment of fifths or twentieths, and of delinquency, a final appeal lay to the Barons of the Exchequer.

To illustrate the fortunes of this period and to afford some insight into the social position of the counsel of the Commonwealth period, I have extracted from the records of the committee the notes of assessment upon as many as I could find of the leading barristers of the day. Those of them, however, who were members of Parliament at the time of their assessment were assessed by the House, and the names of Maynard, Prideaux, St. John, and others are accordingly not to be found in the books. Of those that remain, however, it will be seen that they were most of them men of independent fortune and owners of freehold estates. Their numbers, according to Foss,[1] were—the law officers, five serjeants of the Commonwealth, forty-two serjeants-at-law (including the judges), and sixty-seven barristers — in all one hundred and sixteen counsel in practice. I do not know, however, from what source the learned author drew his list, and it is, I think, very incomplete. One misses the names of Selden, Glanvil, Prynne, and various others.

The value of money during the Commonwealth, as compared with its purchasing power at the present day, is a matter of much dispute. It is generally put at five times the present value. Mr. Palgrave puts it at three times,[2] but Mrs. Everard Green and Dr. Gardiner, who are conversant with the records of this period and have made a study of this question, are of opinion that the purchasing power of money then was four times what it is now. I prefer to adopt their conclusions, and it will therefore be understood that every £100 in the following list represents £400 of the money of to-day.

I have also as a matter of interest added the names of six doctors of medicine.

---

[1] Judges, Vol. VI.
[2] Oliver Cromwell, p. 11.

Counsellors-at-Law.

Serjeant Ailiffe, Serjeant's Inn. 7th June, 1644. £400.

Serjeant Atkins (afterwards Judge). 21st June, 1643. Assessed at £100, to be discharged upon payment of £40.

23rd November, 1643. Assessed at £200, to be discharged on payment of £40, and give Public Bill for £40.

Sir Orlando Bridgman. 28th July, 1644. Assessed at £2,000, respited till the sequestration be taken off his estate.

24th July, 1650. Information that in compounding he had concealed a lease worth £300 a year from the late Archbishop of Canterbury which he had sold.

27th November, 1650. Fine paid, £250, for lands uncompounded for, and £50 (one-fifth) to be paid to informant.

Serjeant Clarke. 23rd November, 1643. Assessed at £500. He had contributed £100 in Kent and lent £30 together with money and horses. £375, being his one-twentieth, he is released on payment of £200 in a month, together with the collector's charges.

Robt. Foster, Justice of Common Pleas. 10th May, 1644. Assessed at £1,000. His house given to poor people driven from home by troops.

Brigg Fountaine, Inner Temple. 30th June, 1644. Assessed at £400.

1st June, 1645. Dischargement for £60, having lent various other sums.

Serjeant Green, Old Jewry. 1644. Assessed at £500, paid £300. Accepted.

Mathew Hale, Lincoln's Inn and Covent Garden. May 1644. Assessed at £300—increased to £400. Respited till his lands be restored.

November, 1644. Again assessed at £800. Assessment vacated, "having been before assessed and respited."

Sir Robert Heath, Chief Justice of King's Bench. June, 1644. £1,000.

July, 1644. Again at £2,000. No proceedings.

Bartholemew Hall, of the Temple. 10th July, 1643. Assessed at £80.

2nd August, 1643. Dischargement on payment of £10, which the assessors certify as his due—one-twentieth.

3rd April, 1644. Again assessed at £100.

26th April, 1644. Assessment discharged, he having been plundered in Dorsetshire.

Sir Edward Littleton, Lord Keeper of Great Seal. 11th March, 1644. Assessed at £1,000. Certain goods, including hangings and other household goods, and his rich robes, etc., found in a trunk, to be sold by the candle. They were sold for £30 on 15th May, 1646.

John Pepys, the Temple. February, 1644. Assessed at £400. Appealed.

March 4th, 1644. He having deposited £100 is to pay £100 more and go and assist Serjeants Rolle and Pheasant in printing Lord Coke's book for the good of the Commonwealth, which being done by him the Commonwealth will either admit him to make his protestation or accept £200 in discharge of his assessment.

7th March. Having satisfied the Commonwealth his sequestration is discharged and a publique Faith Bill ordered for £100 paid.

Serjeant Peter Pheasant, Lothbury. 7th June, 1644. Assessed at £1,000. Discharged on £50 paid and £350 lent, being his one-twentieth on oath.

John Puliston, Middle Temple. 28th August, 1646. £1,200.

16th October, 1646. To be vacated and a former one respited till his estate be reduced from the power of the enemy and come to his possession.

Serjeant Rolls, Old Bailey. 16th February, 1644. Assessed at £400.

21st February, 1644. Order, that as he is well known to have contributed, according to his estate on the proposition, and is wholly deprived of his estates, his assessment to be discharged.

Thomas Twisden, Inner Temple. Assessed at £100 ; discharged on paying £25.

Wadham Windham, Lincoln's Inn. 12th September, 1645. Assessed at £500.

24th October, 1645. Discharged at £62, which is one-twentieth by affidavit.

DOCTORS OF MEDICINE.

Sir Theodore Mayerne (formerly physician to King Charles I.). 4th July, 1643. Assessed at £1,000, as one-twentieth of his estate.

23rd September, 1644. Assessment discharged by order of the House of Commons.

5th March, 1645. Order of Commonwealth to be allowed fourteen days to pay in half his assessment of £1,000. He paid £500.

John Clarke, M.D., Creed Lane, Strand. September, 1643. £250.

Dr. Deodate, Physician. £100.

Thomas Fen, M.D., Aldersgate Street and Amen Corner. £1,000. Ultimately assessed at £260 for his one-twentieth.

John Giffard, M.D., Nugwell Street. £250. Paid £200.

Francis Prugean, M.D. £250.

CHAPTER V.

THE HIGH COURTS OF JUSTICE.

THE High Court of Justice which sat under the
Presidency of Bradshaw was constituted for the trial of the
King and other capital offenders in the Civil War[1] And
this same High Court accordingly met for the trial of
Cavaliers engaged in promoting the second Civil War. There
is little subject for comment in the various trials before this
and other High Courts of Justice constituted under the
Commonwealth and the Protectorate for the trial of cases of
high treason. They partook of the nature of a court-
martial, and the Parliament who voted what persons were
to be sent for trial acted as a sort of grand jury. The
Courts were constituted of some forty to fifty Commissioners, including lawyers, soldiers, citizens and divines, with
a necessary quorum of seventeen, and the respective
Presidents proceeded upon the ruling that the Act of
Edward III. defining the offence of treason was only
declaratory of the Common Law by which any person is
guilty of high treason who compasses the death of the King
or of the Chief Magistrate, by whatsoever name he may be
called, so long as he is the Head of the Executive of the
Kingdom for the time being[2] They sat, except in
the case of the High Court for the Eastern Counties,
which was held at Norwich, in Westminster Hall, occupying the space usually devoted to the Court of Chancery and

---

[1] The reader will find a detailed account of the High Court of
Justice and the trial of the King in " Sidelights on the Stuarts," p. 215.

[2] State Trials, Vol. V., p 848.

their retiring rooms, and other arrangements and regulations were similar to those adopted at the trial of the King.
The first trial during the Interregnum was that of the Duke
of Hamilton, indicted, as Earl of Cambridge (his English
peerage), for levying war against the Parliament and people
of England, and invading this country from Scotland.
Serjeant Bradshaw presided. Mr. Steel, the Attorney-
General, and Mr. Cook, the Solicitor-General, prosecuted,
and questions of law having arisen as to the jurisdiction of
the Court and the terms of his surrender, counsel were
assigned to the Duke for his defence. These were Mr.
Chute, Mr. Hale,[1] Mr. Parsons and Dr. Walker. They
had free access to him in the Tower, with liberty to advise
him generally, and for any one of them to speak for him in
court on any matter of law. They did in fact all speak on
his behalf, and he had in addition a speech from Mr.
Heron, who was not one of those assigned for his
defence. The arguments and the trial lasted from
9th February to the 6th March, when sentence was
given. One remarkable incident of this trial was
the fact that the Reverend Hugh Peters, one of
the Commissioners, of whose character no one has
usually a good word to say, was urgent for saving the
prisoner's life. The Duke contended that he had surrendered on articles which assured him his life, to which
it was replied that the only undertaking given was to
preserve his life for the moment from the fury of the
soldiers, and not to withdraw him from the jurisdiction of
Parliament. The Commission came to a resolution against
the Duke, but Peters interposed boldly and vigorously
on his behalf, declining to accept the finding of the Court,
contending that the most liberal interpretation should
always be given to the articles, and that questions of life or
death should not depend upon a narrow or technical construction. Sentence, however, was passed, and the Duke

---

[1] Afterwards Sir Mathew Hale.

was executed on the 9th March. He was attended on the scaffold by his own servants, who, holding a crimson taffety scarf under his head, caught it as it fell from the block,[1] and removed it with his body for burial. Lords Holland, Norwich, and Capel, and Sir John Owen were tried by the same tribunal and suffered by order of Parliament, as did also Colonel Anderson, Sir John Gell and others, under the presidency of Serjeant Bradshaw.

A High Court was also constituted for trial of the parties engaged in the rising at Norwich and the Eastern Counties, in December, 1650. The President of this Court was Justice Jermyn, of the Upper Bench, and with him were associated Justices Puleston and Warburton, and thirty-two other Commissioners. At this Court sixty persons were convicted and sentenced to death, but nineteen only were executed, the rest being either discharged or left in gaol for short terms of imprisonment.[2] In 1650 Love and Gibbons with others were tried before a High Court, under the Presidency of Lord Commissioner Keble, for participation in the Presbyterian plot. Another High Court was constituted in 1654, under the Presidency of Lord Commissioner Lisle, for the trial of Gerard, Vowell, and Fox for an attempted assassination of the Protector. Others were constituted in 1658, also under the presidency of Lord Commissioner Lisle, for the trial of Dr. Hewet, Sir Henry Slingsby, and John Mordant, engaged in treasonable correspondence with the King. Of these three Dr. Hewet was condemned for contumacy in refusing to plead, Sir Henry Slingsby was found guilty, and John Mordant was, by the casting vote of Lord President Lisle, acquitted for deficiency of proof.[3] Of these courts it is sufficient to say that among the persons of whom they were constituted, there were many

---

[1] See State Trials, Vol. IV., pp. 1155-1194.
[2] *Proceedings in Parliament,* 28th January, 1650-1.
[3] State Trials, Vol. V., p. 907.

thoroughly conversant with the law, and that they appear to have conducted the proceedings with decorum, and with a due regard to the law of high treason as then understood. There would seem to have been no doubt of the guilt of any of the accused. Every facility for defence that the law allowed was given to the prisoners, and if these courts were unconstitutional, it cannot certainly be said of them that they were unjust.

In January, 1653-4, an Ordinance was passed, apparently with the assent of the judges, declaring and enumerating the various offences to be taken and adjudged as treason.[1] In June, 1654, a further Ordinance appointed commissioners for the trial of all crimes and offences mentioned in the Ordinance touching treason.[2] This was afterwards confirmed and enacted by Parliament in October, 1656.[3] But in the meantime many of the judges, though accepting the first Ordinance as necessary for the security of any existing Government, objected to the second as being contrary to the established customs of the country, which provided that all prisoners for high treason should be tried by a jury of their countrymen. And, indeed, the judges of Westminster Hall did not as a rule approve of these proceedings by special High Courts of Justice constituted *ad hoc* for trial of high treason.

There was, however, good reason for these special courts according to the views of Parliament, of Cromwell, who, according to Whitelock,[4] had strong views on the subject of these quasi courts-martial, and of the Council of State. They desired among other things that the same justice in the same form and by the same special tribunal should be meted out to the chief offenders of the King's party that had been given to the King himself, and having

---

[1] Ordinance, 1653, c. 8.
[2] Ordinance, 1654, c. 927.
[3] Statute, 1656, c. 3.
[4] Vol. IV., p. 331.

commenced trials for high treason by a specially-consti-
tuted High Court of Justice, it was considered more
consistent and politic to continue the same procedure
in other cases. The same rules governed all these
trials.[1] The President alone addressed the counsel, the
witnesses, or the prisoner. The judges retired from the
Court to consider of any question raised, and the judgment
delivered by the President was the " sentence, judgment,
and resolution" of the whole Court. The same staff of
clerks and officers was appointed to escort and assist
the President, and they sat in the same part of Westminster Hall that had been set apart for the trial of the
King. Special courts of justice, it must also be borne in
mind, were no new invention, and some still existed. Most of
the State trials in past years had taken place before special
tribunals, and even at the present day it is held that a
Member of the House of Lords can rightly be tried at the
Bar of that House under the presidency of the Lord High
Steward. Although, therefore, we may now consider such
tribunals as arbitrary and possibly unjust, it must be borne
in mind that a court consisting of from thirty to forty
members in regular attendance is in itself a security against
any flagrant violation of the law. Our own practice of
trying a man by a jury commends itself to the country for
many and varying reasons. Among them is the idea that
a prisoner has a right to that chance of escape which is
given to the fox that we chase or the bird that we shoot,
that a human being, to use a common but pregnant expression, is to be pursued like game and not hunted like vermin,
and any attempt to deprive him of this advantage
would be scouted by the country. It speaks, however,
more for the humanity than for the perspicacity of our
people, who even now look askance at the idea of trying a
peer by some hundreds of his peers in the House of Lords.
And yet the doctrine that every man should be tried by his

---

[1] Sidelights on the Stuarts, p. 218.

peers would rather suggest the trial of a nobleman by others of the nobility in the House of Lords than that of a Commoner who might be the Prime Minister of the Crown, by a jury of potwallopers and petty tradesmen in a country town.   Under such a trial, as experience teaches, the criminal has the best chance of escape, but it is by no means certain that it is in all cases the best engine for the administration of justice.   The constitution of these High Courts was very freely and powerfully discussed in a pamphlet attributed to Clement Walker,[1] who compares them to the High Inquisition in Spain, erected by Ferdinand and Isabella to extirpate the Mahometan Moors, and to the Council of Blood in the Low Countries, under the Duke of Alva, to weed out the Lutherans, Calvinists, and Anabaptists. It is nowhere suggested, however, that any of the persons condemned were innocent of the matters laid to the charge, that Hamilton, Capel, and the others did not bring on the Second Civil War, that Gibbons and Love were not engaged in the Presbyterian plot, or that Gerard, Vowell, and Fox had not planned the assassination of Cromwell on his road to Hampton Court.   It is difficult, however, to reconcile their legality with Magna Charta or the Petition of Right, and their adoption can only be defended on the score of necessity.

The various prisoners, whether for trial by the High Court or by a judge and jury, although according to the law of high treason they were not permitted to have counsel except for the argument of points of law, were by no means without assistance in the conduct of their defence.   They were supplied for this purpose with written instructions, which were in every instance, with trifling variations, formed on the same model.   Their best chance, of course, was with a jury, upon whose sympathy or political prejudice they might perchance work.   Their

---

[1] The High Court of Justice, or Cromwell's New Slaughter-House London, 1660.

instructions were, therefore, mainly directed to dealing
with that tribunal, though they were in many points
equally applicable to a trial by a High Court with some
forty or fifty assessors. Thus, they were directed as to the
challenging of the jury, that they might challenge thirty-
five peremptorily, and others for good cause shown ; that
if several prisoners were put up together, then that every
prisoner should allow one juryman that another had
challenged, and challenge one whom others had allowed,
so that each prisoner could thus get a distinct jury
for himself, " which juries will possibly differ in
opinion," and the prosecution be puzzled in the conduct
of their case. For this purpose they were further instructed
to ask for pen and ink, and to take careful notes of the
names of the jurors and by whom challenged. When the
indictment was read they were by no means immediately to
plead, but to except to it at once as not sufficient in law,
and to demand counsel to argue it, and if pressed by the
judge to give particulars, then to say it was neither grounded
on Statute or Common Law, and to ask for counsel to
argue that. Then they were to demand a copy of the
indictment, which, according to law, could not then be given,
and when that was refused they were to except against the
indictment as not being sufficiently precise, and again to
demand counsel. When the judges insisted on it, written
exceptions must be handed in, and then counsel must be
again demanded. If counsel were granted, and, as was
probable, the court overruled their plea, then the same
pleas must be insisted on all over again to the jury, who
must be told they are the true judges to judge between
the prisoners and the judges, and if the jury were
loth to acquit they must be told it is safest to
find a special verdict and let it be argued before all
the judges whether it is treason or not, and so the blood of
the innocent will be upon the judges and not on the jury.
And if the judges are persistent against them they must be

reminded of Chief Justice Tresilian and Justice Belknap, who were hanged in the time of Richard II. for declaring that to be treason which was not, and they were to press upon the jurors the action of the juries in the City of London, who acquitted Lilburn against the direction of the judges. They were instructed as to the mode of cross-examining the prosecutor and the various witnesses; as to objecting to errors of personal description and of time and place in the indictment ; to take the objection that the Statute of Treason did not name a Protector as a person against whom there could be high treason ; to say there were not two credible witnesses to any one overt act, and if indicted for levying war to contend that their offence was only a riot, "for we ought," it is said, " to lose ground by inches." If they were tried by a serjeant, such as Serjeant Glyn or the Recorder of London, they were to say that he was a paid officer of the State sent to take away their lives contrary to law because the sworn judges of Westminster Hall had refused to do it. If they were indicted for felony in stealing arms, ammunition, horses, etc., they were to say there is no felony without a felonious intent, and that they only intended to *borrow* the horses, etc., just as a colonel or a sheriff takes horses, etc., for a special purpose, and no one accounts it as a felony. In short, they were to bring about, if they could, a collision between the judges and the jury, to insist upon every possible objection in point of law, and to keep as far away from the facts of the case as circumstances would permit.

These and many other minute directions and arguments were supplied to the prisoners, who, with this assistance and the occasional help of counsel in court, made for themselves stout and lengthy defences. And it must be put to the credit of the judges and indeed of the counsel of those days, that they went through these various trials knowing each point that was successively coming, and yet dealing with it and deciding it for the twentieth, as if it were for the first time, and giving the prisoners with liberal hand the benefit of counsel if ever any question of law arose. Prosecuting counsel, however, became rapidly familiar with these devices and found little difficulty in circumventing or dealing with them. The prisoners, however, were warned that there must be a limit to their persistency in refusing to plead, or that it might happen that the court would order judgment to be entered against them as mutes refusing legal trial, and so they would be convicted or perhaps be pressed. Mr. Love, in his defence, ran this very close, and the clerk had actually begun to read the sentence when he shouted, "NOT GUILTY!"[1] But Dr. Hewet actually overstayed his time, and argued so long and so hotly through ten pages of the report that the Lord Chief Justice directed the sentence to be read, and he was found guilty for want of a plea.[2] He had at the time some thirteen pages of exceptions, mostly founded on illustrations from the Old Testament, which it is said he intended to present had he not been taken by surprise by the action of the court. He had received, however, frequent and ample warning from the Chief Justice and other members of the court, and it rested with himself alone that his voluminous defence was not produced.[3]

Amongst various notable persons named for trial by the High Court of Justice at this period was Sir William Davenant, who was obnoxious to the Commonwealth, not only as an officer of King Charles and a captain of artillery, but what was to them *anathema maranatha,* a

---

[1] State Trials, Vol. V., p. 66.
[2] State Trials, Vol. V., p. 395.
[3] Whitelock says, "The doctor did not carry himself prudently."
In Thurloe's State Papers, Vol. III., p. 391, is printed a paper extracted in State Trials, Vol. V., p. 784. "The prisoners' plea for themselves, at Exeter, April, 1655." It contains very clear and minute directions for their conduct from the beginning to the end of the trial, and Penruddock's defence, of which we have a record from his own pen, was obviously founded on this paper of instructions.

S

writer and actor of plays and interludes.   And although he
ultimately escaped, there are circumstances in his case
which give it some interest.   His face is as familiar to us
as his name, a fine lofty brow, bound in his statues and in
his portraits, with the laureate wreath, a broad powerful
forehead, with a quick and intelligent eye, but the nose of
a Japanese pug, which he was wont to say had been
disfigured in the wars.   He had courteous manners, was a
brave soldier, and his society was even more courted by
women than by men.   He was born in 1606, the son of a
wealthy vintner at Oxford,[1] proprietor of the Crown
Tavern, a house commonly used by Shakespeare on
his journeys to his native county.   He was educated
at All Saints' School, and afterwards at Lincoln College,
and was in 1638 appointed by King Charles to
the office of Poet Laureate in succession to Ben Jonson.
In due course he received, as Poet Laureate, a pension of
£100 per annum during the King's pleasure.   At the outbreak of hostilities he naturally sided with his friends the
Cavaliers.   He sheathed his pen and drew his sword, and
rendered his Royal master distinguished service in the
camp and in the field. · During the Civil War he occupied,
among other posts, that of Master of the Ordnance to the
Marquis of Newcastle, and took an active and a leading
part as an artillery officer in each campaign.   After the
collapse of the Royalists he joined the Queen in France,
and more than once was the medium of communications
between herself and the King, on the last of which occasions he incurred the Royal displeasure by suggesting that
the question of the Church was not of such a vital nature
that the King might not, for the sake of the peace and
safety of the nation, give way to the Parliament in that

---

[1] His father died in 1622, being then Mayor of Oxford.   He left a
good estate to be divided between his seven children, four sons and
three daughters.

respect.[1]   After this he made no further attempts at
negotiation, and upon the King's death he collected a
company of emigrants, composed of French and English
subjects, and, after the fashion of Columbus and of
Raleigh, sailed for Virginia to open a new career
in a new world.   On his way up the Channel, however, his
vessel was captured by an English man-of-war and taken
as a prize to Cowes.   On the 17th May, 1650, Davenant
was arrested by order of the Council of State and kept in
prison at Cowes, "having been an active enemy to the
Commonwealth."   On the 2nd July the Council of State
reported that William, called Sir William Davenant, was
with five others a fit person to be brought for trial before
the High Court of Justice.[2]   In making this selection the
Council was probably actuated by the fact that in 1641
Davenant, together with Henry Jermyn, Sir John Suckling
and others had been concerned in a scheme to bring a
French army to England to the help of the King.   Most of
the parties implicated, including Sir John Suckling, had
fled, but Davenant was arrested by order of Parliament
and committed to the Tower.   How he escaped from this
position is not very well known, but it was probably through
the good-natured intervention of some of his friends
amongst whom Selden was at that time conspicuous.

The occasion of this State trial, as recited in the Act,[3]
was the murder of Dr. Anthony Ascham, agent for the
Commonwealth in the Kingdom of Spain.   Notice had
been publicly given after the murder of Dr. Dorislaus at
the Hague that if there were any other similar murders the

---

[1] According to Clarendon (Vol. III., p. 32) the King regarded
Davenant as a very unsuitable medium for such a communication;
and, upon the poet suggesting that the Lords Jermyn and Colepepper
were of the same opinion as himself, the King replied that the one
knew as little of the Church as the other did of religion.

[2] State Papers, 1650.

[3] Statute, 9th July, 1650.

Government would proceed to the trial of any Cavaliers
formerly in arms against the Parliament who had not
actually compounded for their delinquency. The murder
of Dr. Ascham, following shortly on this proclamation, led
to the reprisals that brought Sir John Stowel to the block
and nearly compassed the death of Sir William Davenant.
On the 3rd July his case came before the Committee of
Parliament, together with those of the other five recommended for trial, and on the question that he should be
sent for trial before the High Court it was voted in the
negative. "They gave him the noes of the House," said
one, "because he had none of his own."[1]   And indeed,
said the papers, 'twere pity he should die before he had
completed his epitaph, which was then engrossing his
labours in the Tower.   On this report the Council of
State, at the request of Parliament, named Captain
Randolph as a proper person to take the place of
Davenant before the High Court.[2]   On the 4th July, however, the House met again, and repudiating the frivolity of
the previous day, voted that Davenant should be sent for
trial with Sir John Stowel, Jenkins, Slingsby, Brown,
Bushell, and Col. Gerard, and on the 9th July an Act was
passed giving effect to their fatal resolution.[3]   "Thus,"
said *Mercurius Politicus*, "' Gondibert ' will be lost, and a
good jest into the bargain." But " Gondiberts " and good
jests were not too prolific in that age, and Parliament having
retrieved its position in regard to Davenant, no further
steps were taken against him. And, indeed, under the
Commonwealth, which in this respect contrasts favourably
with the Restoration, the bitterness of death was passed
for the man who had once had judgment in his favour. He
had friends among the literary giants of the period. Milton
was said—though on very doubtful authority—to have

---

[1] *Mercurius Politicus*, July, 1650.

[2] State Papers, 1650.

[3] Whitelock, Vol. III., p. 217.

interceded for him, and Whitelock, who in his youth had
wooed the Muses. and was even then a writer of considerable distinction, was amongst his supporters. Accordingly no indictment was presented against him, and
he was not brought to trial, although he still remained
a prisoner in the Tower, where he occupied his thoughts
with the composition of various plays and romances to be
produced at a happier period.   However "Gondibert an
heroic peom by Sir Will: D'Avenant and commended by
Mr. Hobbs," was advertised as just published in December,
1650.[1] Hallam, referring to "Gondibert," describes it as par·
taking more of the character of an heroic romance than of
an epic poem, and as being imperfect, only two books and
a part of a third being completed.   "It is," he says,
"written in a clear, nervous, English style : its condensa-
tion produces some obscurity, but pedantry, at least that of
language, will rarely be found in it. . . . . Its chief
praise is due to masculine verse in a good metrical cadence,
for the sake of which we may almost forgive the absence of
interest in the story, and even of those glowing words and
breathing thoughts which are the soul of genuine poetry."[2]
The critic has hardly taken into consideration the sur·
roundings of Gondibert's production, which almost removed
it from the scope of criticism. It does not
frequently happen that an author has the strength
of nerve and the power of brain to construct and
indite an epic poem of fine masculine verse and metrical
cadence while incarcerated in a dungeon on a capital
charge, with a committee of his enemies arriving at varying
conclusions as to the propriety of his being hanged. Under
these circumstances a paucity of glowing words and breathing
thoughts may perhaps be excused.[3] His confinement in

---

[1] *Mercurius Politicus*, 16th December, 1650.

[2] Literature of Europe, Vol. III., p. 36.

[3] In the autumn of 1650, Davenant writing to Hobbes in reference
to the third book of Gondibert says, "but why do I trouble myself
and you about these things as I am certain to be hanged next week."

the Tower after the trial of Sir John Stowel and the others
seems not to have been too rigorous. He was at all events
accommodated with the services of a French valet, for on
the 15th June, 1651, an order of the Council of State
declared that Jean Bernard, of France, servant to William
Davenant, prisoner in the Tower, should be discharged from
his imprisonment in the Gatehouse, if it were only for not
going as a soldier to Ireland when impressed.[1] In
October, 1652, we find Davenant writing from the Tower to
his old friend, Lord Commissioner Whitelock, with thanks
for obtaining him his "liberty of the Tower"[2]; and again
in September, 1655, asking his perusal of "our opera"—
hot from the press.[3]

In November, 1652, Davenant appears to have had
another narrow escape, for Prince Charles, under the style
of King Charles II., in probable ignorance of Davenant's
position, had issued a commission to Sir William Davenant
to take the command in His Majesty's name of certain
plantations in America. This warrant having been seized
was brought before the Council of State on the 10th
November, 1652. As, however, Davenant had been in
prison ever since May, 1650, the Council treated the
warrant as an idle compliment of the Prince's to one of his
supporters, and troubled their prisoner no further about it.
On 18th April, 1654, Sir William Davenant, then again a
prisoner in the Tower, made a strong and ultimately successful appeal to the Protector in person to consider his
case. It appears from his statement, and that of a small
committee appointed by the Council, of which Sir A. Ashley
Cooper (afterwards Lord Shaftesbury) drew the report,[4]

---

[1] Whitelock, Vol. III., p. 462.

[2] Whitelock, Vol. IV., p. 273.

[3] This was not an opera in the modern sense, but a piece in prose
with some interludes of music, and was afterwards given as an
entertainment at Rutland House in 1656.

[4] State Papers, 18th April and 27th June, 1654.

that having been appointed on the 9th July, 1650, by
Parliament to be tried by the High Court of Justice for
high treason, and no steps having been taken against him,
Colonel Bingham, on 12th November, 1651, made an agreement with Colonel Burgess, Governor of Castle Cornet, in
Guernsey, then holding out for the King, for Sir William
Davenant's exchange for Captain Clark, a Parliamentary
officer, then a prisoner in Castle Cornet. This arrangement was approved by General Blake, and Colonel Clarke
was thereupon released, provided with a pass to London,
and rejoined the service of the Commonwealth. Davenant
was, however, for some reason still kept a prisoner in the
Tower. He therefore petitioned the Court for relief on
Articles which gave him a certificate and liberty on bail to
solicit the issue of a pardon, but put him under engagement
to return to the Tower when so ordered. The result of
this restriction was that he was unable to leave London to
collect his debts, presumably for "Gondibert" and other products of his pen, and being arrested on civil process he was
again committed to the Tower, and thus became a double
prisoner; his imprisonment for debt preventing his leaving
the prison, and the restrictions put upon him by the
Commissioners of Articles of War preventing him going
abroad to collect the monies owing to himself. His
petition to the Protector was strongly backed by
General Blake and Colonel Bingham, who felt that
having pledged their own faith, as well as that of
the army, such an engagement could not be violated
without a direct disparagement to themselves and their
soldiers. The committee appointed to consider Davenant's
petition having reported unanimously in his favour, an
order was made on the 27th June that he be set at liberty
without condition. A warrant was accordingly issued on
the 4th August, directed to Colonel Barkstead, Lieutenant of the Tower, to dismiss his prisoner from custody,
and on the 10th August, 1655, a pass for Sir William

Davenant to France was duly issued by the Council of State.[1]

On the 23rd May, 1656, Sir William Davenant's opera was performed at the Charter House. The price for entrance was 5s. a head, and at least 400 persons were expected, but of these, for some reason, only 150 came, so that the performance was more or less of a failure. The "Entertainment at Rutland House," as it is called, has, like all Davenant's pieces, considerable literary merit. It was written to suit the spirit of the times, and consisted of a short prologue, some interludes of music and two prose disputations. The first between Diogenes and Aristophanes, in rival pulpits, discussed the benefits and disadvantages of public entertainments; the second, which is far the more amusing, was between a Parisian and a Londoner, each extolling his own city by decrying the other, and it gives a very lively and witty description of the various inconveniences of the two cities. It is said that this piece was written in fulsome adulation of Cromwell, but having carefully read the "Entertainment" in the complete edition of Davenant's works,[2] I find nothing to warrant that criticism.

On the 16th August, 1659, according to Whitelock,[3] Davenant obtained his final discharge, and, on the 17th March, 1659-60, he again procured from the Council a pass for France.[4] Whether he joined the Prince and returned with him to this country, I know not; but here, at all events, his political troubles came to an end. He returned to England after the Restoration, reassumed his position as Poet Laureate, and turned his attention to the improvement of the stage by introducing an improved system of lighting and of scenery, and bringing for the first time the opera into England. He also recast several of Shakespeare's

---

[1] State Papers. Warrants, p. 595.
[2] Published by Patterson, of Edinburgh, in five vols., 1872.
[3] Vol. IV., p. 358.
[4] State Papers. Warrants, 1659-60.

plays, for the great playwright was even then more read in the chamber than seen on the stage, and his works failed even then as now to remunerate managers without the costly accessories of mounting, music and dances. He re-wrote " Julius Cæsar," produced a play called " The Law against Lovers," compounded of " Measure for Measure " and " Much Ado about Nothing,"[1] and brought out " Macbeth " with " alterations, additions, amendments, new songs, machinery for the witches, with dancing and singing "[2] and in this form made it a popular play. He also adapted " The Tempest," introducing a female Caliban, together with two new characters, Hippolito, who had never seen a woman, and Dorinda, who had never seen a man. This, added to good scenery, music, and dances, also made a successful play. None of his plays or of his poems, however, are now popular, and the former are said to have derived their success as much from their mounting and other accessories, of which Davenant was the first great master, as from their intrinsic merit.

The story of Sir William Davenant has a peculiar interest by reason of the assistance said to have been mutually rendered to each other by Milton and himself. Milton, it is said, saved Davenant's life under the Commonwealth, and in return for this service Davenant saved Milton at the Restoration. The legend, however, I am constrained to believe, rests upon very slender foundation. It is one of those pleasant traditions that spring up like poppies in the cornfields of history, imparting colour and beauty to the landscape, but growing one hardly knows how or why. It is, however, so much what one feels ought to have occurred, and its occurrence would have been so consistent with the loyal

---

[1] He also brought out " The Rivals," a play founded on the " Two Noble Kingsmen," formerly attributed to Shakespeare.

[2] Published A.D., 1673. Betterton acted Macbeth in this version. He died in 1710.

and patriotic character of the two men, that one naturally hopes it may have been so, and in so hoping would be prepared to accept very slender evidence as sufficient proof. I have found, however, no trace of any intervention of either on the part of the other in the State Papers, the newspapers, or the pamphlets of the period, although with regard to the latter they exist in such prodigious numbers that it is impossible to say what may or may not be found somewhere among them. Davenant, it must be borne in mind, though he had been in arms against the Parliament, had retired at the King's death, had endeavoured to settle the question of the Church in a manner satisfactory to the Parliament, and had held an office, that of Poet Laureate, of an unpolitical and peaceful character. He had also, and this was more important, many influential friends among the heads of the Commonwealth. Among those who interested themselves on his behalf were Hobbes, who admired his character, and puffed his work ; Blake, the greatest of the naval victors ; and Whitelock, the Lord Commissioner, all of them men whose social and political influence far exceeded that of John Milton, who, in 1652, was Latin Secretary to the Foreign Office, at a salary of £200 a year. Public sympathy also, as appears from the papers, ran strongly in his favour, and thus every probability pointed to his safety. Milton, on the other hand, had never been in arms against the King, had taken no part in the trial, and was not within any category marked out for capital punishment at the Restoration. Although he had written stoutly in favour of a Republic, yet he had bowed his head, as to a dispensation of Providence, to the new order of things at the Restoration, and he had, moreover, during his tenure of office, rendered great service to the country, not only in his independent literary efforts, but also in that department of the public service which in the judgment of men of all parties had done great things for the glory and honour of Great Britain. Both of these men might, therefore, very well have

been spared, each on his own intrinsic merit, without the
need of any intercessor.

Davenant died in 1668. His was a life like many of that
period, not without its contradictions. Educated and
illustrious in the arts of peace, and bred up to the enervat-
ing life of the stage, where in early life he habitually played
the part of a woman, he was called upon in after life to
play the part of a soldier on the theatre of actual warfare.
He was justly proud of his early association with his godfather,[1] Shakespeare, but was driven by stress of circumstances in his later years ruthlessly to mutilate Shakespeare's
greatest creations. Being himself somewhat of a solemn
man, living at a solemn and serious epoch ' and among
solemn and serious people, he was the subject of the only
jest publicly recorded during the whole of that dismal
period. He was buried in Westminster Abbey, and his
originality and genius have found no better record than a
gravestone in Poet's Corner disfigured by a commonplace
and vulgar plagiarism of the epitaph on Ben Jonson.[2]

A greater interest, however, attaches to those trials of the
Commonwealth which took place before judges of Westminster Hall, who held their patents *dum se bene gesserint*,
and juries who may be said to have fairly represented the
spirit of the times. With the exception, therefore, of the
trial of Love for the Presbyterian plot, which contained
some matter of special interest, I do not propose further to
deal with these proceedings of the High Court of Justice.

---

[1] It was suggested in Oxford that there was a somewhat closer tie
between them, and it is reported by Oldys in his Choice Notes (printed
in 1862) that on one occasion a tradesman at Oxford, meeting young
Davenant running up the High Street, asked him where he was
hurrying. "To see my godfather, Shakespeare," said he. "Good
boy," said the other; "but have a care that you don't take God's
name in vain."

[2] "Oh rare Sir Will D'Avenant."

CHAPTER VI.

CELEBRATED TRIALS UNDER THE COMMONWEALTH.

I.—The Trials of John Lilburn for seditious libels on the Government.

ONE of the most familiar figures at and about the time of the Commonwealth was that of John Lilburn. Familiar, not from any remarkably good or evil action of which he was capable, nor for any great part that he took in the direction of public affairs, but mainly from the fact that he was tried in almost every court in the kingdom, under varying conditions, during a period of some twenty years, for libels on the Government of the day, King, Parliament, Commonwealth and Protector. And thus it happened that one of the first duties that devolved upon the judges of the Commonwealth was to deal with this gentleman.

Lieutenant Colonel John Lilburn, commonly known as "Freeborn John," from his constant description of himself as a "freeborn Englishman," was one of those vain, pestilent, ill-conditioned persons thrown to the surface by political convulsions, who are invariably to be found at the tail of every popular movement. No great cause has ever existed without the involuntary enlistment of some such recruits. And the misfortune of such connections is that the merits of the cause are apt to be judged and its memory to be perpetually associated with these political mountebanks rather than with the more sober and serious politicians of whom its ranks are necessarily composed. He was of a type discontented and turbulent, the creation of the disorder of the times and in one form or other the terror of the Commonwealth, who found it equally difficult to take him seriously or to treat him with indifference. His only object appeared to be to put in the wrong whatever form of Government might be actually existing, and he was equally certain to bring discredit on the party to which he might be for the moment allied, whatever course might be pursued towards him.[1]

As a striking instance of perpetual discredit brought upon a party and a cause by vain and indiscreet volunteers, let me take the case of our ancient monuments. If there is one thing more than another which has made the memory of the Puritan supremacy perpetually odious to the great mass of English people, it is their dealing with our venerable churches and cathedrals. Into whatever ancient church we may go, with any pretensions to architectural or archæological interest, we find some old monument defaced, some old window destroyed. It is probable that many of these were damaged or removed as early as the reign of Queen Elizabeth, many even after the Commonwealth, and that the carelessness or mischief of succeeding generations has gone far to complete the injury. But people look at the recumbent figures of crusaders, of heroes, and of worthies of the past. They admire the reverent figures of the father and mother of the family, with their sons and daughters kneeling in geometrical progression behind them. They point to their noses and their toes broken, and every available corner of the effigy damaged or removed, and are not wanting in words of reprobation for the Puritans who ordered the destruction of these monuments of antiquity sacred to the memory of the dead and grateful to the pride of the living. These mutilated figures and the blank spaces, where old and

---

[1] Clarendon (Vol. III., p. 500) gives an interesting but inaccurate account of Lilburn and the proceedings taken against him.

beautiful windows may in former days have subdued the
noonday glare, convey to the minds of thousands upon
thousands of our fellow countrymen and women the only
idea they ever possessed of the times and the feelings of our
Puritan fathers. That images of saints and blessed
virgins, and what would even now be regarded by many as
superstitious emblems, should have been removed, and, if
necessary, by force, would not have disturbed their
reason or their sensibility; but a desecration of the
dead, a mutilation of the objects of affection and of
pride, gives a shock to the feelings not only natural but
altogether praiseworthy. But the Parliament who ordered
the removal of superstitious emblems was composed of
much the same class of persons as those who are our
Parliament men of to-day, with much the same feelings
and sensibilities, but being nearer to the evils of Popery they
had a greater fear of its revival and a stronger determination to suppress it. The Act,[1] however, of 1643, under
the authority of which these emblems were removed,
contained a clause expressly excluding from its provisions
" any Image, Picture, or Coat of Arms in glass, stone, or
otherwise, in any church, chapel, churchyard or place of
public prayer, set up or graven for a monument of any
King, Prince or Nobleman or other dead person not being
commonly taken or reputed for a saint; but all such pictures,
images, and coats of arms shall stand and continue as if this
ordinance had not been made." There was, therefore, no
sanction for the wholesale destruction of these works of
art and of piety, either by Parliament, by Protector,
or by Council of State, and had other colonels stood forth
like Colonel Nathaniel Fiennes in Winchester Cathedral,
who vowed that as an old Wykehamist he would not stand
by and see the statue of William of Wykeham mutilated
contrary to law, the monuments of many of our old

[1] Statute, 18th August, 1643. An Act of 19th March, 1644-5,
referring to organs re-enacts the proviso of the Act of 1643.

worthies and warriors might have come to us unharmed, and a somewhat undeserved reproach have been removed from the cause of the Commonwealth. But Freeborn John and his class were the first in their intolerant self-sufficiency to regard every emblem of beauty as in itself an emblem of superstition, and whilst crying aloud for the fullest liberty and toleration for themselves, would only have been able to conceive or willing to concede that peculiar and not yet extinct form of toleration which would give to all the world the freest liberty to differ from everyone else upon every question except that particular doctrine upon which they had for the moment set their seal. To Freeborn John, therefore, and to men of his stamp we owe the melancholy fact that of all our ancient monuments existing during the Civil War hardly one is to be found that has escaped the sacrilegious hand of the fanatic.

This John Lilburn, who is not to be confounded with Colonel Robert or Henry Lilburn, colonels in the Parliamentary Army, who were indeed his brothers, but men of a very different stamp, appears to have belonged to a respectable family in Durham, and to have become early in life connected in some way with literature as either a publisher or bookseller, and like other libellers of a more modern era, to have used his position as a tower for the emission of slanderous volleys, and to have commanded a certain amount of popular sympathy by the very recklessness and audacity of his libels. He was a man of personal courage, and had served with some distinction in the Parliamentary Army, and he either was or assumed to be a lieutenant-colonel. When acting as a captain of dragoons he was taken prisoner by the Royal Army after Edge Hill, and was tried for high treason at Oxford before Lord Chief Justice Heath, who was then holding Assizes at the Guildhall on behalf of the King. At this trial he threw away any possible chance of escape by an excessive laudation of the Parliament and denunciation of the King and his party; but his luck stood him in good stead, for his wife having made known to the Parliament that her husband and other officers were at Oxford being tried for high treason and likely to be hanged for levying war against the King, the Parliament intimated to the King that they should apply the *lex talionis* and for every Parliamentary officer hanged by him they would hang one of the noblemen or gentlemen that they had in their power as prisoners of war. This saved Lilburn's life, and he afterwards managed to escape and rejoin the Parliamentary forces. In 1637 he was tried before the Star Chamber and had heavy fines imposed upon him,[1] which were, however, afterwards remitted by Parliament. In February, 1645, he was before the Lords, where he was defended by those stalwart counsel, Serjeant Bradshaw and Mr. Cook, but was convicted and sentenced to whipping and pillory for libels. After this he appeared before a Committee of the House of Commons, with Mr. Miles Corbet in the chair, on a charge of publishing libels on Members of Parliament, and in August, 1645, he was sent to Newgate by the House of Commons for writing and publishing seditious books.[2] In July, 1646, he was before the House of Lords on a charge of sedition, which he seemed to slight,[3] in consequence of which the Lords sent him once more to the Tower. Thereupon Mrs. Lilburn, accompanied by a multitude of women, made themselves "troublesome and impetuous" by besieging the doors of Parliament and complaining of the tyranny of the Lords in imprisoning the Colonel and thus "divorcing him from his lawful wife."[4] In the summer of 1647 the Commons, in answer to

---

[1] See State Trials, Vol. III., p. 1315.
[2] Whitelock, Vol. I., p. 493.
[3] *Ibid.*, Vol. II., p. 49.
[4] *Ibid.*, Vol, II., p. 70.

various petitions, ordered he should have the liberty
of the Tower, of which he availed himself after his fashion
by making speeches defaming both Houses of Parliament,[1]
whereupon the Commons rescinded their order, recommitted him to the Tower, and ordered his trial at law for
sedition. This was on 18th January, 1647-8, and in the
following February he, with others of the " Levellers," whom
he had then joined as being the latest form of discontent,
published a new and revised edition of the " Agreement of
the People," followed by another seditious book called
" England's New Chains." These papers were drawn on
the well-known political pattern. They contained some
demands which everyone was ready and willing to grant,
coupled with others which no Government conducted by
other than a lunatic could have thought of conceding.
They had not yet, however, arrived at the absurd formula
of Liberty, Equality and Fraternity, the triumph of the great
fabricator of phrases, for even then England was wise
enough to know that though Liberty was a substance for
which all else might be sacrificed, Equality was an impossible
goal, and Fraternity an impalpable shadow. Freeborn
John had also been recently called before Serjeant Bradshaw
and other members of the Council of State for libels on the
Commonwealth, who had committed him with some others
to prison, and ordered their prosecution in the Upper Bench,
with directions to Attorney-General Prideaux to undertake
the case. Add to this catalogue of charges that he was
for ever inciting others to riot, and that his regiment was
always in mutiny, with some of its officers always in prison
and one or two occasionally shot, and it completes the
picture of a thorough goingfirebrand and irreconcilable.

What Freeborn John actually wanted is perhaps as
difficult to say as it has always been with regard to
agitators of a similar class. He had in turns supported
and traduced each phase of the revolution. He alternately

---

[1] Whitelock, Vol. II., p. 263.

T

lauded and libelled the Parliament of which he had been a Member, the army in which he had served, and Cromwell, who had more than once stood his friend. He was a man not only of personal vanity, but of malignant temper, of whom Sir P. Warwick said that he could not live without a quarrel, and if he were the last man left alive he would cut himself in half in order that each part might fight against the other; and being persistently against whatever was the actual Government of the day, he was necessarily supported by every renegade and every malcontent within and without the United Kingdom. His type is familiar to us all in Courts of Justice, where we daily rub shoulders against men who spend their lives in litigation, and who, finding some spark of law in their favour, fan it unceasingly, till they persuade themselves, and, unhappily, also seem to persuade others, that a great cause is involved in their position. Add to this an utter recklessness of statement, unbounded loquacity, and a love of notoriety, and the composition of a professed litigant is complete. And with such persons, as all lawyers well know, there is the greatest difficulty in dealing, for between the natural though weak-minded tenderness which judges feel towards litigants who appear in person, and the inexperience of many juries, who are apt to think that where a litigant appears in person there must be some good in his cause, substantial injustice is constantly done. Juries even now seem unable to accept what experience teaches us is the almost invariable rule, that when a litigant so appears it is entirely from his or her own choice, arising either from a morbid feeling of personal vanity, or from the fact that counsel whom he has consulted, and who may have ascertained the true facts of his case, have declined to be parties to a contest based on pure vindictiveness or falsehood, nor do they seem able to realise the fact that a prepossessing appearance and an easy volubility are by no means inconsistent with a thoroughly dishonest case. The charge against Lilburn was for publishing various pamphlets or small books inciting the apprentices of London to rise against the existing Government, the Army to rise against their commanders, and generally to bring about political chaos. Having been committed by the Council of State in April, 1649, and the House of Commons having approved of their action, it became necessary to decide what course was to be taken with him, and accordingly, as appears to have been the custom at that period, the Council of State ordered[1] the Attorney-General and other counsel for the Commonwealth to confer with the judges of the Upper Bench as to whether the crimes to be objected against Lilburn and others were treasons or misdemeanours, and to cause indictments to be prepared and the usual course pursued touching the examination of the prisoner's witnesses; the fact being, as I assume, that the Attorney-General had doubts whether the publications amounted to high treason, or whether they could only be treated as scandalous libels, and as such punishable under the Acts for regulating the press.[2] What the result of this hugger-muggering, as Lilburn called it, was, we know not, as any doubts as to the form of the indictment were speedily solved by Lilburn himself, who took the opportunity, while in the Tower awaiting his trial, of issuing a series of fresh publications, which undoubtedly came within the law of treason. In the meantime various petitions were signed for his release, and on the 23rd April some hundreds of women, who composed in a great part the following of Lilburn at that time, and many of whom were probably among the deputation that made themselves " troublesome and impetuous " to Parliament in 1646, attended the House of Commons, and in reproachful and scolding language[3]

---

[1] State Papers, 2nd May, 1649.

[2] Statute (24th September, 1649) consolidating and re-enacting these laws was passed while Lilburn was in prison.

[3] Whitelock, Vol. III., pp. 21-22.

demanded his release. On the following day these scolding
women were at the House again, and on the 25th,
having again gone in a procession to Westminster,
the House sent them out the well-known answer
by the Serjeant-at-Arms,[1] that the matter petitioned of
was of a higher concernment than they understood, that
the House gave answer to their husbands, and thereupon
desired them to go home and look after their own business
and meddle with their housewifery. The publication of
these further and more inflammatory pamphlets coming to
the knowledge of the Council of State, they issued a Commission of Oyer and Terminer directed to Lord Commissioner Keble, six of the judges of Westminster Hall,
the Lord Mayor, various aldermen and others, to try
Lilburn for high treason at the Guildhall.[2] On the 19th
September, 1649, an order was issued by the Council of
State summoning the judges to town for their attendance
at Guildhall; and on the 10th October a special summons[3]
was sent to Justices Jermyn and Puleston, who were
named on the Commission. On the 13th October a further
summons[4] was sent to Lord Chief Justice St. John and
Lord Chief Baron Wylde to meet the judges, who had
appointed a meeting at Serjeants' Inn at 9 a.m. on Monday
to consult as to the trial of Lilburn, "being a weighty
matter, although they were not in the Commission for the
trial."

On a Thursday, early in October, the Lieutenant
of the Tower brought his prisoner to the Guildhall
under a strong escort of soldiers, and he was there
handed over to the custody of the Sheriffs of
London and Middlesex. A Special Commission was
directed to Lord Commissioner Keble and Mr. Justice

---

[1] *Ibid.*, Vol. III., p. 22.
[2] State Papers, 2nd May, 1649.
[3] State Papers, 10th October, 1649.
[4] State Papers, 13th October, 1649.

Jermyn of the Upper Bench (who conducted the trial), Baron Gates, Justice Puleston, and some other lawyers, themselves Members of Parliament, and aldermen and citizens, to the number in all of about forty, and the trial took place in the Upper Bench Court at Guildhall by a special jury of the City of London. The whole of the first day was consumed in getting the Colonel to plead guilty or not guilty. According to the report of the trial (which was published from his own notes), the Lord President Keble acted, as appears to have been his wont, with great judgment and moderation, and, indeed, the patience of the Court was very much to be commended, as Lilburn himself appears to have talked nearly the whole time, and to have insulted the judges, the Attorney-General, and everyone except the jury, to whom he expounded fully and frequently the case of Nicholas Throckmorton,[1] tried in the reign of Queen Mary, where the jury, in direct conflict with the law and perverse contradiction to the facts, took it upon themselves, notwithstanding the direction of the judges, to acquit the prisoner. He insisted on having counsel to defend him, a right which was unknown at that time, although he was told if any question of law arose counsel should be assigned. He refused to hold up his hand, according to the common form, when called upon to hear the indictment read. He refused to plead, and at last, after his plea, he obtained an adjournment to the following day. His publication of the papers being then proved, he defended himself by long speeches, making numerous technical objections to the evidence, talking down the judges and complimenting the jury, recounting his own exploits and his sufferings in the popular cause, insisting that the jury were judges of the law as well as of the facts, and that the judges were mere cyphers and " *Norman intruders*," a taunt that was always levelled at the judges when it was sought to disparage them in

---

[1] State Trials, Vol. I., p. 899.

public estimation. In the result he succeeded in obtaining from the jury a verdict of not guilty amid the applause of the people. It may, however, have been the fact, which would go far to account for this verdict, that Milton's plea for an unlicensed press and other less well remembered pamphlets in the same direction, had led the people to sympathize with a victim of what they might regard as the advocacy of a free press, and who were unwilling to see a fellow subject of however objectionable a type sent to the gallows for the mere expression of opinions, however distasteful to the powers of the day, or subversive of order and good government. He was sent back to the Tower, but though his acquittal was a sore grievance to the Government, and was calculated to throw great difficulties in the way of keeping order in the Metropolis, Serjeant Bradshaw, as President of the Council of State, on being appealed to by Lilburn's friends, declared that having stood his trial and been acquitted he was entitled to his release, and on the 8th November, 1649, he signed an order to that effect.[1] Upon his return he was elected a Common Councillor of the City of London an election, however, very speedily set aside[2] for irregularity. He then turned his attention to Justice Jermyn, and on the 29th May, 1651, denounced him to the Committee for the Advance of Money, and Compounding with delinquents, and claimed the judge's estate on behalf of his brother Robert. His charge of delinquency against the judge consisted in an allegation that in 1642, when he was a Justice of the Peace for the County of Sussex, he had sworn in a Royalist High Sheriff with strong expressions of loyalty to the King. As this was a matter affecting a judge, though of so apparently trivial a character, it was referred to Parliament and to the Committees, who both found the charge was groundless, and passed votes of

[1] State Trials, Vol. V., p. 1405.
[2] Parliamentary History, Vol. III., p. 1344.

satisfaction in the judge's fidelity and integrity.[1]   Lilburn
also, about the same time, prompted not by spite, but by
cupidity, denounced one Hoo Games, of the County of
Brecon, on certain specified acts of delinquency in 1648, and
claimed a share of his estate as forfeited thereby.   To this
Mr. Games pleaded that his alleged acts of delinquency were
groundless, and that they had recently on his demand been
publicly inquired into by the Barons of the Exchequer,
who had declared them to be without foundation.   And
this being found to be so, upon inquiry, no steps were
taken by the Committee.   Nothing, however, would keep
Freeborn John quiet, and in December, 1651, he published
a malicious and defamatory libel upon Sir Arthur
Hazelrig, arising out of a claim made by him to a
colliery in the County of Durham.   This was inquired into
by a Parliamentary Committee, who ordered Lilburn to
pay a fine of £3,000 to the Commonwealth, a sum of £2,000
damages to Sir Arthur Hazelrig, and £2,000 damages to
Russell and others.   In the result, the House of Commons
in January, 1651-2, acting on the principle that when
powder is about lucifer matches must be stowed away,
passed an Act for Lilburn's banishment.   He was brought
before the House to hear his sentence.   Being commanded
to receive it on his knees at the Bar, he refused to kneel,
and he was then ordered to leave the country within twenty
days and not to return on pain of death.[2]   On the 29th
January he left London, and many friends, including doubtless the women, accompanied him to the seaside to witness
his departure.[3]   He went to Ostend and thence to
Amsterdam, the home of the exiled Royalists, and there
remained till the summer of 1653, about which time
finding that Cromwell had dissolved the Long Parliament

---

[1] Proceedings of the Committee for the Advancement of Money,
p. 1344.
[2] Whitelock, Vol. III., p. 385.
[3] Whitelock, Vol. III. p. 388.

and had taken the reins of Government into his own hands, he returned to England under the belief, as his friends alleged, that he would be favourably received by Cromwell, whom, however, he had openly denounced in his libels as a murderer and usurper. Cromwell naturally refusing to protect him, he was apprehended immediately on his arrival in the City and committed to Newgate by the Lord Mayor.[1] Certain enquiries having been made into his conduct since he had left England, it appeared from the deposition of witnesses[2] that notwithstanding his protestations of fidelity to the Commonwealth, he had on leaving London made directly for the quarters of Prince Charles, at Amsterdam, put himself into communication with the Stuart party, and, as was alleged, had offered for a payment of £10,000 down to destroy the Lord General Cromwell, the Parliament, and the Council of State, and put the Prince on the throne. No charge, however, was founded on these depositions, but on Wednesday the 13th July, he was put to the Bar of the Old Bailey before Mr. Steele, Recorder of London, the Lord Chief Baron Wylde and a jury, upon an indictment charging him with returning from banishment contrary to the Act passed in 1651. He went through the same performance as at his former trial, insulting the judges and the Parliament, and, according to Thurloe,[3] encountering Mr. Prideaux, the Attorney-General, with so many opprobrious terms, that he was absolutely driven from the court. He was also on this occasion supported by a band of some hundreds of cavaliers, with swords and other arms, whose threatening conduct in the court exercised a very potent influence over the deliberations of the jury. In order, I gather, to quiet him and get on with the case, the court

---

[1] State Trials, Vol. V., p. 415.
[2] Informations and Examinations, etc. State Trials, Vol. V., p. 450.
[3] Thurloe, Vol. I., p. 366

ordered him a copy of his indictment, and at his request
the following counsel were assigned to him, viz., Serjeant
Glynn, Serjeant Earl, Mr. Maynard, Mr. Hale, Mr.
Twisden, Mr. Wylde, Mr. Chute, and Mr. Norbury. None
of these, however, were forthcoming, having all refused to
appear on his behalf. The matter, indeed, was absolutely clear
in law and in fact, nor was the case one in which counsel
could have been of any avail ; certainly none of those whose
names were given would have been willing, or, indeed, have
been permitted, to indulge in the vagaries which are usually
permitted to a prisoner in person. But he produced a
paper purporting to be signed by Mr. Maynard and Mr.
Norbury, containing their opinion that the Act of Parliament banishing him was of no effect, being founded on a
judgment which Parliament was incompetent to give.[1]
What the arguments were, if any, upon the exceptions we
know not. The trial is reported by Lilburn's brother,
who omits all this part of the case, and there seems some
doubt whether Serjeant Maynard ever did, in fact,
sign the exceptions, although it is probable that
Mr. Norbury did.[2] Whitelock refers to the matter no
further than to say that the case went on day
by day at great length. In the course of a very long
harangue, and much time spent in interruptions, Lilburn
insisted (in spite of repeated declarations to the contrary

---

[1] Lilburn handed in one set of exceptions signed by himself alone,
with a fee of *two shillings* for their being recorded, also a further set
purporting to be signed as above stated.

[2] Mr. Norbury was somewhat bitten by the Lilburn complaint. In
August, 1655, he published a broadsheet in the form of a petition on
behalf of the freeholders and other persons who appealed to the Protector. It recognised his position as chief magistrate and his power
with his Council to make laws until the meeting of Parliament. It
referred, however, to the " Ecclesiastical Fifth Monarchy," and was
full of various complaints, for which Mr. Norbury was called before
the Council and his paper suppressed.—State Papers, 10th August,
1655.

from the members of the court) that the jury were judges
of the law as well as of the fact, and that if they agreed
with his exceptions, whatever might be the direction of the
judges, they were bound by their oaths to find a verdict in
his favour. This theory of the jury being judges of law as
well as of the fact, which has sometimes been propounded
by prisoners in person who knew that the law was clear
against them, and that their only chance was in inducing
the jury to override the law, is one which, if admitted,
would be subversive of our entire system of judicature.
The separation of these two questions, questions of law for
the judge, whose peculiar province it is to know the details,
the intricacies and the due procedure of the law, and who
is sworn to administer it, and questions of fact for the jury,
who are sworn to try the issues of fact between the parties,
and whose duty it is to accept the law as laid down by the
judge, is a fundamental principle in our system, and has
worked with the most admirable results. It does no doubt
occasionally happen that the line between what is strictly
a question of law and what a question of fact is very thin
and difficult to determine. In such cases a strong-minded
judge, with a consciousness of his own powers, would be
disposed to withdraw such questions from the jury, and
take upon himself the responsibility of deciding that the
result lies in his own determination. A weak judge, on the
other hand, would probably prefer to put the responsibility
on the jury, and commit to their decision any question as
to which there might be any reasonable doubt as to whether
it were a question of law or not. But on the whole the
practice of some five centuries has shown this division of
the subject matter of legal enquiries to be sound and
eminently conducive to the convenient administration
of justice. The counsel for the Commonwealth
were Mr. Prideaux, the Attorney-General, who from
his important position in the Commonwealth appears
to have sat on the Bench beside the judges, but to

have taken personally very little part in the trial, and Mr. Hall, Attorney-General for the Duchy of Lancaster, whom Lilburn always referred to as "mumbling Mr. Hall," and who, in fact, conducted the proceedings. There were doubtless other counsel, but, as Colonel Lilburn had no special words of vilification for them, their names are not mentioned in the report of the trial. The only question to be tried from first to last was that of identity. Was the Lieutenant-Colonel John Lilburn at the Bar the Lieutenant-Colonel John Lilburn named in the Act of Parliament? Of this fact there was and could be no doubt; indeed, he was identified by Mr. Scoble, the Clerk of Parliament, and yet the Colonel, in the course of a violent tirade, charged the Lord Mayor with having arrested a wrong John Lilburn, and in concluding his speech to the jury, used these words: "I call Jehovah to witness, and do here protest before God, angels, and men, I am not the person intended to be banished by the Act." Influenced, apparently, by this wicked and unscrupulous falsehood, the jury, after a hearing of seven consecutive days, acquitted the prisoner. His friends immediately struck a medal with the head of Freeborn John on one side and the heads of his jurymen on the other, and circulated it through the kingdom.

This acquittal of Lilburn a second time by a London jury was exceedingly distasteful to the Government. It could hardly be regarded as a blow to their authority or a reverse to the Protector, but it was one of those small annoyances which become all the more disagreeable from the undue importance everywhere attached to them by their enemies. And although we may make every allowance for the excitement of the times, for the ignorance of the jury, and it may be for the weakness of the judge, one can but feel that the Government had considerable reason after such a verdict, delivered perversely in the teeth of the evidence, to suspect some undue influence or corruption of the jury. They were accordingly summoned by order of

Parliament, acting on a very bad precedent in the time of
Queen Mary,[1] on the 20th August, 1653, about a month
after the trial, to appear before the Council of
State for the purpose of being questioned as to
the reasons for their verdict. To the questions of
the Council the jury, in agreement with their foreman,
refused to give any definite answer, except that they
had acted in the matter according to their consciences.
But from voluntary statements which in nearly every case
they made to the Council, it clearly appeared that they
believed that they were judges of the law as well as of
the fact, and that many of them accepted Lilburn's statement that he was not the John Lilburn referred to in the
Act.[2]   Nothing further was done with the jury, but
Lilburn himself was recommitted to Newgate, whence
Colonel Hacker, on the 27th August following, supported
by a troop of horse, removed him to the Tower, where he
was ordered by Parliament "for the peace of the nation,"
to be further secured, notwithstanding any order of the
Upper Bench or of any other court of justice. He was
therefore unbailable by any court, but his wife was
allowed to visit him, and it is stated, though on what
authority is not known, that he thenceforward became
a spy of Thurloe's. He did, in fact, receive from
Cromwell, in recognition of their former friendship,
a sustenance of £8 a month, about equivalent to the pay of
a lieutenant-colonel. But however much one may dislike
Freeborn John, and despise him and all his works, I am
not disposed to accept this spy story, nor do I believe that
Cromwell's bounty was dictated by other motives than
that of providing a pittance for a misguided man who

---

[1] Throckmorton's case, A.D. 1554, which, however, was used by
Lilburn to get his verdict.

[2] State Trials, Vol. V., p. 446. Parliamentary History, Vol. III., p.
1413.

had done good service to the · Commonwealth in times
gone by.

Lilburn's position was, however, one of considerable
difficulty to the Government. He had been acquitted by
the jury of having committed any crime in returning to
England, and the jury had thus in effect, though not in
words, found that he was not the John Lilburn contemplated by the Act. If the Government failed to give effect
to this finding, they would be said to have overridden the
verdict of the jury; and if, on the other hand, they recognised it to the full extent, inasmuch as everyone knew that
he was the John Lilburn in question, they would have been
held guilty of weakness and folly. They naturally looked to
policy rather than logic, and refused to shut their eyes to
facts as well known to them as to every other subject. To
keep Lilburn in custody after the prorogation of Parliament
would have been impossible, as the Courts held that though
they had no power to bail a prisoner committed by Parliament during the Session of that body, yet that on a
prorogation their powers revived. A course was thereupon adopted for which Cromwell was severely criticised in
the case of Overton, and for which, in the next reign,
Clarendon was impeached for treason.[1] He was sent to
St. Elizabeth's prison in Jersey, by order of the Council of
State,[2] to which island, according to the decision of the
Courts, no writ of *habeas corpus* could issue. And his
application for such writ was accordingly and rightly
refused.[3] From Jersey, he appears, at some time during
the Protectorate, to have returned without further molesta-
tion to England, where he died at Eltham, in Kent, in

---

[1] The fourth article of his impeachment was that he advised and
procured divers of His Majesty's subjects to be imprisoned against law
in remote islands, garrisons and other places, thereby to prevent them
from the benefit of the law.—Hallam's Constitutional History,
Vol. II., p. 65.

[2] State Papers, 28th March, 1654.

[3] Whitelock, Vol. IV., p. 109.

August, 1657. At this period he had joined the Quakers, who were the chief source of trouble to the Commonwealth by their turbulence and breaches of law and of decency. He was followed by a great number of these people on the 31st August to the "Mouth" in Aldersgate, and thence was carried by them without pall to his grave and buried in a churchyard, which, appropriately enough to Lilburn's career, was immediately adjoining Bedlam.[1] After Lilburn's death the Protector, commiserating the piteous condition of his widow and children, and forgetting her husband's late delinquencies, in recollection of his early services granted her a pension of forty shillings per week. This, after Cromwell's death, was attempted to be made available by some of the assignees of the £7,000 fine inflicted upon her husband by the Parliament of 1651-2. "Your late father," she said in her petition to Richard in January, 1658-9,[2] "professed very great tenderness to me, and persuaded Sir Arthur Hazelrig to return the estate he had taken from me and this he lately did. His Highness also remitted the part allotted to the State and willed the Commissioners to remit the other parts allotted to them. He also granted me a pension, which by your great favour is continued, or I and my children might have perished. Sir Arthur Hazelrig has relinquished £2,000 and Mr. Squibb £500, their shares of my husband's fine, but the other assignees will not follow their example. I beg you to recommend Parliament to repeal the Act, that after seventeen years' sorrow I may have a little rest and comfort among my fatherless children." Mr. Prideaux upon this advised the Council that they might lawfully discharge her of the fine due to the State, but that Parliament alone could compel the

---

[1] *Mercurius Politicus*, No. 379.

[2] State Papers, Vol. CC., p. 53. The £7,000 was thus allotted : The State, £3,000 ; Sir Arthur Hazelrig, £2,000 ; Winslow, Russell, Squib and Mullens, £500 each.

unwilling assignees to release their several claims of £500. A warrant was, however, issued at a later date, confirming her pension of 40s. per week out of public revenue, and ordering her a present payment of £100 in cash.[1]

II.—*The Trial of Christopher Love for Participation in the Presbyterian Plot.*

THE Reverend Christopher Love, a Presbyterian divine, and minister of St. Lawrence, Old Jewry, was brought to trial on Friday, 7th May, 1651, as the scapegoat of what was called the Presbyterian Plot. This was started shortly after the King's death in 1649, the intention being to bring in Charles II. by means of the Scots and their army. Its existence became immediately known to the Council of State, who, finding that its ramifications were by no means considerable, and that the persons implicated were well-known Royalists mostly abroad, allowed their intrigues to continue, with the view of ascertaining how far the reactionary sentiment actually extended, and to what extent the Presbyterians as a party were implicated in it. It thus went on, the minutes of every meeting of the conspirators and copies of all their correspondence being faithfully and duly transmitted to the Council of State, till a vessel carrying despatches, which was seized by the Army in the harbour of Ayr, showed that the conspirators were attempting fresh combinations. Then it was that the net in which they had for two years been enveloped was suddenly drawn in, and some score of persons were arrested. They were all examined, as was the custom of the period,[2] by the Attorney-General, and in the result all those that were in this country, except Christopher Love and one Gibbons, a tailor, received the mercy of the Government, and such ˉof

---

[1] Warrants, 20th March, 1659-60.
[2] " As I am in duty bound to do by my place." Speech of Attorney-General, State Trials, Vol. V., p. 87.

them as were required gave evidence, not without reluctance, against the rest. That the Presbyterians as a party were engaged in this plot is not supported by any evidence, although there is no doubt that a great number of them were averse to the execution of the King, believing that a satisfactory result could have been attained by some means short of his actual death. And the Attorney-General, in the course of the trial, on more than one occasion relieved the Presbyterians as a party of any such suspicion, putting the blame upon those who chose vaingloriously to assume to themselves the title of leaders of that party. Love, who would probably by a timely submission have been spared equally with the others, was a man of violent and ungovernable nature, and probably as much averse to all governments as was his fellow-prisoner, Lilburn. During the Civil War he had shown the most savage animosity toward the King and his party, and he was credited, not without reason, with causing, by his unauthorised intervention, the failure of the negotiations at Uxbridge, where the Commissioners on both sides met to endeavour to arrange a peace and a *modus vivendi.* On this occasion he used the pulpit of Uxbridge to denounce the Commissioners with his utmost vigour, declaring among other sentiments that a truce between Heaven and Hell would be a more holy and possible combination than a peace between the King and the Parliament. Immediately after the King's death, as will be seen, he turned against the Commonwealth and allied himself with the party of whom, up to that period, he had been the deadliest enemy. He was brought to trial on Friday, 7th May, 1651, for high treason in conspiring with William Drake, late of London, mercer; Henry Jermin, late of London, Esquire; Henry Piercy, late of London, Esquire; John Gibbon, late of London, gentleman; Edward Maney, late of London, Esquire; Richard Graves, late of London, Esquire; Silas Titus, late of London, gentleman; James Bunce, late of London, Alder-

man, and others, to subvert the existing Government and
with the assistance of the Scotch to put King Charles II.
on the Throne. Following the precedent of the Duke of
Hamilton, Lord Capel, and others, Love was tried by the
High Court of Justice, composed of some thirty-five
members, presided over by Serjeant Keble, one of the Lords
of the Great Seal. Mr. Prideaux, Attorney-General, had
charge of the prosecution, but the case was opened
and was conducted by the Solicitor-General, Mr. Reynolds,
with the assistance of Mr. Hall,[1] Attorney-General of the
Duchy of Lancaster, the " mumbling Mr. Hall " of Lilburn's
case, and of Sir Thomas Widdrington, junior counsel for the
Commonwealth, who afterwards occupied the position of
Lord Chief Baron of the Exchequer. Love being called to
the Bar, followed the example of Lilburn, with whom he
had chummed in prison, and by whom he had been
instructed in his defence, and occupied the Court for some
hours before he would plead, but, ultimately, on the
President directing the clerk to read the judgment in
default, he interjected a plea of not guilty. This
having been done, evidence was given, chiefly by his
confederates, of the details of the plot. The meetings of
the conspirators, including presumably certain emissaries
of the Government, took place at Love's house, letters were
read from the Prince and his agents, and all the incidents
of a treasonable but hopeless plot were regularly enacted.
Subscription lists were also discussed, formulated and put
forth, but the conspirators, who were willing to risk their
lives, were either unable or unwilling to risk their
money, as, according to the statements of the witnesses,
none of the party in London contributed a penny towards
the funds. Love cross-examined one or two of the witnesses to show that they were unworthy of credit, and
others to show that they were *particeps criminis*, but the

---

[1] Bartholomew Hall, Esq., appointed Chancellor of the Duchy in
July, 1649.

U

case was established beyond the possibility of a doubt. Notwithstanding this, Love spoke at great length on his own behalf. He was then answered by all the counsel for the Commonwealth, including the Attorney-General, and the President was about to give judgment, when Love produced an opinion of counsel signed by Mr. Mathew Hale, Mr. Archer and Mr. Waller, that there was matter of law proper to be argued as against both the charge and the evidence in support of it. One of the features of the trial had been the patience of Serjeant Keble, the President. The prisoner had occupied Friday, the 7th May, in his exceptions to pleading at all. After the evidence for the Commonwealth was concluded, he had been allowed four days to prepare his defence, with full liberty for counsel to attend him in prison, though not to address the Court on his behalf, and he had spoken fully and at great length on every aspect of the case, and yet when, as the Court was about to pronounce judgment, he produced his bill of exceptions, the President, overruling the technical objections of the prosecution and disregarding the threats of the Attorney-General that if so gross a departure from precedent were allowed he should cease to conduct Government prosecutions, declared that if they could be shown to be wrong in law, at whatever time it might be, the prisoner should have the benefit of it,[1] appointed the following Tuesday, 27th June, for the argument of questions of law, and assigned to Mr. Love as his counsel, and at his request, Mr. Maynard, Mr. Hale, Mr. Waller, and Mr. Archer. On Tuesday, 1st July, the counsel for the prisoner accordingly appeared, and were called to the Bar ; but Mr. Archer and Mr. Waller, not having signed the engagement to be faithful to the existing Government without a King or a House of Lords, were disqualified, and Mr. Hale, as the next in seniority, was

---

[1] Walker's impartiality may be gauged from the fact that he hereupon, in his History of Independency, describes President Keble as a "bloodthirsty old cur."

then called in. Being addressed by the Lord President
Keble, who said he had no reason to doubt him, but
thought it necessary to explain why his learned brethren
had been disqualified, " I have done it," said Mr. Hale,
and indeed he had already swallowed the engagement
and every oath that was necessary to qualify him for
the successful practice of his profession. He argued the
exceptions, most of which were found untenable through
his having been furnished with an incorrect copy of
the charge, the law of that period for some not very
intelligible reason refusing to a prisoner a copy of the
indictment on charges of high treason. He then took the
objection that the law, which requires two witnesses in
cases of treason, requires two witnesses to each overt act,
and that there were not in this case two witnesses to any
one act of treason. This was combated by Sir Thomas
Widdrington, who, while admitting that the Act of Philip
and Mary does not repeal the statute of Richard, and that
there were not two witnesses to any one act, contended
that the law was sufficiently complied with if there were
two witnesses, one to one overt act and one to another
overt act, provided that both acts were of the same species
of treason. This was held by the President to be good
law, and it was afterwards so decided and laid down as
Crown law by Sir Michael Foster,[1] and as such is, I
presume, the law of treason of the present day. It is
somewhat interesting to observe during this argument the
courtesy shown even at this period to Mr. Hale, both by
the judges and the Attorney-General, a courtesy which it
is only fair to say was certainly reciprocated by Mr. Hale.
After hearing the arguments on questions of law the
Court adjourned to the 5th July, when Mr. Love was
found guilty, and ordered for execution on the 15th.
Petitions immediately went up on his behalf. He was
popular, a good deal after the manner in which Lilburn was

---

[1] Foster's Crown Law, ch. iii., s. 8.

popular, and one divine, the Reverend Mr. Jackson, who was one of the confederates, and as such summoned as a witness, positively refused to give evidence, and was fined £500, and sentenced to a limited term of imprisonment. One petition, and that the most important, was signed by some hundreds of people, and included the names of many ministers of the City of London. They referred in piteous tones to his wife, now about to become a mother, and prayed in aid the history of Abiathar, the High Priest, who, having borne the ark before King David, and suffered with him in his trials and his afflictions, was afterwards engaged in treasonable practices against Solomon, his successor. "Get thee to Anathoth unto thine own fields," said Solomon, "for thou art worthy of death, but I will not at this time put thee to death."[1]

In the meantime preparations were being made on Tower Hill. An immense concourse of people had assembled to see the spectacle, and as much as 12d. and 2s. were paid for seats.[2] The scaffold was erected, and the prisoner was on the point of starting on his melancholy journey from the Tower, when his brother, having obtained from Parliament a temporary respite by means of the ministers' petition, arrived on Tower Hill, having come direct from Westminster in a boat with four oars, and conveyed the news to the assembled multitude. The prisoner was respited to the 15th August, when it was hoped that his domestic and political troubles might come to an end. Further details as to this case are wrapped in some mystery. Parliament was at first unable to resist the analogy of Solomon and Abiathar, and was probably willing to avoid the shedding of blood. Communications were made to Cromwell, and, according to a passage in the account of the trial, published by Mr. Farthing, the notary,[3] he replied to the Council of

---

[1] I. Kings, ii., 26.
[2] *Mercurius Politicus.*
[3] State Trials, Vol. V., pp. 44, 251.

State "that he was willing the sentence of death should be remitted." According to the same authority, however, Cromwell's letter was intercepted by certain Cavaliers, who, hating Love for the part he had played during the treaty at Uxbridge, and for his persistent hostility to the King, withheld the despatch until the execution had taken place. Whitelock, under date of the 8th August, 1651, says that a petition having gone to the General and the Army on behalf of Mr. Love, the General and the Army would not meddle therewith.[1] Walker, on the other hand, says[2] that both Love and Gibbons were executed at the express suit of Cromwell, who refused to march to Scotland till they were dead. The truth of these various stories is now beyond discovery. We do know, however, that deputations of the army, who were then occupied with the Scotch invasion, and were about to fight the last battle of the Commonwealth, expressed the opinion[3] that after the execution of the Duke of Hamilton and others, the escape of Love, who was at least as blame-worthy as they, would be a public scandal. He was beheaded on Tower Hill, on the 22nd August, the fatal day on which Charles II. erected his standard at Worcester, and on which his father had erected his standard at Nottingham, and he died with many words of self justification, and many prayers for the city and the people. Faithful to the traditions of the party, that punishments should be for an example, and that the death of chief offenders should exonerate their companions, all the other persons engaged [in this conspiracy were pardoned, and did not appear again on the political scene during the life of the Protector.

---

[1] Whitelock, Vol. III., p. 326.
[2] History of Independency, Part IV., p. 17.
[3] *Proceedings in Parliament.*

III.—*The Trial of Major Falconer for Perjury.*

On Friday, 20th May, 1653, one Major Richard Falconer, who had been employed as a spy in Holland in 1650-51, was tried for perjury before Lord Chief Justice Rolle and other Judges of the Upper Bench.[1] This man, who was described as of Westbury, in the County of Southampton, gentleman, and was said to have belonged to a decent family and to have been educated at Oxford, had appeared before the Committee for compounding with delinquents and sworn a detailed and circumstantial statement with the intent to obtain a share of Lord Craven's estate. The substance of his sworn information was that he had seen his Lordship in company with Prince Charles at Breda, that he had overheard their conversation, that Lord Craven had promoted a petition in which the Parliament was described as being composed of barbarous and inhuman rebels, and that arrangements had been made with divers officers of the Parliamentary party of a distinctly treasonable character. Against this it was alleged that at the date assigned by Falconer for this interview, Lord Craven had been to Falconer's knowledge eight hundred miles from England and from Breda, and that he had taken no part whatever in any such proceedings, if in fact they ever occurred. This being brought before Parliament, and it further appearing that Lord Craven's estate had been sequestered and sold by order of the Committee, upon the faith of these statements, it was resolved, after much debate, that Major Falconer be prosecuted in the Upper Bench, and a trial at Bar was accordingly ordered by the Lord Chief Justice.

The indictment was in the first instance found by the Grand Jury of the City of London and removed by

---

[1] State Trials, Vol. V., p. 323.

certiorari into the Upper Bench at Guildhall, but upon the
trial being called on it appeared that the information was
actually filed at Whitehall, and accordingly the Attorney-
General stopped the trial, preferred another indictment
before the Grand Jury at Westminster and had the trial at
Westminster Hall in Hilary Term. The examination of
witnesses lasted from nine in the morning till two in the
afternoon, and they proved that the petition had been con-
cocted by Sindercombe, in whose handwriting it was, and
other officers, in order to get money from the Cavaliers to
pay the score that they had run up for their lodging and
entertainment at Breda.

The trial is remarkable, apart from its historical interest,
for the fact, not generally known, that Mr. Hale (the
future Royalist Chief Justice) was, with Serjeant
Maynard, leading counsel for the Commonwealth, and
prosecuted the defendant in the name of the keepers
of the liberties of England. Falconer's counsel were
Mr. Windham (afterwards Judge of the Common Pleas),
Mr. Latch, Mr. Lechmore and Mr. Haggar. All these
counsel made speeches, and all the judges summed up in
order, as was said, to assist the jury to a right conclusion.
Between the addresses of all these counsel and of the
three judges the jury might have been fairly puzzled, but
for one class of evidence admitted without objection from
any of the judges or of the counsel. It appears to have
been held relevant to the inquiry that the jury should try
the question of the prisoner's character, and for that
purpose that they might receive evidence of his bad
character in other respects. For this purpose witnesses
were called in chief, who proved that on a certain occasion
at Petersfield, in Hants, Falconer went on his knees and
drank a health to the Devil in the open street; that he
commonly used profane language and cursed and swore;
that on one occasion he had obtained £10 from a citizen
by fraudulent personation; that in May, 1648, he was

committed to Aylesbury Gaol by certain Justices of the Peace for the County of Bucks on a suspicion of robbery and murder, and that warrants had been issued for his apprehension as a notorious highwayman. This evidence was only attempted to be met by general evidence of good character. It was admitted that Falconer's charges against Lord Craven were untrue, and the only question was whether they were untrue to his knowledge. The jury, under these circumstances, very naturally convicted the prisoner of corrupt, wilful, false, and malicious perjury. The order of procedure was also remarkable as having been in exact accordance with the present procedure, legalised for the first time in modern days by Denman's Act of 1865.[1] The counsel for the Commonwealth opened the case and called their witnesses; then the counsel for the defendant opened their case and called their witnesses, and then summed up their case, after which counsel for the prosecution replied, and the judges summed up. A long account of this trial, in greater detail than in the State Trials, is to be found in the *Perfect Diurnal* for 23rd May, 1653, but I cannot find in the report any mention of the sentence.

IV.—*The Trial of Don Pantaleone Sa for the Murder of Mr. Greenway.*

DURING the years 1651 and 1652 the Commonwealth had suffered great trouble from the Portuguese, who, while outwardly friendly, were secretly assisting the Prince. They allowed Prince Rupert's ships to shelter in their ports, and at the same time obstructed Blake in his pursuit. The latter accordingly, by way of retaliation, seized various Portuguese merchantmen, and thus brought the relations between England and Portugal to a great strain. The Portuguese, however, like the French and the Dutch, were by no means for coming to open hostilities with Cromwell,

---

[1] 28 Vic. c. 18.

and with a view to an arrangement sent the Conde de Canteneiro as Ambassador in their behalf. He arrived in great state in September, 1652, presented his credentials to Parliament, and was received with the dignity and splendour which, with the Commonwealth, was a point of honour. He took up his abode in London, where he lived in grand style, and incurred liabilities which got him a great reputation at the time, but which, as it afterwards appeared, he was not able to meet. Meanwhile the negotiations for a treaty proceeded as slowly as one of the French King's sieges, and not at all according to the views of either Cromwell or his Council of State. During their progress, however, an event happened which gave rise to the exposition of an enormous mass of learning on the privilege of Ambassadors, and which indirectly brought the treaty to a summary conclusion. Among the numerous suite of the Portuguese Ambassador was his brother Don Pantaleone Sa, a Knight of Malta, and a person of considerable distinction. He lived in the house of the Ambassador, who was attended on State occasions by a large retinue of armed attendants, black and white. On the 21st November, 1653, while the treaty was still under discussion, and the Londoners were becoming daily more incensed against the Portuguese, Don Pantaleone, swaggering with his personal attendants in the New Exchange in the afternoon, let fall some expressions in French derogatory to the English and their political schemes. These were overheard by John, a younger brother of Sir Gilbert Gerard, who, though hating Cromwell personally, was, like most Englishmen of the day, ready to take up his quarrel against any foreign interference. He disputed in French with Don Pantaleone, who immediately gave him the lie. Violent words followed, swords were drawn, and blood flowed, the Portuguese, in the first instance, being in greater numbers, getting the better of it, but ultimately being driven off by the citizens, who quickly assembled in support of their fellow-countrymen. The dispute might well have ended there, but Don Pantaleone, considering he had been insulted by Mr. Gerard, and smarting under the indignity put upon him and his retinue by the citizens, returned to the New Exchange the next day with a large following of Portuguese and others, of whom the black men appear to have given great offence to the populace. They were followed by coaches containing guns, powder and hand grenades, indicating a deliberate intention to do serious mischief. Don Pantaleone and his soldiers soon cleared the Exchange of all peaceable citizens, who, after their kind, went straight home and put up their shutters. They then commenced a search for Mr. Gerard, who, not knowing of their intended visit, had not gone to the Exchange ; and, in the course of the afternoon, Don Pantaleone meeting Mr. Harcourt Greenway, a student of Gray's Inn, walking peaceably and lovingly with his sister on one arm and his sweetheart on the other, mistaking him, as is supposed, for Mr. Gerard, shot him dead on the spot. The noise of firearms rapidly brought crowds to the Exchange, who, on learning that the Portuguese had killed a citizen while walking with his intended wife, immediately attacked the Portuguese party, and even before a troop of horse appeared on the scene had secured many of their enemies. The rest, including Don Pantaleone, followed by the mob, fled to the house of the Ambassador, who barricaded his doors and windows, and threatened to fire on the people if any attempt were made on his house. The appearance of Commissary-General Whalley, a well-known Parliamentary officer, and the Life Guards, appeased the people, who knew that in the hands of the Lord General, as Cromwell was then termed, and his officers, the honour of England was safe. The Colonel demanded of the Ambassador the immediate surrender of all persons concerned in the affray. To this he received the reply that the Ambassador represented his Sovereign, and that in his house all his retinue were sacred from arrest; to which the Colonel bluntly answered that the Ambassador's house contained persons who had murdered an Englishman, and unless they were immediately handed over he would at once bombard the house and carry them off by force. As the Colonel was known to be a man of resolution and obviously in a condition to carry out his threat, a short respite was obtained by the Ambassador till the Lord General himself could be communicated with and his directions received. The latter's reply was stiff and uncompromising. An Englishman, he said, had been killed by the Portuguese. It was thus a matter of public concern to be dealt with by Parliament or by the tribunals of the country, and he advised that Don Pantaleone and all concerned should be given up, adding as a hint (the effect of which coming under similar circumstances from the General had never been known to fail) that if he withdrew his soldiers the temper of the citizens of London was such that they would probably pull down the house and execute justice for themselves.

Don Pantaleone and his fellows were accordingly given up to the troops and taken to St. James's, whence, after being examined by the Lord Chief Justice, they were committed to Newgate on charges of riot and murder, and the coroner and his jury having sat upon the body of Mr. Greenway, the Portuguese were also sent for trial for murder by that tribunal. In due course the depositions were sent before the grand jury, who found a true bill against *Pantaleo De Samensius*, Esquire; *Alvaro Concalves, Pedro Coellio*, gentleman, and *Sebastian Lyte*, gentleman, the first-named for murdering Harcourt Greenway, gentleman, by shooting him in the head, and the others for being present at and aiding and encouraging the said murder.[1]

Having these men in custody awaiting their trial, the

---

[1] Middlesex Records, Vol. III., p. 219.

Council were met with a serious question of law, as Don Pantaleone claimed for himself the privileges of an Ambassador, alleging that he held a Commission from the King of Portugal to discharge the functions of an Ambassador during any temporary absence of his brother, and that he was thus in person an Ambassador from his Sovereign, though with only a contingent right to represent him. And it was contended by him and by the Ambassador, that whatever might be the jurisdiction of the English Courts over the servants of an Ambassador, the Ambassador himself, if in fact guilty of crime, could only be expelled from the country with a view to his being afterwards dealt with as his own Sovereign should determine in accordance with international duties and rights, and the foreign Ambassadors with one accord supported the contention of the Portuguese. But Cromwell, who was always for dealing sternly with principals and shewing mercy to all minor offenders, was determined that Don Pantaleone, as the originator and instigator of the fatal riot, should be brought to trial and punished if the laws of England would so permit. No case precisely in point could be quoted as a precedent, for where questions had previously arisen as to Ambassadors' privileges they had usually been arranged by international courtesy. The case of a foreign Ambassador committing a capital felony was unknown to the lawyers, who, however, were mostly against the privilege, and it was used as an argument amongst others against the Portuguese claim that even under the Levitical dispensation there was no sanctuary for wilful murder.[1] There being, however, some difference of opinion on this question, Chief Justice Rolle and Justices Jermyn and Nicholas holding, in accordance with Lord Coke,[2] that

---

[1] Numerous cases of Ambassadors are referred to in the State Trials, Vol. V.

[2] Coke, 4th Institute, State Trials, Vol. V., p. 503.

if a foreign Ambassador commits any crime such as treason or felony, contrary to the law of nations, he loses his privilege as an Ambassador and may be tried as any other private alien, but that he is not bound by any municipal law or Act of Parliament or custom of the country as to matters not contrary to the law of nations, and some of the civilians being of opinion that the privilege of an Ambassador was absolute and that he was only triable even for murder by the consent of his Sovereign, it was decided to send the chief prisoner for trial before the Lord Chief Justice Rolle in the Upper Bench, associating with him Justice Atkins, of the Common Pleas, Serjeant Steel, formerly Attorney-General to the Commonwealth and now Recorder of London, Dr. Zouch, a learned civilian, brought from Oxford, for the purpose of this trial, Dr. Clark and Dr. Turner, also civilians, Sir Henry Blunt,[1] a great traveller and man of letters, Mr. Lacy and Alderman Tichbourne, whose name turns up on every page of contemporary history. There was thus an even number of common lawyers and of civilians, together with three gentlemen not committed to either view. In the meantime an incident occurred which enabled the Council to put themselves right with regard to one phase of the question, for George Villa, servant to the Portuguese Ambassador, having been arrested for debt and required to give bail for his release, an order was, on the application of the Ambassador, issued by the Council of State on the 2nd December, 1653,[2] to discharge his servant from arrest and his bond from security, the Council finding him to have been arrested in wrong of the privilege of the Ambassador, and requiring all sheriffs and officers to take notice thereof at their peril. They thus gave practical proof that, however they might insist on trying a privileged

---

[1] Knight and Baronet of Blount's Hall, Staffordshire, and Tittenhanger, Hertfordshire. He was one of the Commissioners for reforming the Criminal Law. Evelyn's Diary, Vol. I., pp. 332 and 414.

[2] State Papers, Vol. XLII.

person for a crime committed against the law of nations,
they recognised on the part of the Ambassador's
servants an immunity from arrest on civil process. On
the 13th December, Don Pantaleone made an unsuccessful
attempt to escape.[1] He got out of Newgate, but was re-
taken, and was thereafter put under more rigorous confinement. But his trial, which was then imminent, was, at
the request of the Portuguese merchants in London, postponed till the following month of June.[2]

Misfortune had meanwhile overtaken the other, but less
guilty, participator in the original riot, John Gerard.
He had been discovered to have been, together with
one Peter Vowel, a schoolmaster of Islington, Somerset
Fox, and some others, engaged in a plot to subvert
the Government and restore the King, and for that purpose
to assassinate Cromwell on his way home from Hampton
Court, to seize the City and the Tower, and to shoot the
Council of State and any other opponents. Their plans,
like those of all the conspirators during the Commonwealth,
became speedily known to the Council of State. Cromwell
changed his route from land to water, and before night
Gerard, Vowel, and Fox, together with some forty-four
other persons, were taken into custody and put under
examination in this same fatal month of June. A High
Court of Justice, under the presidency of Lord Commissioner Lisle, was appointed for the trial of Gerard, with
Vowel and Fox, the two latter being charged with undertaking themselves to deal the fatal blow to the Protector.
Arrangements were also made by which the two trials
could proceed in Westminster Hall at the same time,[3]
the High Court sitting in the Court of Chancery to try
Gerard and the others, and the Chief Justice sitting in his
own Court of the Upper Bench, which immediately adjoined

---

[1] Whitelock, Vol. IV., p. 54.

[2] Whitelock, Vol. IV., p. 79.

[3] *Mercurius Politicus*, May and June, 1654.

the Chancery, to try the case of Don Pantaleone Sa.[1] It was thought to shift Justice Atkins, who had considerable reputation as a lawyer, from the Upper Bench, where he was to sit with the Chief Justice for the trial of Don Pantaleone, to the High Court; but, much to his credit, he declined to try Gerard and the others, declaring his opinion that they had a right to be tried by a jury,[2] and equally to the credit of Cromwell such conscientious resolution did not affect the judge's position. And, indeed, the judge to some extent had his own way, for being called in to advise as to the trial of the prisoners in the west and the north in the spring of 1655, these prisoners, together with Sindercombe, in 1657, were all tried by a jury. On Wednesday, the 5th July, each trial commenced and each was finished on the following day. Gerard and Vowel were convicted and sentenced to death. Somerset Fox, in consideration of his pleading guilty and protesting his repentance, was pardoned.

Don Pantaleone, according to the papers,[3] came very unwillingly to the Bar of the Upper Bench, and when he was there they had much ado to persuade him to be uncovered. They desired him to be civil and they would be civil to him and use him as a gentleman of his quality. At last he put

---

[1] State Papers, Domestic, 15th and 19th June, 1654.

[2] Mr. Justice Atkins gave for his reason to the Lord Commissioner Widdrington (who was nominated to administer the oath to all the Commissioners) why he could not take the oath, that "I have already taken several oaths as a serjeant and as a judge to do nothing contrary to the laws of England: the oath that we are to take by this ordinance seems to be contrary to the other oaths I have taken: by the law no man indicted for treason but ought to be tried by a jury: by this ordinance it is otherwise; and therefore this oath seeming contrary to the other oaths I have taken, I desire they may be given in as my reason why I desire to be excused." The other judges, Nicholas, Aske, and the Recorder of London took the oath. Lord Commissioner Lisle's report to the Council of State of the trial of Vowel, Gerard, and Fox. June, 1654. State Papers, Vol. LXXII.

[3] *Proceedings of Affairs* No. 249.

off his hat, and the Court then caused a chair to be brought for him, in which he sate. Being called upon, he refused to hold up his hand, "which they had a little held up for him." The indictment being read and translated to him, he made a resolute fight for his life. He began with the usual demand for counsel, but without avail, as according to the law as it then stood no such request could be complied with except on questions of law. He then asserted his privilege as Ambassador, but the Lord Chief Justice requiring to see his credentials, they appeared to consist only of letters from the King of Portugal, intimating that in the event of the present Ambassador being recalled, Don Pantaleone might be appointed to act in his place. There was no appointment whatever, and hardly even a promise of a contingent appointment. The Court accordingly decided that there were no facts to raise any question of law, and that the Don must be tried as any other alien. He then refused to plead at all, and not until after it was more than once explained to him that in default of plea the Court would be bound in law to sentence him to *peine forte et dure* did he consent to plead not guilty to the charge. An interpreter was then sworn on behalf of the Commonwealth, and one Mouriew Mews for the prisoner, and a jury *de medietate lingue*, composed one-half of Englishmen and one-half of foreigners, was impanelled to try the case. He again applied for counsel, when the Lord Chief Justice, in refusing his request, put for the first time before the country the true relation of a judge to the two parties in a criminal prosecution. "We," said the Chief Justice, "are of counsel equal to you as to the Commonwealth"[1]—a much more accurate and just position than that usually assumed when it is said that in a criminal matter the judge should be counsel for the prisoner. A judge has no more right to be counsel for the prisoner than for the prosecutor. His duty is limited to

---

[1] Whitelock, Vol. IV., p. 115.

seeing that the proceedings are regular, and if the prisoner is undefended that he does not suffer in law from the want of counsel to protect him from inadmissible evidence or faulty procedure. Don Pantaleone was found guilty by the jury and sentenced to be hanged, but he obtained a short reprieve till the 10th of July, and the sentence was altered to beheading at the entreaty of the Ambassador, who declared he would rather kill his brother with his own sword than see him suffer so ignominious a death as that of hanging.[1]

Don Pantaleone was not, however, without personal friends among the fair sex, two of whom made a determined attempt to effect his release the very night before his execution. On this Sunday night he was visited, according to the lax regulations of the prison, by a Mrs. Gourdon or Mohun and her maid. The latter, under her woman's clothes, had on a foot-boy's suit, and the two women being left alone for some time with Don Pantaleone, the maid slipped off her woman's clothes, in which they dressed up the Don. Downstairs he came with Mrs. Mohun, and would have got out of Newgate as he did on his first attempt, but the keeper, "narrowly prying under the maid's hood," recognised the features of the prisoner, and so discovered the whole business. The Don was reconducted to his apartment, and Mrs. Mohun and the maid in the boy's suit were locked up to await the further orders of the Council of State.[2]

Monday, the 10th July, was celebrated in the annals of the Commonwealth. The intervention of the Ambassadors, not only of Portugal but of the other Powers, had been unavailing to save the life of Don Pantaleone. At eight o'clock in the morning the Portuguese Ambassador, on behalf of his Sovereign, signed the treaty demanded by England, conceded all her claims, and then, unwilling to be

---

[1] *Perfect Diurnal*, 9th July, 1654.
[2] *Perfect Diurnal*, 17th July, 1654.

V

in London at the hour of his brother's death, set out at ten o'clock in his coach for Gravesend on the way to his native land.[1] He owed, however, many thousands of pounds in London, for which his goods had been attacked and his servants threatened with imprisonment, and he himself was followed on his journey by clamorous creditors seeking satisfaction for their debts. For these claims certain London merchants went bail, but finding after a time that he had no means to meet his liabilities, they had him arrested in the month of August to prevent his leaving the country. "Thus," says the paper, "nothing but ready money can get him out of England."[2] The Council of State, however, had when they first heard of these proceedings, instructed their officers to enquire into the facts and " endeavour such conclusions, as that the Ambassador may have no dishonour or breach of privilege, and that the creditors be not prejudiced."[3] Under these instructions he was ultimately got out of the country, but whether through the intervention of England or that of Portugal, I am unable to say.

At Tower Hill at four o'clock on the afternoon of the 10th July, both Gerard and Don Pantaleone were beheaded. Gerard, a young enthusiastic Cavalier, only just of age, was much lamented by the people, who wept as he laid his head upon the block. But when Don Pantaleone fell beneath the stroke of the headsman " they gave a great and general shout as applauding the justice of the Portugal's death." That shout settled Cromwell on his throne. Down to the very falling of the axe, those who knew Cromwell but little doubted his stiffness in this matter. The Portuguese and their friends had calculated and boasted that an Ambassador's brother could never be killed for the death of " a mechanic," and even the friends of the Lord

---

[1] *Perfect Diurnal*, 17th July, 1654.
[2] *Perfect Diurnal*, 7th August, 1654. Whitelock, Vol. IV., p. 128.
[3] State Papers, 12th July, 1654.

General appear to have thought that by some means the prisoner would have secured his escape. But when the axe at last had fallen and the citizens realised the fact that not only was their trade protected and their name feared abroad, but that in their own homes and in their own city an even-handed and fearless justice was dealt out in a fashion not known since the days of the great Queen, they gave in an allegiance to Cromwell that no slanders ever shook, that survived even his death, and secured the unanimous acceptance of his well-meaning but incompetent successor. He had shown his invincible prowess in the battlefields of England, Scotland, and Ireland. He had raised the position of England to its former height of power among the nations of the world. He had set on foot and was urging on schemes and reforms in the interest of the poor, the helpless, and the oppressed, and now he had vindicated the honour of England and avenged the blood of an English citizen by seizing the malefactor in the house of a foreign Prince, and dragging him like another Joab even from the horns of the altar. One must almost have lived in the London of 1654 to appreciate the effect of this trial, so great and widespread does it appear to have been ; and yet it decided no contested point of the law of nations, it disposed of no great question of English jurisprudence. There were no special incidents of the trial, and the crime itself was one of vulgar egotism and of stupid brutality. But the bearing of Cromwell and of the nation during that period, the unflinching pursuit of justice, even at the hazard of a war, were the admiration of all the kingdoms of Europe. Two centuries and more have passed away since this shout went up from English throats in approbation of Cromwell's work. And no one who has studied the changes of his country's life, and loves the great passages of its history, can fail to accord a meed of praise, in this respect at least, to the

great soldier and statesman who at that period held its
destinies in his hand.

The chief offender being punished, all the other Portuguese were pardoned; but the English boy, who accompanied Don Pantaleone and assisted at the fray, was made
a victim to the spirit of impartiality and hanged at Tyburn.
The two women who had plotted the escape were, according
to their sentence, brought near the New Exchange on the
last day of August to stand together for the space of an
hour on a little scaffold by the side of the pillory;[1] the
Council possibly coming to the conclusion that for a woman
to plot the escape of her lover was not, under any dispensation, a peculiarly heinous offence.

V.—*The Trial of Miles Sindercombe for an attempt to
assassinate the Protector.*

ON Monday, the 9th February, 1656-7, Miles Sindercombe, a cashiered trooper of General Monk's regiment,
formerly apprenticed to a surgeon in the parish of St.
Catherine's, London, was tried at the Bar of the Upper
Bench in Westminster Hall, before Lord Chief Justice
Glynn, Justice Warburton, and a special jury, for an
attempted assassination of the Protector.[2] The plot was
to shoot the Protector as he went to open Parliament in
September, 1656, and then to burn Whitehall, cause a
general rising, and bring back Charles II. Several fellows
of the same stamp as himself were joined with Sindercombe in the undertaking, and they were paid by the
Royalists abroad, through the medium of the Spanish
Embassy. They had filled their house with arms and
explosives, were well supplied with money, and had the
sanction of the Prince for their undertaking. Thurloe,
however, as usual, had full information of the plot, and on

---

[1] *Proceedings of State Affairs*, No. 258.
[2] State Trials, Vol. V., p. 842; *Mercurius Politicus*, Nos. 345, 347,
348, 349.

the day before their intended operations arrested the whole
party, with their money, guns, pistols, arms and explosives.
One Colonel Sexby, a former officer of the Commonwealth,
but afterwards an Anabaptist Cavalier, was subsequently ascertained to have been the manager of
the affair, and agent for the foreigners in this
country. Sindercombe made no defence, but "carried
himself insolently to the court," and being found guilty
by the jury of an attempt to murder the Protector,
was sentenced in the usual form. After his sentence he
tried to bribe his keepers with large sums, £200 and £700,
to connive at his escape, and this failing, he contrived to
kill himself after some fashion that no physician of the
time could explain. He was guarded by a captain, a
lieutenant, and a company of soldiers, in addition to the
warders of the Tower, all of whom were warned to take
special precautions against any attempts to escape or
obtain poison. According to the humane practice of those
days he was permitted, the night before his execution, to
receive the visits of his two sisters and his sweetheart, and
having been at his request left alone with them for a short
time, it is supposed that they gave him some mineral
poison, of which he availed himself to avoid his sentence.
Some hours after the women had left he was found by his
keepers breathing heavily, and shortly afterwards he died
in the presence of the surgeon, without recovering
consciousness. An inquest was immediately held, but
the doctors who examined the body not being able
to account for the death, it was adjourned, and
the assistance of Sir Richard Napier, M.D., and Dr.
Fern, Reader of Anatomy at Gresham College was called
in, together with that of three wardens of the College of
Surgeons. These all agreed that though the symptoms
somewhat resembled apoplexy, they did not consider that
he died of that disease, and they accordingly certified that
they believed he had committed suicide, though they could

not specify the means of his so doing. After this the coroner's jury were taken to the house of Lord Chief Justice Glynn, who as chief coroner of the kingdom, directed them "touching matters of form," in the result of which they found that Sindercombe had committed suicide by snuffing up into his head through his nose certain powdered poison. The Chief Justice and the jury may have been and perhaps were right in the detailed conclusion at which they arrived, but there is no record of any evidence to support such finding. A paper purporting to have been written by Sindercombe was found in his room two days after his death. In this he said, " I do take this course because I would not have all the open shame of the world executed upon my body, etc.," but it was stoutly alleged then and afterwards that the paper was forged, and the strict supervision and constant searches made of his person and of his cell to prevent any concealment of poison tend to negative the suggestion that the paper could have lain in his cell for two days without being discovered. Colonel Sexby's theory that he was smothered by the orders of Cromwell seems to me to be irrational. There was no question whatever of Sindercombe's guilt, no one could doubt the justice of the sentence, and there was hardly any conceivable object to be attained by Cromwell in killing a man over-night who was to be hanged early the next morning. His sisters and his sweetheart were examined, but their depositions threw no light upon the case except that according to their statements he repeatedly declared he would rather kill himself than undergo the disgrace of an execution. Having thus been found guilty of self-murder his body was dragged on a hurdle at a horse's tail and buried at the foot of the gallows erected for his execution. A stake was then driven through him, with the top end cased with iron standing out of the ground, as a warning to other malefactors.[1]

---

[1] *Mercurius Politicus*, No. 349.

Sindercombe's death, however, was followed by one of the most remarkable publications of the age, "Killing no Murder." It appeared from Thurloe's enquiries to have been printed in Holland and imported in great numbers by one Sturgeon, formerly a Life Guardsman but now a Leveller, who had a hand in Sindercombe's business and for a time fled to the Hague. Sturgeon, when arrested, had 300 copies of the pamphlet about him, 1,400 more were seized in St. Catherine's Dock, 300 were found in a haberdasher's in Smithfield, and 140 copies in the Minories.[1] It was logically, vigorously and eloquently written, being the work, as was afterwards discovered, of Colonel Sexby, who confessed to its authorship, but professed to have altered his views when the Protector as such was adopted by Parliament.[2] It was a clear and direct incitement to the murder of Cromwell, and it contained unequivocal suggestions that for some inexplicable reason Sindercombe had been privately slain. "Let him take away the stake from Sindercombe's grave, and let him send thither the pillows and the feather-beds with which Barkstead and his hangman smothered him. But let not this monster think himself the more secure that he hath suppressed our great spirit; he may be confident that *longus post illum sequitur ordo idem petentium decus.* There is a great roll behind even of those that are in his own muster-rolls and are ambitious of the name of deliverers of their country, and they know what the action is that shall purchase it. His bed, his table is not secure, and he stands in need of other guards to defend him against his own. Death and destruction pursue him wherever he goes : they follow him everywhere like his fellow-travellers, and at last they will come upon him like armed men." Language such as this, printed and circulated with impunity through the

<hr />

[1] Thurloe, Vol. VI., pp. 311-15, 16-17.
[2] Thurloe, Vol. VI., p. 560. After Sexby's death the authorship of the pamphlet was claimed by Captain Titus.

kingdom, the author unknown, the distributors undetected, the printers and publishers concealed from the vigilant eyes of his detectives, caused Cromwell, as we are told, many an hour of unspeakable trouble, and the doubts it must have raised in his mind of his own popularity, not only with the people but also with his beloved soldiers, may well have saddened his later days. His own somewhat sudden death in the following year showed that his hold upon the country and the Army was as great as ever, and that the unanimous congratulations he had received from Parliament on the occasion of his escape were not a mere matter of form.[1] To a man of his power and judgment, however, it must by that time have become apparent that from whatever causes it may have arisen, the benefits which he had hoped to confer upon his country had not been achieved, and that its future was one which could not be contemplated without anxiety.

It is difficult to say what suggestions may not be made to the discredit of Cromwell by persons who take persistently adverse views of his motives and his actions ; and in regard to these various Royalist plots, with their uniformly feeble conception and melancholy results, it was hinted at the time by the Venetian Sagredo, an Ambassador not too friendly to the Protector, that they were promoted by Cromwell for the purpose of attracting sympathy to himself and discredit to the Cavaliers, a suggestion which derived some colour from their universal failure and want of support from the masses of the nation. Charles was himself also so far implicated in most of these attempts that without taking any active part in them, a position which as he expressed it would discredit him in the eyes of the Sovereigns of Europe, he knew of their institution and prosecution, and would gladly have taken advantage of their success as doing his business more effectually than any general rising, against which he warned his followers

---

[1] Carlyle, Speech VI.

as premature and impracticable during the life of the Protector. It was therefore an obvious act of policy, which was adopted after the Restoration, to clear the Prince from the discredit of any such complicity by minimising the position and suggesting that the plots were in fact the device of his enemies to injure his friends. The cry, however, "got up by the police," has never been a successful defence, either in politics or in law, and there were few people, I suspect, even during the fever of the Restoration, who accepted this violent theory except that class of persons who are at all times and in all ages ready to believe anything, however absurd, to the credit of their friends, and anything, however gross, to the discredit of their opponents. To enunciate the proposition that Cromwell instigated plots against his own life is almost to refute it; but the sanction which it has recently received from Mr. Reginald Palgrave,[1] whose position, official and literary, entitles his views to respectful consideration, renders it necessary that the topic should not be passed over in silence. The suggestion, as I understand it, is that the Protector, through Thurloe and others, procured certain discontented Cavaliers to get up plots against him and his government with a view to frighten the nation with the terrors of a third civil war and thus to concentrate all authority more completely in himself. I have carefully read Mr. Palgrave's interesting discussion on this subject, but I fail to find any evidence directly inculpating the Protector in these attempts. It is not suggested that any of these plots were unreal or that the intention of the conspirators was not to assassinate the Protector and restore the Stuart Dynasty, and the absence of any such suggestion is in itself strong evidence of the genuineness of the plots. With regard to the action of Thurloe and others, I find evidence of very

---

[1] Oliver Cromwell, The Protector, 1890.

continued and pronounced attempts to discover all the plotters before arresting any, so as to bring them all red-handed to justice, but of instigation or invention of any of these plots on the part of Thurloe or of the Protector I find no evidence whatever. That they both knew of these plots and allowed them to proceed, as described in the case of Love, until they could lay hands on all the parties implicated, is beyond a doubt ; that Thurloe had early information as to Sexby and Sindercombe also appears certain, and that he delayed taking action until he had a complete case against them is also clear. But Mr. Palgrave appears not to have sufficiently recognised the moral difference that exists between originating a plot for the purpose of murdering a man otherwise innocent of offence and taking measures, secret, inquisitorial, and long-delayed, in order to bring a malefactor and his accomplices securely to justice. The one is the act of an assassin, the other is the course of every-day police. That the danger of these plots was exaggerated by Thurloe and others in the supposed interest of the Protector is likely enough, but the argument that the Protector was a party to instigating plots against himself, apart from its apparent absurdity, is open to obvious and adverse criticism. It is alleged, and, as I believe, with truth, that the Protector was much alarmed lest some one or other of these attempts should succeed, and that he enlisted for his protection a large body of Life Guards picked from his favourite regiments, without whose escort he rarely went abroad, and who attended upon him at Whitehall. He also carried arms for his own protection, as was shown by the explosion of a pistol in his pocket when thrown from his coach in Hyde Park ; and, according to Clarendon,[1] he constantly shifted the hours of his excursions and the rooms in which he slept. That he should, under these circumstances, have invited

[1] Vol. IV., p. 646.

attempts upon his life seems hardly within the bounds of probability. But, in addition to this personal reason, there is a far more potent objection to be found in his political aspirations. I have shown how, from his elevation to his death, he endeavoured to gain the confidence and the affection of the multitude by his exertions in further-ance of trade, in relief of poverty, and in mitigation of punishments. The success of these attempts would have much depended upon his own personal popularity, on which, more than on repressive measures, he relied to secure the goodwill of the populace and to protect him-self against his enemies both at home and abroad. To these appeals a series of plots made public to the world would necessarily have been disastrous, as tending to dis-credit the very popularity he was then endeavouring to estab-lish. To charge the Protector under these circumstances with instigating plots to attempt his life and undermine his authority is to suggest that he loaded Sindercombe's pistols, and revised the proof-sheets of "Killing no Murder." I can-not but think that the universal failure of these plots, their lack of support in England, and the speedy conviction of the plotters alone led to the suggestion of the times, which the more it is investigated the more certainly it will be found to be based upon little more than the fertile imagina-tion and distorted reports of a foreign agent.

CHAPTER VII.

CROMWELL.

WHEN Cromwell dissolved the Parliament of 1657 he left the issue between them and himself to the arbitrament of the Highest Power: "God be judge between you and me." Men arguing from different premises have given their judgments, and have pronounced the Protector either a saint or a scoundrel according to their preconceived predilections. In the meantime the period indicated by Marchmont Needham,[1] "when (Envy being laid asleep by Time) Posterity would pay him more honour than his contemporaries could express" should have arrived, and we may, leaving the political and sectarian views of his character to be propounded by the politician or the religionist, consider whether in regard to the material and social interests of the people of this country he did his duty to the best of his ability as a ruler and a governor over them. Truth demands that this question should be answered in the affirmative. By his military prowess and his bold diplomacy he secured for England an unassailable position and a prospect of permanent peace. For the furtherance of trade and of commerce he pushed boldly forward on what was then conceived to be the true road to national prosperity and wealth. He secured the protection and the encouragement of native industries by subjecting competing shipments

---

[1] *Mercurius Politicus*, 9th September, 1658.

The latest instances of this divergent criticism are to be found in the rival biographies of Oliver Cromwell, by Frederick Harrison (1889), and Reginald Palgrave (1890).

of foreign goods to import duties fluctuating with
the rise and fall of prices in England, accompanied by a
strict enforcement of the legalised rates of wages and of
food, and by the discouragement of the middleman and
the usurer. He secured our trade abroad by asserting
and maintaining our supremacy at sea. He inaugurated a
scheme for equal and sound Parliamentary representation.
For the advancement of education he attracted to himself
and his Court persons of learning, of science, and of arts, and
he had under his consideration when he was called away a
scheme of general and gratuitous education. In the interests
of true religion at home he restored the Bible to its original
purity and put it within reach of all; and for the advancement of religion abroad he chartered, for the first time in
the history of England, a corporation with common seal
and perpetual succession to propagate the Gospel in New
England and other colonies of the empire by the spreading
of religious and secular education among the natives and
the settlers that occupied and surrounded our possessions.[1]

By the establishment of a General Post he promoted the
free circulation of information and intelligence, and thus, combined with his care for all country roads, he put every man
within reasonable limit of expense in communication with
his fellows in all parts of the United Kingdom. Our English
Justinian, King Edward I., spent thirty-five years over the
reform of our laws, while Cromwell during his short
tenure of office purified the administration of justice by
the appointment of learned, just, and independent judges,
and reformed the law itself by the introduction of numerous
amendments, which the judgment of posterity has indorsed
with approval and acceptance. He endeavoured to remove
the disabilities attaching to sincere but unpopular religious
conviction, and to inaugurate an era of religious toleration.
He struck off the fetters from many hundreds of

---

[1] The Enabling Act was passed 27th July, 1649.

helpless captives at home and abroad ; he wielded the sceptre of mercy whenever the supreme safety of the State would seem to have permitted its exercise, and he was personally blameless in his private life. Of how many monarchs or rulers can we say so much? And yet in immediate effect his administration was a failure. His early death occurring at the moment when the country was comparatively quiet, when "all things seemed to be going well with him," and when the beneficial effect of his many reforms would have just begun to bear fruit, was the one great cause. The misrepresentation and vilification of the Protector and all his works in which the Royalist presses were incessantly engaged during the whole period of his rule, was probably another. For although he had raised England to the pinnacle of power among nations, had constituted her the great champion of the Protestant World, and had rendered her shores impregnable by attack, it was only to bring her in the near future under the heel of a Sovereign of the hated faith, to have her arsenals captured by the foe, and her Ministers in the pay of foreign Kings. All benefit of the Protector's legislation was lost to the people through the jealousy and the incapacity of his successors, his very statutes were torn from the Journals of Parliament, and such only as it was impossible to ignore were, like the gold mace of the Commonwealth, adapted to the use of the Monarchy and credited to King Charles as acts of thoughtful and beneficent legislation. The carefully sown seeds of civil and religious liberty were uprooted and scattered to the winds, and every effort was made to treat the Commonwealth as if it had never been. But waters that gather on mountains and hill-tops spring again to the surface in distant valleys and plains, and good seed though scattered to the wind is likely in some time or place to find congenial soil, and in secluded and unlooked-for spots to germinate and flourish. And so these underlying principles of the Commonwealth—the Protestant Cause, the Command of the Seas, Freedom of Conscience, Popular Power, Equal Representation, Irremovability of Judges, Amendment of the Law, Moderation of Punishments—for a time lay dormant and apparently dead. But they had taken root in the hearts of many in the nation, and one by one, as years rolled on, they blossomed into fruit, until we now enjoy in their fulness the rights which the Commonwealth struggled to attain. Cromwell was often in the time of his prosperity described as the Joshua of the New Dispensation, who led the people of England under the wing of his army out of the desert of slavery and doubt into the promised land of freedom and grace. The comparison, however, hardly bears the test of criticism. We may, perhaps, picture him to ourselves gazing earnestly at the passage of his people through the River of Trouble. The army, always faithful, passes over and joins him on the farther shore, but for the rest, a motley and disorganised multitude, of whom the common people believe in and press on to his standard, while of the captains of hundreds and of thousands some envy his position and undermine his authority, while others break away from the cause when there appears a prospect of its quiet and peaceful realisation. He was, in truth, rather the warrior who, after many battles, dies on the field when he first sees the prospect of a victory, than the general who has brought home his followers after a long and victorious campaign.

A complex character, such as that of Cromwell, is impossible of creation, except in times of great civil and religious excitement, and one cannot judge of the man without at the same time considering the contending elements by which he was surrounded. It is possible to take his character to pieces, and, selecting one or other of his qualities as a corner-stone, to build around it a monument which will show him as a patriot or a plotter, a Christian man or a hypocrite, a demon or a demi-god as the sculptor may choose.   It should also be possible at this lapse of time to discuss his motives and his career as critically and as dispassionately as we can discuss the dimensions and the architecture of an ancient ruin, or the bones and vestments of a discoffined prelate.   But experience teaches that such time has not yet arrived, that the problems of the seventeenth century are not yet solved, and that the character of Cromwell is still enveloped in clouds of prejudice and of uncertainty, which, like the mists of the Adriatic, magnify the outline while they obscure the detail. For my own part, I am content, while not ignoring his failings on the one hand nor accepting him as an inspired prophet and lawgiver on the other, to recognise his love for England, his ambition and his courage on her behalf, and his zeal as a reformer of her laws, and for these and other merits of his, to have added a tributary stone to the cairn which the patriotism and the impartiality of the nineteenth century are rapidly raising to the memory of the Lord Protector.

CHAPTER VIII.

A LIST OF THE CIRCUITS DURING THE COMMONWEALTH, 1649 TO 1660; WITH THE NAMES OF THE JUDGES ATTENDING SO FAR AS THEY CAN BE ASCERTAINED FROM THE STATE PAPERS, ACTS OF PARLIAMENT, WHITELOCK'S MEMO-RIALS, THE NEWSPAPERS OF THE DAY AND OTHER SOURCES.

HIEMAL, 1648-9 (March, 1648-9).

Northern—Serjeant Thorpe and Serjeant Puleston.[1]

Western—Chief Baron Wilde[2] and Francis Swanton.[3]

AUTUMPNAL, 1649.

Northern[4]—Baron Thorpe[5] and Justice Puleston.

---

[1] He died 5th September, 1659, but had not been reappointed by the Protector in 1654.

[2] "Capital Baro de Scaccario publico."*j*

[3] Francis Swanton, according to various entries in the Shaftesbury papers, was a J.P. of the quorum for the Counties of Wilts and Dorset (p. 84). He regularly sat at Quarter Sessions both before and during the Commonwealth, frequently as Chairman. He swore in Sir Anthony Astley Cooper as a J.P., and subscribed the engagement with him and thirteen other Justices of the County of Wilts on 17th January, 1650 (p. 85). In 1654-5 he was informed against by the Rev. J. Donington, Rector of Yerlington, as having been a party to Penruddock's affair. The information shows nothing but a quarrel with the rector, and no steps were taken against him.—Thurloe, Vol. II., p. 331.

[4] The question of the judges to go circuit was referred to the Council of State. Ordered that in consideration of the great inconvenience accruing by delay of justice in the Bishoprick of Durham, the judges who ride the Northern Circuit do hold Assizes at Durham, so that justice may be impartially executed.—*Moderate Mercury*, 21st June, 1649.

[5] Upon information of the good service done by Baron Thorpe in the last Northern Circuit, ordered that he do go the same circuit this

W

Western—Chief Baron Wilde[1] and Baron Rigby.
Gloster, etc.—Justice Jermyn[2] and Justice Nicholas.

HIEMAL, 1649-50.

Western[3]—Lord Chief Justice Rolle and Justice Nicholas.

AUTUMPNAL, 1650.

Western—Lord Chief Justice Rolle and Justice Nicholas.
Surrey,[4] etc.—Baron Gates and Baron Rigby.
Northern—Baron Thorpe[5] and Justice Warburton.

---

vacation.—Whitelock, Vol. III., p. 54. He tried Colonel Morris at
York, 16th August, 1649. Baron Gates, by reason of his sickness, was
excused of riding this circuit, and Serjeant Green was ordered to go
judge in his place.—*Ibid.*, p. 60.

[1] State Trials, Vol. V., p. 1315.

[2] State Papers, 22nd June, 1649.

[3] 27th March, 1650. Letters of a charge by Judge Nicholas at the
Assizes at Sarum, in vindication of the proceedings of Parliament and
of their and the people's power and the origin of it.—Whitelock,
Vol. III., p. 167.

30th March, 1650. From Exeter, of the solemn reception of the
Judges of Assize by the magistrates and military officers, and of the
conducting them through the several counties by the troops of horse,
and of the great respect showed by the soldiery to the civil magistrates.
That the Judges of Assize had much settled the people's minds as to
the present government in their charges to the grand juries, wherein
the Lord Chief Justice Rolle and Judge Nicholas were very much
commended.—*Ibid.*, pp. 168, 171.

11th April, 1650. From Chepstow, that at the Assizes was as great
an appearance of gentlemen and freeholders as ever was seen in that
county.—*Ibid.*, p. 174.

[4] These two judges were attacked by the plague while on circuit at
Croydon, and died; Baron Rigby on 18th August and Baron Gates on
19th August, 1650.—Foss's Judges, Vol. VI., pp. 433-470.

Serjeant Parker was sent to finish the circuit.—Haydn Dictionary
of Dates, p. 232.

[5] Statute, 30th July, 1650, empowered them as judges of Northern
Circuit to try cases at Durham on 12th August, 1650.

HIEMAL, 1650-1.[1]

Western—Lord Chief Justice Rolle and Lord Chief Baron Wilde,[2] or Justice Nicholas.[3]

AUTUMPNAL, 1651.[4]

Northern—Baron Thorpe and Serjeant Parker.[5]
Western—Lord Chief Justice Rolle and Justice Nicholas.
Hereford, etc.—Lord Chief Baron Wilde.[6]
Berks, etc.[7]—

HIEMAL, 1651-2.[8]

Western—Lord Chief Justice Rolle and Justice Nicholas.

AUTUMPNAL, 1652.

Western—John Wilde, Chief Baron of the Publique Exchequer, and Edward Atkins, a Justice of the Common Bench.[9]

---

[1] Barons Gates and Rigby being dead, two serjeants were sent the circuits in their places.—*Proceedings in Parliament*, 4th February, 1650-51.

[2] State Papers, 11th January, 1650-51.

[3] "To Salisbury Assizes Judge Nicholas Chief Justice."—Shaftesbury Diary, p. 86.

[4] Dates and places set out but not names of the judges.—*Proceedings in Parliament*, 16th June, 1651.

[5] Statute, 9th July, 1651, appointed those as Judges of the Northern Circuit to try Causes at Durham.

[6] This day concludes our Assizes, and we thank God to see the day when justice and judgment are executed in the land. Baron Wilde in his charge gave very excellent information and instruction for our country.—Letter from Hereford. *Proceedings in Parliament*, 31st July, 1651.

[7] These judges, whoever they were, tried Captain James Hind, the most celebrated highwayman of the century, who had been captured and examined by the Council of State.

[8] To commence on 2nd March, 1651-2.—*Proceedings in Parliament*, February, 1651-2.

[9] Western Records.

HIEMAL, 1652-3.[1]

Western[2]—Chief Baron Wilde and Justice Atkins.

AUTUMNAL, 1653.

Western—Chief Baron Wilde[3] and Justice Atkins.

LENT, 1653-4.[4]

Western—Lord Chief Justice Rolle[5] and Serjeant Glynn.
Berks, etc.—Lord Chief Justice St. John and Justice
Atkins.

---

[1] To commence 10th February, 1652-3. *Proceedings in Parliament.*
No names of the judges are given.

[2] Here is the first record during the Commonwealth of the cause
lists of this circuit. The judges took the civil business at alternate
towns. The Chief Baron tried causes at Winchester, Justice Atkins
at Salisbury, etc. The entries were as follows: Winchester, 17
causes; New Sarum, 49; Exeter City, 32; Taunton, 118; Dorchester,
87; Launceston, 75; Exeter, for the County of Devon, 112; total,
440. They appear to have been all tried, and there were no remanets.
The name of each cause is given with the number on the list, and the
party to whom the postea is delivered. The cause of action is not
stated.

[3] On this circuit the Chief Baron at Salisbury sentenced a witch,
Alice Bodenham, to be hanged.—Sidelights on the Stuarts, p. 165.

[4] *Proceedings in State Affairs,* 16th February, 1653-4. These were the
Judges appointed by the Protector. Chief Baron Wilde was not
reappointed.

[5] 10th February, 1653-4, Lord Chief Justice Rolle to be one of the
Justices of Assize for the Western Circuit and Justice Atkins, of the
Common Pleas, to be Judge of Assize for the next Oxford Circuit, although
they be the countries of their respective birth, and their commissions to
be issued accordingly.—State Papers, February, 1653-4. By Statute 8,
Richard II., c. 2, it was provided that "no mann of lawe shall be
Justyce of Assyse in hys countrey." It was, therefore, necessary for
judges going circuit into their own county to obtain a dispensation
from penalties.

Chief Justice Rolle is thus described in the commission: "Henry
Rolle, Chief Justice, assigned to hold pleas before the Lord Protector
of the Commonwealth of England, Scotland, and Ireland, and the
dominions thereto belonging in the Upper Bench at Westminster."

Sussex, etc.—Justice Aske[1] and Serjeant Newdigate.

Midland—Baron Thorpe and Serjeant Pepys.[2]

Bucks, etc.—Baron Nicholas and Serjeant Conyers.

Northern—Justice Hale and Serjeant Windham.

SUMMER, 1654.[3]

Western—Lord Chief Justice Rolle[4] and Baron Thorpe.

Berks, etc.—Lord Chief Justice St. John and Serjeant Glynn.

Hertford—Baron Pepys.[5]

Bucks, etc.—Justice Atkins and Justice Aske.

Northern—Justice Windham[5] and Justice Newdigate.[5]

Warwick—Justice Hale and Baron Nicholas.

LENT, 1654-5.[6]

Western—Lord Chief Justice Rolle and Baron Nicholas.[7]

Bucks, etc.—Lord Chief Justice St. John and Justice Atkins.

Berks, etc.—Baron Thorpe.

Surrey, etc.—Justice Aske and the Recorder of London (Steele).[8]

---

[1] He died 23rd June, 1656.

[2] In June, 1655, Baron Pepys was acting Chief Justice of the Upper Bench in Ireland. He died 18th March, 1658.—Foss, Vol. vi., p. 467.

Samuel Pepys, the diarist, was his youngest son, and Lord Chancellor Cottenham was his lineal descendant.

[3] *Proceedings in State Affairs*, July, 1654.

[4] 21st July, 1654, Lord Chief Justice Rolle to go to the Western Circuit and Baron Pepys the Essex Circuit, without incurring penalties. —State Papers, July, 1654.

[5] Serjeants Pepys, Windham, and Newdigate were made judges on 2nd June, 1654.—Whitelock, Vol. IV., p. 109.

Justice Jermyn died 18th March, 1654-5.—Foss, Vol. V., p. 443.

[6] *Proceedings in State Affairs*, 16th February, 1654-5.

[7] He had been moved from the Upper Bench to the Exchequer.

[8] Justice Aske and Recorder Steele applied to the Protector on 14th March, 1654-5, for a guard of horse during their circuit, which was granted.—Thurloe, Vol. II., p. 244.

Northampton—Justice Hale[1] and Justice Windham.

Northern—Justice Newdigate, with Serjeant Hatton and Serjeant Conyers to be the other two.

APRIL, 1655.

A Special Commission of Oyer and Terminer and Gaol Delivery, for trial of Penruddock and others in the West, was issued in April, 1655. The Commissioners sat at Salisbury on the 16th and at Exeter Castle on 18th April, where the hall was prepared for their reception by the Sheriff. An order was subsequently made by the Commissioners that he be repaid by the county his expenses attending the preparation of the hall for the Assizes. The following were the Commissioners named, but the Chief Justice and Baron Nicholas being the persons on whom the assault was committed did not take any part in the proceedings. John Lisle, one of the Lords Commissioners of the Great Seal of England ; Henry Rolle, Chief Justice, etc.; Robert Nicholas, Baron, etc.; Hugh Windham, one of the Justices of the Common Bench ; John Glynn, Serjeant-at-Law to H.H. the Lord Protector ; William Steele, Serjeant-at-Law and Recorder of the City of London. Justice Windham presided at Salisbury, and Serjeants Glynn and Steele tried Penruddock and others at Exeter.

SUMMER, 1655.

Western—John Glynn, Chief Justice, Justice Hale, and Francis Swanton, Esq.[2]

---

[1] Complaint was made to the Council of State that Justice Hale referred a cause at Warwick instead of trying it himself, and the arbitrators would not go on with the arbitration.—State Papers, Domestic, May, 1655.

[2] "Francis Swanton, Esq., was associated with Chief Justice Glynn, Mathew Hale, one of the justices, etc., not being expected."—Western Records.

·I find no record of the judges of this Summer Circuit. Chief

LENT, 1655-56.[1]

Western—Lord Chief Justice Glynn, William (?) Swanton associated to him by form of Statute.

Norfolk—Lord Chief Justice St. John and Justice Aske.

Oxford—Lord Chief Baron Steele and Justice Atkins.

Northern—Justice Windham and Baron Parker.

Surrey, Sussex, etc.—Unton Croke, Esq.,[2] and Justice Warburton.[3]

Midland—Justice Hale.[4]

Justice Rolle had resigned. Baron Thorpe and Justice Newdigate had retired, and no appointment had been made to the post of Lord Chief Baron, *vice* Wilde, but there were numerous serjeants-at-law, some of whom could have been and probably were sent as Commissioners.

[1] "To commence 28th February, 1655-6."—*Public Intelligencer*, No. 21.

April, 1656. Letters of great appearances of the country at this Assizes, and that gentlemen of the greatest quality served on the Grand Juries.—Whitelock, Vol. IV., p. 233.

[2] Bencher of the Inner Temple.

[3] Formerly Justice of the County Palatine of Chester. He died in 1659.

[4] "After the Assizes at Warwick be over, which is the last of Judge Hale's Circuite, I shall acquaint your Highness, by Mr. Levy, what we have done and what is desired in reference to public good and indeed my Lord I cannot but inform you that Judge Hale hath so demeaned himself in the counties under my charge, both in reference to your Highness's interest, as also for his justice to all, and in a special manner taking care of poor men in their causes, without which some had suffered, and I desire that when he shall wait upon your Highness you would be pleased to take notice of it, and if it seem good to you, to give him more than ordinary thanks."—Warwicke, 31st March, 1656. Major-General Whalley to the Protector.—Thurloe, Vol. III., p. 663.

"I must add this much to what I formerly have writ. I never knew any at his own cost more willing to serve the present Government than he. He has reprieved some horse-stealers and robbers, and confined them to gaol, so as to be sent out of the country, if His Highness and the Council think well, a course of which the country much approves.—Nottingham, 9th April, 1656. Major-General Whalley to the Protector.—Thurloe, Vol. III., p. 686.

Summer, 1656.[1]

Berks, etc.—Lord Chief Justice Glynn and Justice Windham.

Norfolk—Lord Chief Justice St. John and Justice Atkins.[2]

Southampton, etc.—Lord Chief Baron Steele and Baron Nicholas.[3]

Warwick, etc.—Justice Hale and Serjeant Hill.[4]

Hertford, etc.—Justice Warburton and Serjeant Croke.

York, etc.—Baron Parker and Serjeant Earle.

Lent, 1656-7.[5]

Hampshire, etc.—Lord Chief Justice Glynn and Justice Warburton.[6]

---

[1] *Public Intelligencer,* No. 29.

[2] At this Assize Judge Atkins affronted the Sheriff of Suffolk by saying to him, " More of your purse and less of your courtesie." But " my Lord Atkins said it was a usual expression of his, and he meant no evill in it."—Major-General Haynes to Thurloe. Bury St. Edmunds, 19th July, 1656.—Thurloe, Vol. IV., p. 230.

[3] William (?) Swanton was associated with the Chief Baron, as Baron Nicholas was absent till the Assizes at Taunton.

[4] " The judges and lawyers have much less business than formerly, but twelve trials at Nottingham Sizes. . . I need say nothing of Judge Hale. I assure you that Judge Hill gave a very honest charge, and very much to the advantage of the present Government at Lincoln."—Major-General Whalley to Thurloe. Newark, 9th August, 1656.—Thurloe, Vol. IV., p. 296.

" 22nd August, 1656. The Protector and Council reprieved, for three weeks, four men convicted and sentenced for coining, and in the meantime desired a report from the judges. 5th September, 1656. Serjt. Hill (late Justice of Assize) reported that one should be reprieved, and the law take its course as to the other three."—President Laurence to Mat. Hale and Serjt. Hill, Justices of Assize for the County of Northampton.—State Papers, CXXIX.

[5] *Mercurius Politicus,* No. 350. Chief Baron Steele was appointed Lord Chancellor of Ireland in September, 1656, and his successor was not yet named.

[6] The Lord Chief Justice was not expected though named in the Commission, so Mr. Swanton was associated with Justice Warburton.

Norfolk, etc.—Lord Chief Justice St. John and Justice Atkins.

Berks, etc.—Baron Nicholas and Serjeant Fountain.

Chelmsford, etc.—Justice Hale and Serjeant Hill.

Northampton, etc.—Justice Windham and Serjeant Croke.

York, etc.—Baron Parker and Serjeant Earle.

SUMMER, 1657.

Berks, etc.—Lord Chief Justice Glynn and Serjeant Earle.

Bedford, etc.—Lord Chief Justice St. John and Justice Atkins.

Hertford, etc.—Justice Hale and Justice Warburton.

Hampshire, etc.—Baron Nicholas and Justice Newdigate.[1]

York, &c.—Baron Parker and Serjeant Croke.

Northampton, &c.—Justice Windham and Baron Hill.[2]

LENT, 1657-8.[3]

Surrey, etc.—Justice Hale and Serjeant Croke.

York, etc.—Justice Warburton and Baron Parker.

Ailsbury, etc.—Lord Chief Justice St. John and Justice Atkins.

Berks, etc.—Baron Nicholas and Justice Newdigate.

Hampshire, etc.—Lord Chief Justice Glynn[4] and Justice Windham.

Northampton, etc.—Baron Hill and Serjeant Fountain.

---

[1] Reinstated after his resignation in May, 1655. Justice Newdigate made orders at Taunton, on 3rd August, 1657, that the Statutes for destruction of crowes, rooks, and other vermin be put into operation, and that "ducking-stooles" be set up in parishes where they formerly existed and are not now.

[2] Serjeant Hill, of the Inner Temple, was appointed a Baron of the Exchequer, and sworn in on 10th July, 1657.—*Mercurius Politicus,* No. 367.

[3] *Mercurius Politicus,* No. 403.

[4] The Lord Chief Justice left the Circuit at Launceston, and his place was supplied by Mr. Swanton.

x

SUMMER, 1658.[1]

Hampshire, etc.—Baron Nicholas and Serjeant Fountain.
Surrey, etc.—Lord St. John[2] and Justice Hale.
Bucks, etc.—Justice Atkins and Justice Warburton.
Southampton—Lord Chief Baron Widdrington[3] and Justice Windham.
York, etc.—Baron Parker and Justice Newdigate.
Berks, etc.—Lord Glynn[2] and Baron Hill.

LENT, 1658-9.[4]

I find no trace of any Assizes held in the spring of this year.

15th February, 1658-9. An order was made by the Council of State that the Assizes be postponed.—State Papers, Vol. CCI.

13th May, 1659. Newdigate, Atkins, Archer, and Parker were made judges.—Whitelock, Vol. IV., p. 346.

16th June, 1659. The judges were voted by Parliament for the Summer Circuits.—*Ibid.*, p. 352.

10th July, 1659. Hugh Windham was made a judge.—*Ibid.*, p. 354.

These were judicial appointments made by Richard Protector.

SUMMER, 1659.

Northern—Justice Farwell.
About London—Sir Thomas Widdrington.
Western—Justice Newdigate.

---

[1] *Mercurius Politicus*, No. 422.

[2] The two Chief Justices Glynn and St. John were now members of the House of Lords.

[3] Sir Thomas Widdrington, Knight, was appointed Lord Chief Baron on 26th June, 1658, in place of Lord Chief Baron Steele, promoted to Ireland.—Whitelock, Vol. IV., p. 334.

[4] State Papers, 16th June, 2nd to 8th July, and 5th August, 1659.

Gloster—Lord Chief Baron Wilde[1] and Serjeant Hill.

The other judges who went circuit were Baron Thorpe,[1] Justice Nicholas,[2] Justice Atkins, Justice Archer,[3] Baron Parker, Justice Windham and Serjeant Earle. Serjeant Bernard went as Chief Justice of the Isle of Ely.

January 17th, 1659-60. The following appointments were made to the Courts :—

UPPER BENCH—Newdigate to be Chief Justice; Hill and Nicholas to be Judges.

COMMON BENCH—St. John to be Chief Justice; Windham and Archer to be Judges.

EXCHEQUER—Wilde to be Chief Baron; Thorpe and Parker to be Barons.—Whitelock, Vol. IV., p. 389.

February 6th, 1659-60. Orders for Lent Circuits.—*Ibid.*, p. 393.

February 25th, 1659-60. Lent Circuits postponed.— *Ibid.*, p. 400.

I find no account of any Assizes held this spring, though criminal business was transacted by the Quarter Sessions. In the summer the King's Judges went circuit, and the records relapsed into a mixture of English and Latin.

---

[1] Restored by the Parliament.

[2] Put back into the Upper Bench.

[3] Rev. Jos. Glanvil gives an account of Justice Archer trying a witch, Julian Cox, at Taunton, in 1668, on his reappointment after the Restoration, and adds that he was much attacked for allowing her to be executed.—Sadducismus Triumphatus, pp. 326-336.

INDEX.

Y